Walking a Blues Road

Walking a Blues Road
A Selection of Blues Writing
1956–2004

by

Samuel Charters

MARION BOYARS
NEW YORK · LONDON

First published in the United States and Great Britain in 2004 by
MARION BOYARS PUBLISHERS LTD
24 Lacy Road, London SW15 1NL

www.marionboyars.co.uk

Distributed in Australia and New Zealand by Peribo Pty Ltd
58 Beaumont Road, Kuring-gai, NSW 2080

Printed in 2004
10 9 8 7 6 5 4 3 2 1

'Slidin' Delta', by J. D. Short and 'Let It Be', by Champion Jack Dupree, are
published by Stainless Music. The following selections first appeared as notes
for albums released by Prestige Records: Furry Lewis, Memphis Willie B. and
Jesse Fuller. The extended essay on Lightnin' Hopkins first appeared as an
introduction to the collection of Prestige albums released by Fantasy Records.

A CIP catalogue record for this book is available from the British Library.
A CIP catalog record for this book is available from the Library of Congress.

ISBN 0-7145-3107-3

Set in Bembo 10/13
Printed in Great Britain by Biddles Ltd King's Lynn Norfolk

CONTENTS

For Marion, in memory –
with thanks.

Acknowledgement

Much of the writing that has made its way into this book appeared first as liner notes or as longer essays for more ambitious record releases, but the excerpts from the books *The Legacy of the Blues* and *The Roots of the Blues* were first published by Marion Boyars, who ran her publishing company, Marion Boyars Publishers, from a series of small, cluttered offices in London, though she herself was originally from the United States. She, her husband Arthur, who is a poet and an enthusiastic, discerning listener to music of every style and era, and their daughters Susan and Catheryn, became close friends. Ann and I and our daughters Mallay and Nora met them in various familial combinations to drink wine, eat in surprising restaurants Arthur had discovered and talk or argue in more different cities on more occasions than I can remember. Someone who writes as I do, without any of the commercial adjuncts such as agents and long-term book contracts, needs to find, somewhere, a publisher like Marion, who will at least consider anything within reason. Marion was emotional, determined, shrewd, generous and forgiving – and she could also be exasperating, unyielding and unpredictable. Once on a walk across the fields in the south of France, when Ann and I and our daughters had driven down from Paris to visit Marion and Arthur and their daughters in her country farmhouse, she said most decidedly that she wanted to publish everything I would ever write – and then she turned down the next two manuscripts I sent her. She published six of my books, including three of my works of fiction, for which I will always be grateful. One of the books, *The Roots of the Blues*, went on to win an important literary prize, and a number of reprint contracts, but it was also a book that presented some difficulties in finding its final form. At those moments she was a skillful and patient editor.

For our last book together, *The Day Is So Long And The Wages So Small*, she called me in Stockholm a few days after she'd received the manuscript and said with some decisiveness that 'It wasn't at all what I expected, but I like it very much and I certainly want to publish it.' Then she added, 'And, Sam, it's such a wonderful love story.' I had never realized as I was writing it that it was a love story, but, of course, she was right. Then she said with some satisfaction, 'I'm not really going to edit it. It doesn't need it. I'm just going to go to typesetting.' A few months later, when Ann and I saw her for a last afternoon, she was close to death from cancer, and we sat around the bed, with Arthur stretched out beside her. The gentle talk was about times we'd met and dinners we'd eaten and ideas we'd shared – but at the same time she also was concerned about some of the production details of the book, which she was determined would come out, whatever happened to her. Her daughter Catheryn took over the burdens of the publishing company, and the book, indeed, was published just as Marion intended it. I am certain that it was Marion's presence and her support that made some of my writing possible over the long, rich years of our association.

Also:
I couldn't have done the writing for the record companies I worked for without the interest and the response of Moses Asch at Folkways, Bob Weinstock at Prestige, Maynard Solomon at Vanguard and Dag Haeggqvist of Sonet and Gazell Records in Stockholm. Dag and I have been associated for more than thirty years and he has continually presented me with new challenges and new musical possibilities to explore. Our most recent project was the biography of Cuban pianist Bebo Valdes, which Dag suggested I write, and then published with the small imprint that he manages, with his partner Henry Denander, as part of their commitment to music they love. Also, in recent years, I have worked closely with Bill Belmont, an old friend in Berkeley, California. Bill is a vice-president of Fantasy Records, a large and successful independent label that acquired many smaller jazz and blues labels, including Riverside and Prestige. We have produced dozens of CD compilations from the material in the Fantasy archives and Bill has given me the opportunity to write about artists and styles I had never had a chance to consider before.

The photographs in this book were taken by Ann Charters and Samuel Charters.

What We Write About When We Write About The Blues

It might have been the next year, but I am almost certain that I first heard a blues record in 1937. I grew up with a mother and father and an extended family of aunts and uncles who either played or were closely attuned to jazz and popular music, but this was the first time I was told that what I was listening to was something different. The recording was Bessie Smith's 'Nobody Knows You When You're Down And Out'. The economic struggles of the Depression had forced my mother, along with me and my younger sister, to move back to the upstairs bedrooms of her mother's house in Pittsburgh, and my mother's teenage brother Bill, who was only eleven years older than I was, played it for me on the large, mahogany wind-up cabinet phonograph in the living room. Bill's father, my grandfather, had died of a heart attack at the beginning of the Depression, and my father had just been taken by his mother to Los Angeles in the hope that he would be able to deal more successfully with his own problems. The bond that grew between Bill and me — both of us confused and fatherless — was closer than if we had been brothers, since we didn't have sibling rivalry to work our way through. Everything Bill introduced me to in the years I lived there in the big house on Bayard Place in Pittsburgh became part of my life later. Through Bill I began to understand the adult world of jazz — since he shared this with his older brother — through Bill I learned about writing and about poetry — since he was already writing poetry in high school — (one of the handful of poems I know from memory is a love poem he wrote for his class year book) — and through Bill I had my first glimpse into the world of the blues.

Bill, who in the old family photos was the tense and sensitive teenager I still remember, played Bessie Smith for me because he had decided to take the record over to the house of a girl who lived in the neighborhood. His plan was to wind up the phonograph that sat in her family's living room and play the song for her, in the hope that it might make her notice him. If you've heard the record you know that the song only has a verse and a chorus, and to extend it to the length of a side of a record you have to repeat the verse, and add some kind of instrumental solo to fill out the rest. Bessie's solution was to hum the second verse in an impassioned, despairing vocal sound that is much more expressive than the song's words. As she hummed, the tuba player – whom I learned many years later was Cy St. Claire – played the melody on his deep voiced instrument. It is one of the great moments in Bessie's recording career.

Bill was too upset when he came back to tell me what had happened, but the next day he told me sorrowfully that after the record was over the girl had taken a moment to think of something to say, and then she had suggested brightly, 'She certainly can hum!' He understood, without anything else being said, that there was no hope for him.

When I turned into a tense and sensitive teenager myself only a few years later, my family, reunited now, moved to Sacramento, California and I found myself completely without friends or any other relatives. The jazz and the blues I had known all my life suddenly *became* my life, and with my family's typical way of dealing with a difficult situation I retreated to the downtown local library. Nobody had written a book about the blues, but I found the first book which presented jazz as a musical experience that reflected what I had grown up with. It was titled *Jazzmen*. It had been published in 1939 and despite wartime paper restrictions it had been successful enough to make its way onto most public library shelves. The concept of the book – that jazz was an expression of African American culture – and its way of responding to its subject – with portraits in the lyrical prose of the musicians themselves and evocations of the cities and neighborhoods where they had played and lived – became the template I was to use in everything I came to write about jazz and the blues, and about all the other musical styles I've written about in the years since. Charles Dickens consciously chose a Victorian boxing writer, Pierce Egan, as his literary model; my model was Charles Edward Smith who, with Frederic Ramsey Jr., was one of the editors and contributors to the book, and whose sensitive interludes, capturing the feel of New Orleans and its veteran musicians, became the only school of writing I tried that left any real impression on me.

I first began writing about the blues in the early 1950s, as I was completing the biographical dictionary I was writing about the New Orleans musicians I had met when I followed the path of Smith and Ramsey to New Orleans, with its fast fading memories of the first years of jazz. By now I'd met them and we'd become friends, though Charlie was drinking so heavily that no real friendship was possible. At first I was only writing album notes for the recordings I had begun to do in the rural South in 1954, but when I realized that there was no book about the blues, particularly about the acoustic rural blues, it was obvious that what I had to do was write one. When I came to write *The Country Blues* in the spring of 1959 I had never written anything like it before – since the New Orleans book was a collection of many, many short biographical sketches – but it was a book that seemed to write itself. I simply translated what I had absorbed from those years of teenage reading into the new book. A few years later, when I was expanding and rewriting it, I asked Fred Ramsey, as a gesture of acknowledgement, if he would mind if I called the new book *The Bluesmen*, and he was pleased that his early book had meant so much to me. *Jazzmen* was the most important book he was to finish, though he and Charlie did assemble a guide to jazz records, and Fred wrote a sensitive text to a collection of the photographs he had taken on his southern journeys.

I didn't think of writing anything for the record releases themselves, since I grew up in the era of the 78rpm single. They didn't have notes. They came in a paper sleeve printed with the company's name and a decoration and sometimes a list of a few other titles. Since there was no way to know what they sounded like, the shops that sold them had listening booths, and I spent most of my after-school hours in Sacramento in the much battered booths of a tiny shop that an older friend, Russ Solomon, had opened in the back room of his father's drug store. It took its name from the movie auditorium that filled most of the building. The name of Russ's first little counter operation was Tower Records, and as it grew it was to play a decisive role in the expansion of the world's music audience two decades later. I had the good fortune to begin writing about jazz and the blues just as the LP was introduced; although the first LPs weren't much better than the 78s for their notes. I have facsimiles of some of the first 10" LPs of early Miles Davis and Thelonius Monk recordings, and in the beginning the back space was blank, then catalog listings began to appear and finally there were short, promotional pieces that eventually evolved into the album notes that were so useful in helping the buyers understand what they were buying.

I was also fortunate that I had begun doing field recordings when I was living in New Orleans, and I met Fred Ramsey there. Fred introduced me to the man who was bringing out most of the documentary recordings he was doing – Moses Asch of Folkways Records. Moe's interests were musical, literary, political, social, educational, linguistic and scientific – his dream was to document every sound that was created by every form of living creature on the planet, from tree frogs to Woody Guthrie, and he extended his universe of sound to include flash floods in the Arizona desert or the splatter of rain on the leaves in a tropical forest. Thirty years later, when Moe and I looked back at what we had done together, our only real sense of disappointment was that we hadn't caught it all on film as well. I did my first blues writing for Folkways albums that began to be released in the middle of the 1950s. The first of the documentations was the search for Blind Willie Johnson that took me through much of East Texas with my first wife Mary, recording blind singers and local preachers who had known him. The search had ended with a meeting with his widow in her poor shack on the outskirts of Beaumont, Texas. Moe printed the notes just as I wrote them, and added evocative drawings by a young African American artist, Ernest York. When I took the first copy of the album out of the carton Moe had packed it in to send to me in New Orleans I realized that – whatever other ambitions I might have had – this was probably going to be my life.

The first years of writing for Folkways were useful for me since there were no limitations on what I wrote. Moe's vision of what he wanted to document was so encompassing that he accepted what those of us who were associated with the company did without question. Our only problem was getting paid, since Moe simply put out what he thought should be documented, and the company never really had much money. I remember once in the 1960s he held out a new album for me, telling me with genuine excitement that it was something I had to listen to. It was an album of unaccompanied songs by a survivor of one of the Nazi death camps. The man's voice was tired and broken, and he was singing in Yiddish, but, yes, it was something that had to be included in the legacy of the human spirit that Moe was creating.

It was also at Folkways that I became associated with the Harlem poet Langston Hughes. He was producing children's records about jazz for Moe, but Moe had already recorded him on 78 singles reading his poetry, and he was in and out of the office on other projects, just as I was. It was Langston who helped me to overcome the uncomfortable feeling I had that what I was doing with the recordings and the writing

14

about African American music was an unwelcome intrusion into the privacy of another culture. One night when we met at a Folkways party after *The Country Blues* was published he told me with spontaneous enthusiasm how much he'd liked it. I said lamely that he, as a black man, must know much more about the blues than I did. He only laughed and answered, 'Tell me something I don't know about Schubert!' It was Langston who, with Moe Asch, Fred Ramsey and Charlie Smith, made my life possible.

Folkways Records notes were, in another way, not as useful as they might have been in providing a writing course on musical experiences. For Moe the texts of the songs, as well as the backgrounds of the folk music from everywhere in the world that he was releasing, were important to understanding the music, so he had created a packaging for his albums that provided a separate space for lengthy album booklets. This meant there was no particular limit on what we might write, though if we went on for too many pages Moe would patiently remonstrate. When other companies began sending me to the South to do blues recordings in the 1960s I found myself dealing with the space limitations of the commercial LP. If somebody would have asked me what I was writing about in all the LP album notes I wrote over the next thirty years – until CDs arrived with their more spacious booklets – I would have said, without thinking, that I was writing about four and a half double spaced pages.

But what *was* I writing about in all of the books and notes and essays, for what has now been almost fifty years? As I wrote in an introduction to a new edition of *The Country Blues* in 1975, the writing had become my modest soap box to attack the racism that I encountered when I first went to the South in 1950. I had grown up in a family that had always been completely at ease with black life and culture, and although Pittsburgh certainly was not a city with an easy exchange between the races, the schools I attended were integrated, even if there were only what would be considered a 'token' number of black students in the classrooms with me. The United States has never been any more gentle with minorities than any other society, and what I remember from those young years were the tiresome Jewish jokes, the coarse smell of the burnt cork I had to wear when as a nine year old I sang in a minstrel show, and the fear I felt when, as a nervous adolescent of Scottish American background, I had to walk through a hostile Italian neighborhood to get to high school. But I wasn't prepared for the oppressive fear and the intense racial feelings I encountered when I first went to Louisiana and Alabama. Simply riding the New Orleans street cars involved moving the barriers marking the white and black sections of seats back and forth so that no person of color would ever sit in front of a white person. When I first began meeting New Orleans musicians in 1950 I had to be told that I should pretend I was an American Indian if I was caught in a bar in a black neighborhood, and I was warned against even displays of friendship on downtown streets.

The 1950s were a breathtaking time for anyone who was fascinated, as I was, by the world's musical cultures. With my second wife, Ann, I recorded the songs and instrumental music of the sponge fisherman of Andros Island in the Bahamas. I recorded Mexican Indian dances, Scottish shepherds, Japanese koto music, Greek bozouki orchestras, ragtime opera, and Irish bagpipe players. Ann and I even did an album with the militant Orangemen of North Ireland, who played the world's largest and loudest marching drums. The thunder of the drumming deafened us for the better part of a week. When I began to work for other New York companies in the 1960s I was still asked to go back to the blues, although I was now producing everything from acid rock to the songs of Charles Ives. With the blues, however, I could continually say something about the racial dilemma, so I always kept the door open to new projects.

This consciousness of the blues writing as a social agenda also shaped the way that I wrote. I was, from the beginning, trying to add my voice to the struggle against racism. I wanted someone listening to the blues to be conscious that this was another individual who was singing – not simply a representative of a social minority or an economic class. I also felt that the real thrust was not toward unit record sales, advertising campaigns, or marketing strategies – my concern – however I expressed it – was human respect, and particularly in lifting the veil of fear that hung over every African American I met in the South. At the same time it was so important to document what still survived of a fast disappearing musical culture, and I couldn't help but be sensitive, also, to the economic ambitions and the hopes of the many blues artists I recorded. Most of them were poor, and any kind of recording session, any effort to protect the copyrights for their part of the treasury of black vernacular song that they had helped to create, made a crucial difference to their lives.

I think this consciousness that I needed to support and present the artists themselves was the main reason why I didn't write reviews. I wrote everything else, but no reviews. After *The Country Blues* was published I was approached by a number of music publications and asked if I would do record reviews for them. I made a tentative effort with the first records I was sent, but I immediately realized that I could never bring myself to write a negative review. Within the specific context of a book I could criticize artists and styles, but when it was a new product and a singer's career was on the line I couldn't dismiss the effort, however dreary the record sounded. Also, I had been severely attacked for *The Country Blues* by English blues writers, particularly Derrick Stewart-Baxter and Paul Oliver, and I had found the experience so painful that I couldn't inflict it on anyone else. Liner notes, of course, are never critical, which can make a collection of them rather tepid reading.

So how much writing has there been over all these years? The truth is I don't really know. Certainly much more than has made its way into these pages. It isn't only that there were many notes which repeated themes and responses to artists that I had written about often before. One reason I'm vague about how much I've written is that, like many other writers who do considerable work for hire, I used pseudonyms. I look at something that I might have written forty years ago, but I can't really remember if it was me. I think I was so casual about the use of pseudonyms because virtually all of the early blues artists had released records – and even signed contracts – under a variety of names. Also, in the years that I was a recording director at Vanguard Records in New York, I worked with the company's in-house writer, jazz critic Sidney Finkelstein. Sidney used his own name for music that needed a certain imprimatur, but for budget LPs, or pop material that was out of his field he was 'S. W. Bennett'.

I was almost as casual about using pseudonymns for recording sessions. In November 1955 I spent an evening with Virgil Perkins and his wife and sister in Houston, Texas. Virgil had been the washboard player for a country blues group I had recorded in Mobile, Alabama in May of the previous year. He had moved to Houston before I found them, but they gave me his address, and on a trip back through Texas from Berkeley, where I had been a student, Mary and I stopped by Virgil's apartment. When I listened to the tapes later I found an exuberant version of 'John Henry' with a churning acoustic guitar accompanying Virgil's washboard, kazoo, and vocal. We had all had so much to drink that I had no memory of joining him for the song, but I had an old acoustic 12-string guitar in the trunk of the car and the guitarist on the tapes was at about my level of skill. At one point in the song Virgil said, 'Old guitar Jack, I hear you,' so I gave myself the name 'Jack Sims' in the notes to the album – it was titled *American Skiffle Bands* – that Moe released the next year. A few years later I found, to my dismay, that Charles Edward Smith, who, like Fred Ramsey, was also one of the Folkways family, had used the song to open a two LP boxed set titled *American Folk Music*. Somewhat shaken, I told Moe, and I apologized for compromising the set by playing on what was supposed to be a genuine folk performance. Moe just laughed and shrugged, 'That only makes it more ethnic!'

When I go through some of the albums I was involved in during the 1960s I know that I was 'John Frederick,' who wrote the notes to a Prestige album *The Art of the Jug Band*. I am certain about that, because I also played guitar, washboard, cornet and jug on the record under two other different names, 'John Friedman' and 'Darrell Innes.' 'John Friedman,' on some numbers, was guitarist and harmonica player Danny Kalb, and on most of the album the washboard player 'Darrell Inness' was my wife Ann. The reason for all the subterfuge was that Danny and I, along with mandolin and violin player Artie Rose, were under contract to Mercury Records for another jug band led by Dave Van Ronk, and it was necessary to conceal our identities.

I am also reasonably certain that I was the 'Walt Crane' who wrote the notes to Geoff Muldaur's first solo Prestige Record, *Sleepy Man Blues*. I was doing a literature series for Moe at the time and I was particularly interested in Walt Whitman and Stephen Crane. I also suspect that among the names I used for other Prestige albums were 'Art Weiss,' 'Geoff Gregory,' 'Werner Lind,' and 'Walter Avery.' If these are the names of people who really wrote these notes, please let me know! I have a vague memory of writing the notes for an album including songs by Pete Seeger, and to give the notes the right spin I gave myself the name of 'Rachel' something. Again, if someone knows what the album was I would be pleased to know something about it. After I moved to Europe and became associated with Sonet Records in Stockholm I continued to use a variety of names, since the company used me to write about such a range of music that I had to come up with new personalities to deal with all of the different styles.

There was a particular problem with a long series of Sonet albums I made with Cajun and zydeco artists in Louisiana. As a promotional giveaway our London office decided to publish a Cajun 'newspaper' to discuss the culture, the Louisiana setting, and the music. I managed to get an article from British scholar John Broven, and a piece from Revon Reed, a Louisiana school teacher who presented a 'Cajun Hour' from Fred's Lounge every Saturday morning in Mamou, but to fill out the rest of the paper I had to write the rest of the articles myself, using a variety of styles, and resorting to two or three other names. One pseudonym I used often for Cajun and zydeco pieces was 'Freddie Crozier.' I couldn't keep appending long, scholarly notes to what were essentially very happy, uncomplicated albums, so 'Freddie' wrote most of those. I became fond enough of Freddie that I have included one of his short pieces that introduced a Rockin' Dopsie album.

If someone who is reading these selections has the original notes or the original chapters from the books, they will find that I have often rewritten them, and sometimes the rewriting has been extensive. Many of the notes from the 1960s felt cramped by the space limitations, so I have simply written them the way I would have done if there hadn't been the problem of fitting the writing onto the back of an album. Also, since each album was a separate release, I had to repeat some of the generalized comments about the place of the blues in black culture for every introductory note, since a new purchaser might not pick up any other record. Reading essentially the same sociological background again and again can become a little wearying. Another problem, particularly with the book *The Poetry of the Blues*, was that in our first excitement over discovering the blues world, many of us who were writing about the songs overstepped the boundaries of fair use of copyrighted material. As I looked at the old chapters I was aware that with today's increased consciousness of copyright the song texts couldn't be used again in their original form. What I have tried ultimately to do is to put together a book that focuses on things I've written about on the blues that might be of interest to new readers, as well as to someone who might have encountered some of the pieces at the time they appeared. As I said, I can't, at this point, even be sure of a few of the things I wrote, although I am certain about everything I have gathered here. What I have collected are pieces that I still felt like reading myself, even though almost a half-century has gone by since I produced some of the writing.

I have also included three or four essays that, for one reason or another, were not published at the time I wrote them. The blues continues to absorb and fascinate me, and I often find myself responding to a new aspect of the music that I want to comment on. I usually don't make an effort to publish any of these pieces unless someone has asked me for them. There has been a great deal of writing about the blues in the last few years, and I'm very conscious that there is already so much there for us to read and study that there is no way for anyone to become familiar with all of it. My hope is that no one will mind if I add these pieces – some of them written so many years ago – to the pile.

Samuel Charters
Storrs, 2004

I

Lightnin' Hopkins' Texas

1. Beginnings

It is true that, technically, this set of notes shouldn't be included in a selection of blues writing, since Blind Willie Johnson was a guitar evangelist and, unlike other religious singers including Reverend Gary Davis, the thirty titles he recorded between December 1927 and April 1930 were, without exception, sacred songs. Three years after these notes were written, I explained my reasons for including a chapter about his life and songs in *The Country Blues*:

'Of the other singers on the Columbia 14000 series, the religious singer, Blind Willie Johnson, is the only other important figure. Perhaps he does not belong in a discussion of the blues, but as jazz historian Frederic Ramsey Jr. said many times to justify including his 'Dark Was The Night (Cold Was The Ground)' with a collection of blues performances; he seems to belong with these other men. Like them he was an itinerant guitar player, a blind street beggar, and his sacred songs were an expression of the religious music he had grown up with in the Central Texas cotton country. He was one of the most intense singers to record in the late 1920s, and his style left a deep imprint in the singing of both sacred and secular singers who heard his recordings.'

These notes were written for the Folkways album that presented the documentary recordings I had made of the search to find Blind Willie in Texas over the two or three previous years. The notes were written in November, 1956, when I left the tapes with Moe Asch at the Folkways office on W 46th Street in New York City. This was the first writing I did with the blues as its subject. Folkways released the album the following spring.

In 1993 Larry Cohn, who was directing the 'Roots n' Blues' reissue program for Columbia Records, asked me if I would write a longer introduction to a complete CD collection of the Blind Willie Johnson recordings. It was an opportunity to reconsider an artist whose music had been important to me for so many years, and the 'booklet' format meant that I had a chance to write more fully. Someone who reads the booklet carefully will notice that I had already corrected one of the errors in the old Folkways notes. Blind Willie's last session was recorded in Atlanta, not Beaumont, and the woman who sang with him was someone named Willie B. Harris.

The notes won an award for the year, but ten days after I had been notified of the honor I received a package of notes and xeroxes from a persistent young researcher in Houston named Randy Harper, who had finally tracked down Blind Willie's family, conducted extensive interviews with friends and family members, and located the death certificate in the state archives, with its invaluable information about the date and the cause of his death. Thanks to Harper's efforts we now know that Blind Willie died in Beaumont on September 18th, 1945, and the cause of death was malaria, with complications from syphilis. I hope that someone else will have a chance to write the notes to a new collection of the songs, and they will be able to work with this rich hoard of material which Harper and other researchers have added to the story of the greatest of the guitar evangelists, Blind Willie Johnson.

Blind Willie Johnson
from the notes to the *Folkways* Album

When Blind Willie Johnson died in Beaumont, Texas in 1949 he had been a legend for many years. Between 1927 and 1930 he had recorded thirty magnificent religious performances for Columbia Records; then as far as anyone knew he had disappeared. The recordings were successful; widely distributed and reissued on subsidiary labels. Willie knew nothing about this. He was living in Beaumont, trying to provide for his family in the hard Depression years. The storekeepers along Forsythe Avenue, in the colored district, remember him as a tall, heavy man, not dark in color; a dignified man and a magnificent singer. A small picture of him taken in the late 1930s or 1940s shows a square, heavy face, a thin straight mouth. His head was shaved, the blind eyes were closed.

In 1947, when the first reissues of early jazz recordings were becoming relatively common, reissues of a handful of Blind Willie's recordings were among the first to become available. The first definitive series of jazz reissues, the Folkways multi-volume *Jazz* series, edited by Frederic Ramsey Jr., included Blind Willie's haunting 'Dark Was The Night – Cold Was The Ground' in the second volume. In Beaumont Willie was attending church every Sunday at the Mount Olive Baptist

Church, playing his guitar to accompany young people at evening services and preaching to small meetings.

In the winter of 1949, as a major study of jazz which included a discussion of Blind Willie was beginning to reach a large audience, Willie's house at 1440 Forest caught fire. He, his wife Angeline, and the children got out safely, losing only a few furnishings and Willie's guitar. The house was filled with water, but Angeline spread newspaper over the wet bedding, and they slept in the house that night. Willie was a restless sleeper and turned over onto the soaked mattress. He was sick the next morning, but he tried to sing on the streets and earn a little money. He died of pneumonia a week later. Angeline had tried to get him into a hospital, but he was not admitted, probably because of his blindness. As she said sorrowfully, 'Blind people has a hard time…'

In the spring of 1954 I was living in New Orleans, and a close friend, Richard B. Allen, told me that he had talked with a blind singer begging at the bus stop on South Rampart Street who had said that he had known Blind Willie in Texas. I interviewed the singer, Elder Dave Ross, the next week, and he said that he thought Blind Willie was still living in Dallas. With my first wife, Mary, I drove to Dallas and began asking in the streets for Willie Johnson. A year later we had traced him to Beaumont. We walked along Forsythe Avenue on a cold November afternoon asking if anyone had seen a blind gospel singer. 'Which one?' they asked me. I said an older man who played a guitar. They asked me, 'Which one?'

Late in the afternoon I talked with the druggist at Fowler's Pharmacy, at the corner of Forsythe and Neches, and he was able to place the man we were looking for. He sent us to Angeline, who was living in a shack at the outskirts of town. Until we reached Beaumont we had no idea what Willie looked like. Every person we talked to in northern Texas who had known him was blind.

Blind Willie was born outside of Temple, Texas about 1900. His father, George Johnson, was a farmer. There was at least one brother, Robert. Willie's mother died when he was a baby, and his father married again. The second wife had a lover, and in a fit of anger after an argument with Willie's father she threw a pan of lye water in Willie's face, blinding him. He was seven years old.

Angeline said that Willie always wanted to be a religious singer, but Adam Booker, a blind preacher who lived outside the little town of Hearn, Texas, said that when he first met Willie in 1925, he was singing a few secular songs. Every Saturday Willie's father would bring him into Hearn, where Booker was pastoring, and Willie would play on the streets. As Booker remembered, 'He wouldn't hardly miss.' Willie was singing 'If I Had My Way I'd Tear The Building Down' on the streets of Dallas when Angeline heard him in 1927. They lived in Dallas and Waco, then settled in Beaumont after two or three years of wandering. His first recordings were made in Dallas in December 1927, and included some of his best known songs, 'It's Nobody's Fault But Mine', 'Mother's Children Have A Hard Time', 'Dark Was The Night...' and 'If I Had My Way...' He sang alone, with his own guitar accompaniment. A year later he recorded four more songs in Dallas, and in December, 1929 Columbia brought him to New Orleans. He recorded ten additional songs, and he stayed in the city for nearly a month. Elder Dave Ross, the blind singer who sent us to Dallas, had first met Willie in 1929 in New Orleans. There is a woman singing with Willie on some of the songs, perhaps from one of the local churches.

Richard B. Allen has heard a story in New Orleans about a blind religious singer who was arrested in 1929 for trying to incite a riot. The singer was standing in front of the downtown Customs House singing 'If I Had My Way . . ,' a highly emotional version of the Samson and Delilah legend. The chorus is sung, 'Oh Lord, if I had my way I'd tear this building down.' If the story is true the singer was very probably Blind Willie.

Angeline sang with Willie on the last group of recordings, done in Beaumont. They never heard from Columbia again. They stayed close to Beaumont, except for occasional trips to Houston to sing for a few days. They were in Houston from August 11th to 18th, 1936, for the encampment of the 'South Texas Missionary Baptist Association of Texas.' Angeline led Willie through the streets in later years, singing with him. She is still living in Beaumont, making a poor living as a midwife and day nurse.

The thirty songs Willie recorded give a clear picture of his stylistic range as a singer and his technical abilities as a guitarist. Some, like 'If I Had My Way' and 'Jesus Is Coming Soon,' are sung as rough, chant-like songs, half shouted in harsh, growling tones. 'Mother's Children Have A Hard Time' and 'Nobody's Fault But Mine' are sung with a stronger, clearer voice, with the harsher tones used for emphasis. 'Dark Was The Night' is a wordless cry. In later recordings he sang in both a falsetto soprano voice and a false bass voice.

Angeline Johnson, Beaumont, 1955
(Photo: Samuel Charters)

The guitar accompaniments are as varied in style as his voice. He played in at least three tunings; the standard E-B-G-D-A-E, 'Hawaiian' tuning, E-C#-A-E-A-E, and an open E tuning, E-B-G#-E-B-E. The E tuning is used for the chants, 'If I Had My Way' and 'Jesus Is Coming Soon.' The guitar is played with finger picks and a thumb pick. The sound is an intense and highly rhythmic ostinato, complex and unvarying, a superb stylistic complement to his harsh, rough voice. There is no harmonic movement in these accompaniments. Melodic elements are introduced in the upper strings, but they are completely subordinated to the relentless rhythm. A dominant chord is very difficult to finger when the guitar is in this tuning, so there are no harmonic cadences. He generally ends a piece by playing a full chord.

The 'Hawaiian' tuning was introduced into the United States before the first World War by touring Hawaiian troupes who were a vaudeville favorite, and whose records sold in large quantities everywhere in the country. The guitar was laid across the lap while a small steel bar in the left hand slid up and down the strings. Finger picks and a thumb pick were usually used on the right hand. Country musicians used a variety of objects to slide along the strings, from small bottles to pieces of tin. It was the 'Hawaiian' style, considerably modified, that was a characteristic of the Mississippi blues style. The musicians used a broken bottle neck or a piece of metal tubing on the little finger of their left hand, and used it to slide on a single string. Blind Willie used a pocket knife.

With the use of the slide on the upper strings it is easier to play melodies, and the accompaniments to his pieces like 'Motherless Children', 'Nobody's Fault But Mine', and 'Dark Was The Night' are in this style. He uses his voice and the guitar in a highly developed melodic interplay. The guitar plays the first phrase, the voice sings the second, the voice sings the first three lines, the guitar plays the last. One of the possibilities of this tuning is the repetition of melodic material an octave above or below its first statement, because of the three E strings. He makes beautiful use of this in both 'Nobody's Fault But Mine' and 'Dark Was The Night'.

The harmonic possibilities of the 'Hawaiian' tuning are limited, since it is an open A chord, but with a selective use of superimposed harmonies over the unvarying tonic in the bass a feeling of subdominant and dominant can be suggested. The accompaniments are usually more varied harmonically than those in the E tuning. The standard tuning is used to accompany songs of obvious white derivation. Willie plays them with a flat pick. There is considerable melodic material played on the bass strings, with conventional harmonies on the upper strings. The rhythm is the swinging, relaxed dance beat of a lot of white country music recorded at the same time.

The songs themselves came from a number of sources. Some were credited to Blind Willie, but the others were widely known in Texas. Adam Booker, the Hearn preacher, said that the words for 'If I Had My Way' came from the 'Doctor Watts' hymnal. Other songs were from late Baptist sources. The hummed cry of 'Dark Was The Night' is unlike anything else recorded in that area. There is a recording by Leadbelly, who lived in East Texas for many years, in which he hums a melodic fragment similar in mood to Blind Willie's recording. He said that this type of singing was used in Baptist services out in the country, and this is probably the background for the song. Angeline sang a version of it that was completely different from her husband's. Her performance was a completely realized solo, including both a song leader's call and a group's response. In this kind of 'lining', a line is sung and immediately followed by a set response.

Angeline taught Willie many of the songs he sang in the streets. There were over a hundred song books in an old trunk beside Angeline's shack in Beaumont. The weather and roaches had destroyed all but a few of them. I bought one from her for 25 cents. It was the *Redeemer's Praise, for the Sunday School, Church, and Family* by T. C. Okane, published by Walden and Stowe in 1881. It contained words and music for over 500 hymns. These trite, commonplace songs came to life in Willy's voice and guitar. He brought to them fire and excitement. In superbly creative, imaginative performances he expressed his faith in his God.

(1956)

The following is one of the first notes I wrote about a blues singer, and it set the tone for much of the writing I did later. Every now and then, as I found myself writing more and more about some of the same subjects, I made a half-hearted effort to be either more colorful with language or more academically nuanced, but it was always the places and the people of the blues that interested me. I was to go on and write about Lightnin' often again, and I often retold the story of our first meeting. This is also the only time I can remember a reviewer including the album notes as part of their comments. A New York writer described them in a magazine as my 'I-Love-A-Mystery-Notes,' referring to a popular radio program of the era. The morning I met Lightnin', and the day that we did the recording in his room, was January 16th, 1959. The notes were written when I returned to New York from the research trip to the South, probably in March. A month later I began writing *The Country Blues*. A reader today will notice that most of us who were discovering the blues at that moment still didn't include the Chicago electric style in our definition of the blues idiom.

The Legendary Lightnin'
The Texas Blues of Lightnin' Hopkins

On a windy winter morning in January 1959 I was driving along Dowling Street, in Houston, Texas. I stopped at a red light and a car pulled up beside mine. The window was rolled down, and a thin, nervous man, wearing dark glasses, leaned toward me.

'You lookin' for me?'

'Are you Lightnin'?'

'Lightnin',' I said, 'I sure am.'

I had been looking for Lightnin' Hopkins, off and on, for the five years that had passed since I first heard him on record.

Lightnin' is one of the last of the great blues singers, like many of them almost a legend in his own time. His records sold widely and his name was very well known, but there was almost nothing known about him. I first heard one of his records in New Orleans in the summer of 1954, 'Contrary Mary' on the Jax label. It was around town on the juke boxes and a musician I knew, the trombonist Paul Crawford, heard it and found a copy in a shop on Rampart Street. It was a brand new record, but it sounded like a record that could have been made in 1924 as well as 1954. He was accompanying himself on an unamplified guitar, singing a mean, unhappy blues in the long, irregular rhythms of a man who learned his singing in the fields or along dusty southern roads. I asked around New Orleans, but about the only thing I could find out was that he was living in Houston. A distant cousin was cooking in a restaurant in the French Quarter and he had an old Houston address for Lightnin'.

I was in and out of Houston for the next five years, recording, interviewing musicians, and asking about Lightnin' Hopkins. When I'd come from California to Houston I'd find out that Lightnin' was out in California, when I'd get to California I'd find that Lightnin' had gone back to Houston. I didn't make a determined effort to find him. He was recording for three or four Rhythm and Blues labels and it was easy to pick up his records. Most of the R&B stations would play the new ones, and an afternoon's listening every month or so made it easy to keep even. I wasn't the only record collector who was interested in Lightnin's playing, He was attracting more and more blues fans who were interested in the old style of singing and playing the guitar.

Since nothing was known about Lightnin' he became more and more of a legendary figure. His name was mentioned in articles on the blues and some of his old records were selling for nearly the same prices that records from the 1920s were bringing. His early recordings, done in 1947 and 1948 for Gold Star Records, a small company in Houston, were particularly prized. There wasn't much anyone could say about him, except that he was a very exciting blues singer, and it was the confusion about Lightnin' himself that shaped the legend as much as his music did.

The records continued to come out, but he had begun recording for companies in New York, and something was being lost as Lightnin' turned out more and more singles that were simply designed to sell to the teenage R&B audience. He was using a loud amplified guitar and there was usually a loud drummer and bass player to do away with the subtle rhythm that had made his earlier records so memorable. By 1957 he was losing much of his popularity, and in 1958 his records weren't played much on the rock and roll shows that had taken over afternoon radio. The record labels seemed to have dropped him. Suddenly it was very important to find him and record him singing as he'd been singing when he made his first records, only ten years before.

Since the last address I had for Lightnin' was in Houston, that seemed to be as good a place to start as any. I had seen a letter to jazz historian Fred Ramsey from a young playwright in Houston named Mack McCormick, mentioning that Lightnin' was somewhere in the city. When I drove to Houston and talked with Mack he shook his head.

'You can record him if you can find him.'

'You don't know where he is?'

'I've been trying to find him for five months.'

Mack had about given up on Lightnin', but he took me down to Dowling Street, the main business street of Houston's black section, and we retraced his steps, asking about Lightnin'. Mack's last contact had been a waitress at a bar a month before. She was off work, but she didn't live far. She opened the door part way, a beautiful young girl wearing a rumpled slip.

'Lightnin' left. I ain't seen him in two, three weeks.'

Cab drivers didn't know anything. After one look at us they decided we were either police or collection agents and they were vague about things as simple as the weather. Mack finally had an idea. Pawnshops. The first one we tried had Lightnin's address.

'Sam Hopkins. Electric guitar. He's in and out of here all the time. You want his address?'

It is probably just as well that the pawn broker had never tried to get in touch with Lightnin' at the address on the pawn card. It was a weathered building in a tenement section off Dowling. After much knocking a little boy came to one of the doors.

'Lightnin' don't stay here.'

Lightnin's sister was living across the street. He was willing to tell us that much. After a lengthy explanation an older woman said to go around back and try the doors there. Lightnin's sister was as carefully evasive.

'What you want him for?'

She was a tall, thin woman, her face hard. Finally she said to try a house with a red chair on the porch two blocks away. At the house a heavy, gray haired woman looked nervously out of a dark living room with a television set flickering in the corner. She said that Lightnin' stayed in a room in her house and she'd take a message for him. The next morning, after Mack had gone off to his job and I was driving again along Dowling, Lightnin' found me.

As we talked later I learned that he had been born Sam Hopkins on March 15th, 1912 on a farm outside of Centerville, Texas. He grew up on the farm, working from the time he was in his early teens. Centerville is north of Houston, on the road to Dallas. It's small – two or three hundred people – its buildings scattered around a mud lot that does as a town square. It's on a little rise, with a creek running beside the road near town, then crossing under the road a few miles north of town. The family is scattered, but an uncle still has a small farm just beyond the square and Lightnin's mother lives in a room over the feed store.

Sam – he didn't get the name Lightnin' until 1947 – began playing the guitar when he was very small, and one Sunday when the family went up to Buffalo, Texas for a Baptist Association picnic, he took his guitar with him. The singer hired for the afternoon was a fat, blind singer named Lemon Jefferson. Lemon shouted at him when Lightnin' finally got up enough nerve to play along, but when Lemon realized it was a little boy he laughed and showed him some of the things he knew on the guitar. Sam saw him from time to time when he was in Waxahatchie and learned little things from Lemon about his playing.

The area of Texas where Sam grew up has always had singers and a highly developed singing style. He picked up the intense, half-crying way with the blues that is associated with the empty farm country of Central Texas. The style is different from the strong work song rhythms of Louisiana's Leadbelly, or the harsh, droning sound of the Mississippi bluesmen. Lightnin' had a cousin who had a farm near Leona, Texas, five miles from Centerville, and it was his cousin who taught him what he needed to know about blues singing. His cousin was 'Texas' Alexander, one of the distinctive, talented blues artists who had recorded for OKeh records in the 1920s.

Sam got through the lean years of the depression working on the farm; then during the second World War he took his wife onto a large farm north of Houston run by a man named Tom Moore. Moore was the man Sam was singing about in his sardonic 'Tim Moore's Farm,' recorded in 1947. The change in the name from 'Tom' to 'Tim' was Lightnin's way to keep himself out of trouble. He went back to Centerville after the war, but an uncle, Lucien Hopkins, talked him into moving to Houston and trying to become a singer. Lightnin' worked around Houston accompanying Texas Alexander, then finally recorded himself for Hollywood's Alladin label, late in 1946. He was working with a piano player named 'Thunder' Smith; so they became 'Thunder' and 'Lightnin'. Early in 1946 he was back in Houston, and a singer working for a local record company, Gold Star Records, heard Lightnin' sitting on the curb, playing his guitar. He got him over to the studio and Lightnin' began recording for Gold Star. These were his first recordings as a solo blues singer, and despite the noisy surfaces on the records – it was still the period of material shortages following the war

– the new releases sold as many as eighty thousand copies of some of the more popular numbers.

The owner of Gold Star, a sincere young war veteran named Bill Quinn, still remembers Lightnin' with some wonderment. Lightnin' was as expensive to maintain as a small steamboat. Four hundred dollars, paid to him on Tuesday, would be gone on Thursday, and Lightnin' would be back in the office, asking for enough money to pay a bill at a bar where he had just bought drinks for everybody in the neighborhood. After a year and a half with Quinn, Lightnin' finally ran out of reasons to ask for more money. He travelled to New York and recorded most of his big hits for another small label with a blues line. This isn't done in the record business, and Quinn fired him. Over the next ten years Lightnin' recorded more than one hundred and ninety blues for several record companies. Most of the songs were original, but others were more or less derived from songs he had learned from listening to phonograph records. He sang Leroy Carr's 'How Long Blues' as 'Ain't It A Shame,' changing most of the words and the last part of the melody. He recorded one Lemon Jefferson song, the hymn 'See That My Grave Is Kept Clean', as 'One Kind Favor' on RPM Records.

When I finally found him he was anxious to begin recording again, and after I'd rented an acoustic guitar for him I carried the tape recorder I had in the trunk of my car into his shabby room on Hadley Street. He sang all afternoon, becoming more emotional and even more musically exciting as the hours passed. He sat for a moment, thinking, then he began humming and singing the Texas prison song 'Ain't No More Cane On This Brazos.'

> You ought to been on the Brazos in 1910,
> Bud Russell drove pretty women like he done ugly men…
> 'Smoky Hogg got a little of it, but there hasn't been nobody done it right.'
> My mama called me, I answered, 'Mam?'
> She said, 'Son, you tired of working?'
> I said, 'Mama, I sure am…'

Lightnin's expression was thoughtful as he drank more raw gin out of the cap of the bottle. Then he nodded his head and sang 'Penitentiary Blues,' creating a personal blues out of the old work song.

'Uumh, big Brazos here I come…
It's hard doing time for another man when there ain't a thing
poor Lightnin' done…

It was very close to the genesis of the blues.

As Lightnin' was finishing his last song we could hear people laughing and joking in the kitchen, right outside his room. When he sat back with his guitar the door opened and his sister looked in,

'How's it going, honey?'

Lightnin' was still subdued from the long emotional hours of singing. He shrugged. Three or four people came in as Lightnin' was counting his money. His sister was there, there was a younger girl, his sister's boyfriend, and a friend of Lightnin's. The landlady was looking over their shoulders as Lightnin' straightened up, looking very tired and alone. Finally all of them left for a small, noisy saloon at the corner, Lightnin' trailing along behind them with a quiet friend who had been with us earlier in the afternoon.

Lightnin', in his way, is a magnificent figure. He is one of the last of his kind, a lonely, bitter man who brings to the blues the intensity and pain of the hours in the hot sun scraping at the hardened earth, humming and singing to make the hours pass. The blues will go on, but the country blues, and the great singers who created from the raw melodies of the work song and the field song the richness and intensity of the country blues, will pass with singers like this thin, intense man from Centerville, Texas.

(1959)

2. The Country Blues

Robert Johnson

My first book, *Jazz: New Orleans, 1885-1957*, was published by a jazz researcher and amateur publisher named Walter C. Allen. This was in the spring of 1958, and in the fall, after Ann and I had returned to New York from the trip to Andros Island in the Bahamas, the writer Nat Hentoff called and asked if I wanted to talk about the book and play some of the New Orleans recordings that Folkways had released on a radio program he presented with composer and jazz historian Gunther Schuller. At the end of the program Nat asked me what I was working on next, and I said I was going to write a book about the country blues. He looked thoughtful and told me to send a sample of what I was doing to the editor, Ted Asmussen at Rinehart Publishers. I hadn't begun the writing, but I had been planning a book that would present the country blues since 1954, when I had begun interviewing veteran blues musicians in Louisiana, Alabama, Texas, and Tennessee. Over the next ten days, when I could put together a few spare hours, I sat in the littered artist's studio on Broadway, just below Union Square, where I slept on a seamy couch I'd borrowed from sculptor Waldemar Baronowski, and wrote four or five very short sample chapters. I dropped them by the Rinehart office on a Thursday, and the next Monday morning there was a telegram in my mailbox at the bottom of the staircase saying that Rinehart would be pleased to publish the book, they also had an English publisher for it, and would I please come by the office and sign a contract.

There was an advance, but it was small, so I continued to talk to publishers, and I soon had a contract to write a history of jazz in New York City for Doubleday, ostensibly with a friend, Leonard Kundstadt, who was co-editor of a two-man jazz record magazine called Record Research. With the second contract there was enough money for me to plan the travelling I had to do in the South. There was also enough money for me to make the first payment on a better tape recorder – an Ampex, to replace my much-travelled 1953 Pentron – and to give up the day job I had packing art reproductions for the Dollar Print Club

Ghetto homes in Birmingham, Alabama, 1964
(Photo: Ann Charters)

on Hudson Street, where some nights I slept on the floor under the shipping table. I borrowed Ann's green Chevrolet coupé, packed the tape recorder, the microphones and tapes in the trunk, and drove South, stopping first in Atlanta, then Birmingham, and going on to New Orleans, Houston, Dallas, Mississippi, Memphis, St. Louis, and Chicago. At the end of the journey, in February, 1959, I had enough new material to begin the book.

I was so immersed in the blues – so overwhelmed by the prolonged glimpse I had into this now familiar world of the other America – that the book was written in one sustained burst of thirty-six days in the one-room basement apartment I had rented for Ann on E 46th Street in Brooklyn after our marriage in April. I spent the days in the newspaper archives of the Schomburg Collection in Harlem, or sorting through notes and deciding what I wanted to use in the next chapter. I wrote all night at a small table in our little kitchen alcove while Ann slept a few feet away. When I took the manuscript to Rinehart I put the notes away, took a deep breath, and turned to the jazz history for Doubleday. I left the new manuscript with the editor in September, when we moved out of the apartment and drove to California. We stayed in Memphis for a few days to complete the album I had begun the winter before with Furry Lewis, then continued to Los Angeles to spend the rest of the fall with her parents before we left for a year in Europe.

The Country Blues has remained in print for almost fifty years, despite its naivety and the many mistakes I made in the very sketchy historical backgrounds that I had at that time. I conscientiously set out to correct the errors in two later books, *The Bluesmen* and *Sweet as the Showers of Rain*, but although they are much more detailed and historically more accurate they have never been as popular. They have now been reprinted together in one volume titled *The Bluesmakers*. Despite the faults of *The Country Blues* it seemed to express the excitement so many of us felt at discovering the beginnings of the blues, and the book's approach, which was to present the country blues as its African American audience had responded to it, presented an outline for the history of this new idiom which is still largely followed today. Also, with the book I tried to make a romantic story of the journey to search for the older blues artists. In the long months that I spent driving endless miles through the South on that winter's research trip I found myself feeling very alone, realizing that I was trying to do a job that was much too ambitious for one person. I decided that if, with the book, I could make readers see what there was to be found, they might become enthusiastic enough to take on some of the research. The book did this part of its job – when Ann and I returned to New York in 1961, after our year that we spent mostly living and writing in a bedsit in Edinburgh, we discovered that everywhere in the South excited young blues collectors had tracked down nearly every one of the old blues artists who could still be located, and over the next few years other collectors found the rest.

Although I tried in the book to present the country blues artists in terms of the popular tastes and responses of their own audience, I made one exception, for which I apologized in the chapter itself. The exception was Robert Johnson. As is evident from the chapter, almost nothing was known about his life, but I had first heard his music in 1948, when I was rehearsing with a traditional jazz group led by trumpeter Dick Oxtot in a back-garden shingle house in Berkeley, California. There were two records that we used to end the rehearsals – one night we would end with the worn single Dick had of Blind Willie Johnson's 'Dark Was The Night (Cold Was The Ground)' and the next night would end with an acetate copy someone had given him of Robert Johnson's 'Stones In My Passway'. I hadn't found any trace of Johnson when I was gathering material in Texas in the 1950s, but I didn't feel that I could write the book without including him, since he was one of the most breathtaking blues artists I had ever heard. As far as I knew, this chapter was the first description of Johnson and his blues, and the album that was released with the book in September 1959 included his 'Preachin' Blues', the first reissue of one of his 1930s recordings.

From *The Country Blues* (1959)
Chapter 16. Robert Johnson

I got stones in my pathway [sic]*, and my road is dark as night.*

The young black audience for whom the blues has been a natural emotional expression had never concerned itself with artistic pretensions. By their standards, Robert Johnson was sullen and brooding, and his records sold very poorly. It is artificial to consider him by the standards of a different audience that during his short life was not even aware of him, but by these standards he is one of the superbly creative blues singers.

Almost nothing is known about his life. In 1941, Muddy Waters, a young singer who was recording for the Library of Congress, said that Johnson had been raised near the Mississippi, north of Clarksdale, but he had never seen him. Will Shade, the Memphis musician, was playing in a roadhouse in West Memphis, Arkansas, and Johnson came in and played with the band. He was murdered in San Antonio, Texas in 1937, a few weeks after his last recordings. From the little that Muddy Waters and Will Shade have remembered, Johnson seems to have been about thirty years old when he recorded. In the early years of the depression he went into Arkansas, then moved to San Antonio. There is a story that his first recordings were done in a billiard parlor and a drunken fight broke out after he had recorded. Someone threw a billiard ball at one of the engineers and smashed several of the masters. The company ledger sheets for the recordings, November 23rd, 26th and 27th, 1936, list only a single recording for the second session; so the story may be true.

The next spring, June 19th and 20th, he recorded in Dallas; then returned to San Antonio. Sometime during the summer he was poisoned by his common-law wife.

It seemed possible that he might have lived in Clarksdale, about thirty miles south of his home, but he seems to have moved north, into West Memphis. His name was not known to anyone in Clarksdale. San Antonio is a large, sprawling city, and despite weeks of questioning, no one could be found who remembered him. He is only a name on a few recordings.

In three days of recording in 1936 and two days in 1937, Johnson did twenty-seven sides for the American Recording Corporation. Three were rejected, but twenty-four were released on the Vocalion label in 1937 and 1938, and six sides were used on the cheaper Conqueror label. There were probably other sides released on the ARC labels – Melotone, Perfect, Oriole, Romeo, and Banner – but the records are very rare and it is difficult to determine which sides were used.

There was almost every kind of blues on the records. Robert Johnson is an artist like Blind Willie Johnson; the intensity of his own performance reshaped the songs into searing, harsh poetry. There is a suggestion of Scrapper Blackwell's guitar style in his playing, but he uses the guitar as a thin, droning undertone or as an extension of his singing, and his style is distinctly his own. For many of his accompaniments he uses a bottle neck to slide on the strings, giving the guitar an insistent, whining sound.

He was consistently brilliant, but there are four or five records that seem to be identified with him. These are '32-20 Blues' and 'Last Fair Deal Gone Down' on Vo 03445; 'Preachin' Blues' on Vo 04630, 'Stones in My Pathway' [sic] on Vo 03723, and 'Hellhound on My Trail' on Vo 03623. They are among his finest blues, but many of the other blues have a superb sexual imagery. 'Terraplane Blues' on Vo 03416, is an extended sexual image, elaborated until the blues is an imaginative poetic image, rather than a thin series of double meanings. 'Come on in My Kitchen', Vo 03563, is another sexual blues,

> Come on in my kitchen, it's raining outside,

but he sings it in a gruff, heavy voice, as though he were unsure of himself with the girl, then his voice falls and the guitar almost stops, playing a halting series of notes on the upper strings. He mumbles, almost inaudibly,

> Can't you hear that rain … don't you hear that rain outside…

and the notes from the guitar suddenly seem to evoke the smell of a summer rainstorm, and the water streaming down a shadowed window pane…

A blues that was the first of the Dallas recordings, 'Stones in My Pathway', seemed to express the brooding pain of his short life:

> I got stones in my pathway, and my road is dark as night…

(1959)

Fifteen years later I was in a little Mississippi delta community on a warm Sunday morning, standing beside the road, listening to the voices of people gathering for services in the shabby wooden building that was their church. The cluster of shacks against the Mississippi levee was called Commerce, and it was at the end of a hazy road that went a few miles to the larger town of Robinsville. Robert Johnson was no longer only a name on the label of some old blues singles. The older Mississippi singers like Son House who had been rediscovered in the 1960s had told us enough so we knew now that Robert Johnson had been one of the children playing on the levee back of the shacks, and that his father had walked the unpaved road to Robinsonville so many times that he had been given the nickname 'Robert Dusty'.

Johnson's name is so much part of the story of the blues today that blues history is continually being revised to enlarge his very small role in the story. It might be more accurate to say that it was Johnson's influence on the electric blues of Muddy Waters, and through Muddy, the next generation's rock and roll, that has shaped the story. The naive chapter in *The Country Blues* seems almost have be written in a different language, but I sometimes look at it again to remind myself of how little I knew then, and of how much we have learned about the blues over the forty years. In the time that has passed since that Sunday in the delta, Johnson's records have been reissued as bestselling CDs, and he has become a tourist attraction in the Mississippi countryside where he grew up and was murdered. Visitors can see at least two cemeteries where he is buried, and if they show enough interest someone will probably repeat for them the earnest story that became one of the myths of 1960s – that Johnson learned his guitar skills by selling his soul to the Devil by the crossroads.

Certainly the most exciting new glimpse of Johnson was the discovery of two photographs. In them he looked like the bluesman he had been when he recorded. He was young, he had an air of easy confidence, and his fingers – as the first A&R director who recorded him remembered – were long and beautifully shaped. His new audience, which came of age in the 1970s and 1980s, wasn't concerned that much of the style of his blues was borrowed from Kokomo Arnold, or that the 'Preachin' Blues' was his effort to copy a recording done several years previously by Son House, the older man who taught him some of his style, or that some of his memorable guitar fills were borrowed from Lonnie Johnson or Scrapper Blackwell. They were also not concerned with the series of law suits and claims and counter claims that for many years were argued over the rights to his song copyrights. Since the publication of the chapter in *The Country Blues* more than forty years ago, the nearly forgotten, obscure Mississippi singer Robert Johnson has become an American icon, and that, in itself, adds a new dimension to what the blues has come to mean in today's culture.

3. The 'Crazy Blues'

A few days after I had taken the manuscript of *The Country Blues* to Rinehart, I began working on the history of jazz in New York City that Leonard Kundstadt and I had signed a contract to write for Doubleday. Len's role in our collaboration was to sort through the mountains of research material on jazz and popular music in New York City that he had been collecting for years as part of his work as co-editor of *Record Research Magazine*. The entire staff of the magazine consisted of Len and his partner Bob Colton, and they managed to put together issue after issue from crammed office spaces they found in rundown buildings in Brooklyn, the last of their offices on Grand Avenue close to Atlantic Avenue. Ann was the only employee I ever saw in the office. For a few cold winter months she sat in the middle of piled records and heaped newspapers and magazines and typed their auction lists, wearing gloves, since there wasn't enough money to heat their little space.

Len was a warm, genuinely sincere man with almost frightening nervous energy. He travelled everywhere with his dog, Whiskers, who lived in the back seat of his old-model car. After he met blues veteran Victoria Spivey he became her enthusiastic supporter and established a record label for her, Spivey Records, which brought back-up musicians like Lonnie Johnson, members of the Muddy Waters band and a very young Bob Dylan into the studio for her sessions. At her death he had been her companion for several years. In that summer of 1959 Len came by early every morning – standing outside our street level window and playing a Johnny Dunn-style blues chorus on his kazoo to wake us up. He would leave me with the pile of material he'd found in his archives the day before and drive off with Whiskers to continue his eternal search for old records to list in their magazine's columns of auction items. *Jazz: A History of the New York Scene* was written in another excited burst in a stretch of forty-two days over the rest of the summer. Two of the book's early chapters were devoted to the sudden and unexpected blues boom of the early 1920s.

After the long, lean years of blues record sales, when even a Muddy Waters or a B. B. King barely nudged the sales charts, it was difficult in the beginning for me to imagine myself back in those brief, dizzying days when the blues was its day's equivalent of rap or grunge rock. All the usual things we know from today's music business went on – money in uncounted amounts, avid attention from the press, law suits, temperaments, more law suits, and even a prison sentence for one of the leading figures in the blues craze, composer Perry Bradford, who wrote the 'Crazy Blues.' None of the storms reached the level of the murderous rivalry between the two major hip hop labels of the 1990s, which culminated in the murder of two of the style's biggest artists, Tu Pac Shakur and Notorious B. I. G., but things might have stayed a little calmer because the blues bloom lasted only three or four years, and after the first flurry the money at stake was less tempting. Certainly the record industry rushes down some of the same winding back streets every time a new style makes its presence known, and there is a flash of young talent looking for some of the heavy business deals and the dazzling attention that had been paid to the old stylish trend they've just pushed off the pop world's unsteady throne.

In part it was possible to write this chapter, and the following chapter in the book, 'If You Crave Those Jazz Moanin' Blues…', in such detail because of two articles which Len Kundstadt found in the Harlem newspaper, *The Amsterdam News*. A persevering reporter named Dan Burley did two extensive profiles, one of Mamie Smith and the other of Perry Bradford, which appeared in the paper in January and February 1940, when Burley had the chance to talk to both veterans of those colorful years. Of course, Len and I also had to deal with Perry himself, who hung over us so watchfully that I decided I would document his brief jail sentence with direct quotations from the newspaper articles that reported it. If Perry decided he wanted to sue someone over our disclosure he'd have to go to the newspapers themselves. Again, as in *The Country Blues*, this was before the flood of reissues that brought the world of African American music to a new generation of listeners, so I was careful to list the original label and catalog number of the recordings I mentioned in the text. In those years this was all we had to listen to.

From *Jazz: A History of the New York Scene* (1962)

Every afternoon an edgy, slightly built young entertainer named Perry Bradford dropped into the Colored Vaudeville Benevolent Association clubroom at 424 Lenox Avenue and spent two or three hours working over new songs on the piano. Usually no one paid much attention to him, but if he started to play a blues someone would call him to the phone or ask him to go over a number for them. If he persisted, someone would even buy him a drink. In 1919 the New York musicians didn't care for blues songs. To them the blues stood for everything they had tried to leave behind them. Perry was from Mississippi, by way of Georgia, but he felt that blues songs had commercial possibilities, and he kept playing over his little tunes. Will Marion Cook, the concert violinist, was the only musician who encouraged him. Cook had spent much of his youth in Berlin, studying the violin, and his European training seemed to have made it possible for him to create a little distance for himself from the racial climate in the United States. The blues, despite their rough vernacular language and their expression of an even rougher social atmosphere, didn't make him uncomfortable. When someone would ask Perry why he kept playing that kind of music he would just smile and keep right on playing. Like many other young men who had been drawn to the glitter of New York, Perry had determination to spare. After a few months the others nicknamed him 'Mule,' and the name stuck.

Usually Perry spent every morning walking the streets from one record company to another. He was trying to interest a recording director in some of his songs, and he was trying to interest someone in a young singer, Mamie Smith, who was singing one of his songs in a show called *Maid of Harlem* at the Lincoln Theatre on 135th Street. She was a 'heavy-hipped, heavy-voiced' woman, light complexioned, with wavy brown hair. She wasn't from New York either. She had left Cincinnati when she was ten, dancing with a troupe called The Four Dancing Mitchells. When she was fifteen, Tutt Whitney had offered her a job in the chorus of his *Smart Set* company, and after a season she came into Harlem with the show. After some weeks she decided to stay in New York and began singing in some of the cabarets – Barron Wilkin's, Leroy's, Edmund's, and the popular Gold Grabbin's. About this time she was married to a comedian named Gardner. Perry heard her singing in one of the cabarets and took her into the *Maid of Harlem* show with him. She was a sensation with Perry's song, 'Harlem Blues'.

Perry had gotten so used to being turned down at the record companies that he could just look at the expression on the secretary's face, nod his head, and walk out. He walked the streets through the summer and fall of 1919; then in the winter, when he was beginning to wonder if he was ever going to find someone who would listen to him, Otto Heineman, the president of OKeh Records, unexpectedly told Perry they might be interested in a blues, since white artists like the 'Red Hot Mama' Sophie Tucker and the popular recording star Marion Harris had been featuring blues songs for three or four years. Harris at one point advertised herself as the 'Queen of the Blues', and her singles were selling in large quantities. OKeh was a new company, and their struggles to get the name established had not been very successful. At this point Heineman was ready to try an unknown singer, who was at least appearing locally. Perry played a few of his numbers for Fred Hager, the recording director. Hager decided against doing a blues, but he was willing to try two of the other songs Perry had, and he told him to bring Mamie Smith to the studio on W 45th Street.

A few weeks later Mamie recorded two of Perry's songs, 'That Thing Called Love' and 'You Can't Keep A Good Man Down'. Hager supervised the recording and used the house orchestra, the Rega Dance Orchestra. Working with him was a young assistant, Ralph Peer, who was to go on to direct the recording activities in the South for Victor Records in the late 1920s, and with his discovery of Jimmy Rogers and The Carter Family at a series of sessions in Bristol, Tennessee in 1927 set the country music recording industry in motion. The record that Hager did with Mamie, OKeh 4113, was released without any sort of publicity in July 1920. OKeh seemed almost reluctant to advertise that they were recording a black singer. The record was listed as by 'Mamie Smith, contralto,' in their July release lists. Although the title suggests a love ballad, Mamie sang with a strong blues feeling and within a few days the word had gotten around Harlem, 'Mamie's on a record.' So few black artists had been recorded, a release by someone like Mamie, who was well known and very popular, attracted considerable attention. The busy Harlem newspapers soon began mentioning the record, and OKeh finally woke up the fact that they had something with commercial possibilities.

The company was still not convinced that it was Mamie who was selling the songs, and Hager spent the summer trying to tempt Sophie Tucker away from her other contracts to record Perry's 'Harlem Blues.' Perry would drop by and play it over on the studio piano. He decided to change the title to 'Crazy Blues', at Mr. Heineman's suggestion, and the Pace-Handy Music Company published it in the fall. A few months later this was to cause Perry considerable trouble, but at that moment he wasn't worried about it. He realized that success wasn't far away.

His immediate obstacle was the song's new publisher, Pace-Handy Music. The Handy in the partnership was W. C. Handy, who had helped set the blues craze going with his 'St. Louis Blues' in 1914. He and his partner Harry Pace continually advertised that they were the 'only genuine colored house,' with their goal a new interest in the African American artist and his music, but they tried to stop Perry from recording the tune with Mamie Smith. They were more excited about a proposed Victor Records recording of the tune by one of the new white 'blues' singers, Aileen Stanley. They thought they could make more money with it. Perry, however, had come too close to be headed off, and he went ahead with his recording. He had finally talked OKeh into letting him use a Harlem jazz band for the accompaniment, arguing that the Rega Dance Orchestra wasn't very rhythmic. Even Otto Heineman had to admit that much, and he told Perry to get his band together.

In November 1920, Okeh released 'Crazy Blues' and 'It's Right Here For You (If You Don't Come Get It – 'Taint No Fault O'Mine)' on OKeh 4169. The label read 'Popular Blues Song' with the artists 'Mamie Smith and Her Jazz Hounds'. The Jazz Hounds were a noisy five-piece band with Addington Major, cornet; Ernest Elliot, clarinet; 'Dope' Andrews, trombone; Leroy Parker, violin; and Willie 'The Lion' Smith, piano. Before the recording session Hager took Perry aside and explained to him that it was very important to have a sweet, singing accompaniment for Mamie's voice. A little rhythm was all right, but keep it light. Perry nodded, went into the studio, and just winked at the musicians. When the recording light flashed on, they backed off a little from the old-fashioned recording horns and played the piece with a raucous cheerfulness. Mamie shouted the lyrics into the horn, and the startled OKeh engineer found himself recording the first actual blues-styled performance by a black artist with a black accompaniment.

When the record was released, Perry took a few copies, put them in his brief case, and took them to shops in Harlem. A few days later he left New York on tour with a Shubert production, *Dearie,* doing a comedy routine. At the end of the month someone at OKeh noticed that 75,000 copies of 'Crazy Blues' were listed on the books as having been sold to Harlem record shops in a little less than four weeks. Mr. Heineman and Fred Hager looked at the figures and decided there must be a mistake somewhere. They called their shipping director and he assured them that 75,000 copies of the record had been distributed. Still dubious they sent a salesman named Stanford up to Harlem to see what was happening to all the copies of 'Crazy Blues'. Stanford came back with the news that the copies were selling, thousands of them. That was enough for OKeh. They began wiring theaters playing the Shubert show to try and find Perry. They got him back to New York and Mamie into the studio, and they began turning out records. Perry replaced Smith at the piano, a violinist named Parker was added, and the cornetist Johnny Dunn replaced Addington Major. Dunn was the third side of the triangle – Mamie, Perry, and Johnny – who for a few years were to turn the blues record industry into a million dollar business.

Dunn had come up from Memphis a few months before Perry hired him for the Jazz Hounds, and he had been introduced to Harlem audiences on the stage of the Lafayette Theatre, doing his specialties with W. C. Handy's blues orchestra. His tone was thin and hard, and his technique was limited, but he could play more blues than anyone else in New York. He was the first real blues instrumentalist to record, even releasing solo sides with just rhythm accompaniment. He was the first cornet player to use a plunger, an ordinary plumber's toilet plunger, for a mute, and he introduced the 'wa-wa' style which is still a standard effect for jazz trumpet and trombone. He had studied with Professor Hamilton at Play Street High School in Memphis, then learned his blues with bands in the city. Handy heard him and brought him to New York, featuring him on two Handy compositions, 'Bugle Blues' and 'Ole Miss Rag.' Johnny was a tall, thin man, dark-skinned, with deep, searching eyes. He dressed sharply, with a flair for fashion. He was respected and admired for his revolutionary cornet style, but he had few close friends. People around him considered him a conceited dandy, and despite his success most of the musicians in New York were pleased when Louis Armstrong came to New York in the fall of 1924 and took over the spotlight. Today Dunn is mostly remembered by jazz historians for a classic date he made with Jelly Roll Morton in New

York in the late 1920s, his acid trumpet tone working brilliantly against Morton's solid, steady arrangements.

In 1921 the three of them, Perry, Mamie and Johnny, had the blues world in the palms of their hands, but there was so much money coming in and so much sudden attention that everything became very confused. OKeh neglected to sign Johnny to an exclusive contract, and after hearing him from the audience at the Lafayette Theatre a representative of Columbia Records went backstage and signed him to a contract. Several of Dunn's most interesting blues records were made accompanying Edith Wilson, a fine early blues singer who was recording exclusively for Columbia. The early blues recordings still lacked the emotional fervor of the recordings that were made a few years later, but Edith's recording of 'What Do You Care?', Columbia 3674, with a series of brilliant cornet breaks by Dunn, is one of the classic early blues releases.

Sometime during these years Mamie's husband, the comedian Gardner, died in Chicago. For a time she was interested in a singing waiter named 'Smitty' who worked at the Sugar Cane on Fifth Avenue, then a piano player from Philadelphia, then a hefty business manager named Ocey Wilson. Mamie was jealous and very quick tempered, and at the first sign that her current favorite was interested in someone else she would rush out the door looking for him, her curls flying, and her maid trailing along behind, trying to slow her down. When Mamie was excited she just walked up to her errant lover and opened fire with a revolver that she kept for such emergencies. She never hit anyone, but Ocey Wilson and a man named Sam Walker once dodged Mamie's errant gunfire on 135th Street. She fought with the musicians in the band and the sidemen came and went with disturbing rapidity. Dunn's replacement was a young New York cornet player named Bub Miley, who didn't have Dunn's fire, but had the flexibility that Dunn lacked. When her stage show was playing in St. Joseph, Missouri Mamie heard a young tenor saxophone player named Coleman Hawkins and finally induced him to join the band. Later both Miley and Hawkins, one with Duke Ellington and the other with Fletcher Henderson, were to leave a lasting imprint on the development of jazz.

Mamie's band was making considerable money during the years between 1921 and 1923, her years of greatest popularity. She could sing any kind of song, and her name on a record was enough to sell it. She couldn't read music, but she picked up a tune quickly, and if she were in the mood she could record nine or ten songs in an afternoon in the studio. Her musicians were paid fifty dollars a side, so they considered part of their job was teaching Mamie as many tunes as they could. They'd spend most of a road trip feverishly playing songs for her, so they could pick up fat recording checks in New York.

Mamie herself made so much money she never really counted it. It is estimated that she made nearly $100,000 in recording royalties alone. She was making between $1000 and $1500 a week in the large theaters in New York and Chicago and nearly as much in the smaller theaters in the new Theater Owners Booking Agency, the T. O. B. A. circuit, which had been set up to handle black acts exclusively. She played the circuit '...from end to end and over and over again.' For a one-night appearance in Billy Sunday's evangelist tabernacle in Norfolk she was paid a high of $2000. There were a number of motion picture shorts, the most successful a one-reel affair called 'Jail House Blues' with Porter Grainger, Billy Mills, and the comedian Tutt Whitney, who had brought her into New York with his *Smart Set* show.

The money that Mamie made was spent almost as fast as she made it. It went into riotous years of sumptuous living, and despite the occasional storms with her current favorite she didn't regret a minute of it. She bought large houses on 130th Street, St. Nicholas Place, and Long Island. Visitors at 130th Street remember lavish furnishing, with an electric player-piano in every room. The closets were stuffed with player-piano rolls. She bought ermine robes, silver gowns, gowns of gold cloth. For an engagement at the Bal Tabarin in Atlantic City she spent $3000 for a cape of ostrich plumes. Standing in a spotlight on a darkened stage, the silver gown shimmering, the ostrich plumes gently swaying, the diamonds on her fingers and around her neck glittering, Mamie was a breathtaking sight. She didn't even have to sing. She just walked grandly across the stage and there were storms of applause. In the spring of 1922 the OKeh company proclaimed a 'Mamie Smith' Week.' She received gifts from many of her admirers, several proposals of marriage, and her royalties from the company.

Perry was making almost as much money as Mamie was, despite the confusion. With her unpredictable temper he had to struggle continually to keep her band together. Over the months he hired, and had to fire, dozens of promising young musicians, including Buster Bailey and Bob Fuller, both clarinet players, and the pianist Charlie

Matson. He finally decided to turn Mamie's affairs over to someone else, and he sold the management contract he had signed with her to Maurice Fulcher, a white booking agent. Fulcher also made considerable money with Mamie, but between her temper, the continually changing orchestra, and the endless recordings, he earned every cent of it.

Perry and Mamie had a stormy relationship. At one point he is said to have walked into the OKeh studios and declared, 'Mamie, you've made me a rich man. Here's $1000 for you.' But a few months later they had a 'misunderstanding' over some of Perry's songs. He tried to serve her with a summons to appear in court, but she refused to accept the papers. He decided he'd serve the papers himself and climbed across the rooftops on W 135th Street to Number 44, where Mamie was then living. As soon as she saw him she went for her revolver and Perry had to beat a hasty retreat. They were able to settle their differences, but Perry soon found himself in considerable legal difficulty.

Perry's troubles started with the original 'Crazy Blues.' When he interested OKeh in it, it was called the 'Harlem Blues', but it seems to had other names before that. In June, 1921 the song publishing house of Frederick V. Bowers, Inc., sought an injunction restraining Perry Bradford, the 'colored song writer and publisher', from publishing and selling the song 'Crazy Blues', and also asking that thirteen mechanical companies be restrained from paying Bradford royalties on the song. Bowers claimed that Perry had sold them the song under the title 'The Broken Hearted Blues' in 1918. Max Kortlander of the Q. R. S. company also tried to bring suit again him, claiming that Perry had sold him the same song under the title 'Wicked Blues'. Perry finally settled out of court with the various claimants, and on December 21st, 1921 the New York *Clipper* reported:

> Perry Bradford…has settled all suits which have been filed against
> him for royalties on his song, the 'Crazy Blues'.

The next year he was in more serious trouble. He published Lem Fowler's song 'He May Be Your Man But He Comes To See Me Some Time', even though Fowler seems to have already sold the song to the Ted Browne Music Company in Chicago. The song was so successful that nearly $10,000 in royalties were involved by the time the suit brought by the rival music company reached court. At the hearing both Fowler and Spencer Williams, also testifying in Perry's behalf, perjured themselves in their testimony, which was a criminal offense. The *Clipper* reported:

> Later Williams and Fowler admitted that they had committed perjury and made false affidavits at the instigation of Bradford. Perry was tried for subornation of witnesses the first week of January 1923. He was convicted and sentenced 'to serve four months in the Essex Country Penitentiary'.

Perry was always quick to challenge any infringement of his own copyrights. One night he was sitting down front at the Standard Theatre in Philadelphia when a girl named Valaida Snow performed her act singing and playing the trumpet. The song was by another composer, so Perry paid no attention to it; but when she started to play the trumpet she played a melodic figure that Johnny Dunn had used on one of Mamie's records.

Perry leaped to his feet, shouting, 'You can't use that! That's copyrighted!'

Mamie's first great record, 'Crazy Blues,' which Perry had written, under whatever title he'd given it, sold and sold. In seven months it has sometimes been estimated that over a million copies of the record were sold everywhere in the United States, though this figure was probably closer to 350,000. Its success had opened up new areas of commercial possibility that the record companies hadn't dreamed existed. Virtually every company recorded Perry's tune; even the very respectable Edison record company brought Harlem entertainer Noble Sissle into the studio to sing the 'Crazy Blues' for them. Edison, who had invented the phonograph almost fifty years before, probably wouldn't have approved of the song, but the recording director finally decided that the company was going to have to try recording the blues to stay alive in the competitive record industry of the early 1920s. They just didn't tell the venerable old man about everything they were doing.

For some reason Columbia Records was not aware of the OKeh recording of 'Crazy Blues' for several weeks after its release. They had picked the tune up from the publisher's catalogs and were interested in recording it. An entertainer who had been doing some recording for them, Mary Stafford, recorded it with a small instrumental group; then the Columbia attorney, a man named Gomez, wrote to Perry:

> I'm going to make the 'Crazy Blues' a big hit for you, if you'll waive your royalties.

At this point the OKeh record, on which Perry was getting two cents a copy royalty, had sold over 100,000 copies. He answered with a classic show business flourish,

> Yours of even date and so important that I am even answering right away, which is – please be advised that the only thing Perry Bradford waives is the American Flag.

Yrs.
Perry Bradford

(1962)

4. Faces of the Blues

In the first years of the blues rediscoveries there was a heady level of excitement just at finding that the blues was more than names on old phonograph records. For any of us who had come to the blues through our interest in classic jazz or through our involvement in the folk movement, the modern electric blues was considered with some wariness as an intrusion on the 'folk' spirit of the blues. For myself, there was also a sense of urgency. The younger blues artists in places like Chicago or Detroit could wait – whatever we thought of their style of the blues. The older blues artists who still were living in rented rooms or tenement apartments in cities like Memphis or Atlanta didn't have so many years ahead of them, and if we didn't save their stories and their music their rich legacy would slip away from us.

In the early 1960s, after the publication of *The Country Blues* I travelled again and again to the South, often for Prestige Records, which had started a Bluesville series for the country blues, sometimes on my own to record other blues artists, either with the thought that Folkways Records might be interested in what I was finding, or for the documentary film *The Blues* that Ann and I made in 1962. It was during these years that *The Poetry of the Blues* was published and the first chapters were written of *The Bluesmen*. Much of the writing, however, was for record companies, and many of the notes and promotion pieces were a series of blues portraits, still wide-eyed with wonder that here were the faces and the songs of artists who had seemed as lost to us as the passenger pigeon or the herds of buffalo that had once darkened the hills of the West.

Furry Lewis

One of the most influential introductions to the acoustic country blues in the early 1950s was the three volume set of reissues of commercial singles from the 1920s and 1930s, *American Folk Music*. It had been compiled by a film artist and record collector named Harry Smith and

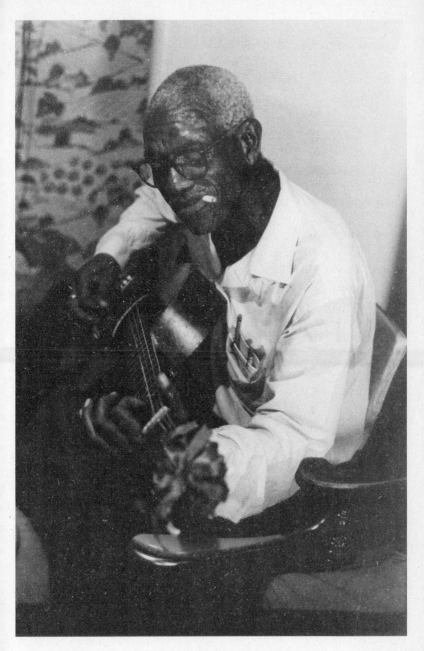

Furry Lewis in his kitchen, Memphis, 1962
(Photo: Ann Charters)

Moses Asch for Asch's Folkways Records and released with Smith's idiosyncratic notes in 1952. The six LPs in the set were a wonderful melange of folk styles, including everything from mountain ballads to cowboy songs, cajun dances, singing evangelists, and blues singers. When Ann and I began living together in her Berkeley backyard cottage, our first purchase was the set of all three double LP albums, which at that time cost the very daunting sum of $34.

Of the blues artists who were included on the set, two of them, Furry Lewis and Mississippi John Hurt, turned out to be very much alive and still playing almost as well as they had thirty years before. Sleepy John Estes, who was also included on one of the albums, was blind and in poor health when he was found again in a shack outside of Brownsville, Tennessee, but following his rediscovery he also performed and toured again, although his playing never recovered its early fluency. John Hurt, with his gentle songs and his flowing acoustic guitar accompaniments, was to become a much loved performer at the Newport Folk Festivals and a major stylistic influence on a generation of folk blues guitarists. Furry influenced almost as many young instrumentalists with his slide guitar style, and his 'John Henry' became a popular acoustic slide style piece for many young musicians.

I first recorded Furry in February 1959 with a portable tape recorder in his room on a back street in Memphis, as part of the long trip to search for the backgrounds for the book *The Country Blues*. Ann and I returned to Memphis in October to add enough material to fill out an album. The album was released in 1960 by Folkways Records. When I returned from Europe in 1961 Ken Goldstein, who was supervising the Prestige Records Bluesville series, sent me back to Memphis to do two more albums with Furry. For the 1961 recordings I used Sam Philip's Sun Studio, and the engineer was Scotty Moore, the guitar player who had done the first singles with Elvis Presley, and who was still working with him when there was a movie in production. The sessions with Furry were a long series of discussions between the two guitarists about Furry's Mississippi tunings. We would begin a song and I would hear Scotty's voice over the studio loudspeaker, 'What's that tuning you're using, Furry?' and I would sit waiting while Scotty came into the studio and sat with Furry until they'd figured it out. Sun Studio, as I found when I listened to the tapes later, also had an echo chamber built into their sound system, and Furry's old blues took on a modern tone that I thought was only on the studio's playback system.

When I investigated, I found that the echo chamber was a closet in the hall beside the control room. The sound from a small speaker in the ceiling of the closet was picked up by a cheap microphone on the floor. I was upset with myself for not becoming aware that I was making recordings with what I thought was an unnatural sound, but I was the only one who seemed to notice. The notes to Furry's albums were written in 1960 and 1961.

From the Folkways record *Furry Lewis*, and the Prestige Records *Back On My Feet Again* and *Done Changed My Mind*

The last time I saw Furry Lewis he was chopping weeds on a highway embankment near the outskirts of Memphis, Tennessee, the town he has lived in since he was six years old. He was wearing faded denim overalls, a khaki work shirt, a bright red handkerchief tied around his neck. It was a hot day, and his sweat soaked shirt clung to his back. He was chopping at the heavy plants with a hoe, stopping every now and then to wipe off his face. Furry has worked as a laborer for the city of Memphis for nearly thirty-five years. He chops weeds, cuts grass, rakes leaves, picks up trash – whatever needs done around the city's streets and parks. He limps a little, but watching him work it's still a surprise to notice that he has only one leg. He lost his left leg in a railroad accident in 1917 and he's worn an artificial limb ever since. His hair is gray, his body is thin and bent, his face is lined, but in many ways he is still a young man. He was wearing a shapeless, tan felt hat, the brim turned up all around and there was a note painfully lettered on the front with a pencil, 'KID FURRY – Have Gun, Will Travel.'

Will Shade, the guitar and harmonica player who had organized the Memphis Jug Band for Victor Records in 1927, had remembered Furry in a conversation in February, 1959. Will and I were sitting in his room, passing the bright winter afternoon talking about the blues and the older blues singers. I looked out of the window, over the roofs toward Beale Street, and said to him, thinking out loud as much as anything else, 'I certainly would like to have heard some of those old singers, Jim Jackson, Furry Lewis, John Estes, Frank Stokes…'

Will leaned out of his chair and called to his wife, Jennie Mae, who was working in the kitchen.

'Jennie Mae, when was the last time you saw that fellow they call 'Furry'?'

Jennie Mae, a slight, worn woman with a gentle expression who was Will's age, came into the doorway, thinking.

'Furry Lewis, you mean? I saw him just last week.'

Jennie Mae said that Furry was working for the city, so I called the Memphis City Personnel Office and found out where he was working. It was too late in the afternoon to get him at the job, but later in the evening I found someone who could take me to where he was living. He and his wife Stella had had a little difficulty, and Furry had moved into a furnished room in a run-down neighborhood on the north side of town. When we came in he was sitting in bed, writing letters, the light coming from a bare bulb hanging from the ceiling in the center of the room. The children of the house ran in and out of the room, jumping on the bed to watch him write his letters, then calling him 'MISTER Furry' when he looked up. He seemed withdrawn at first, but his reserve soon gave away to a warm friendliness. He no longer had a guitar and he hadn't played much in twenty years, but when I asked him if he could still sing and play he straightened and said, 'I'm better now than I ever was.'

With Furry it was clear again that many of the singers who were recorded on the first sweeps that the 'race' record labels made through the South in the 1920s had been young when they made their singles. The blues they were performing were a new style of music, even though there were elements from the older work song traditions, and it was the younger musicians like Furry who were at their creative peak when they went into the companies' improvised recording facilities. Furry had been born in Greenwood, Mississippi on March 6th, 1900. His childhood name was Walter. We talked about it several times, but he never was able to explain how he got the nickname everyone knew him by. When the Depression ended most of the recording in the South the musicians were left with their instruments, a few phonograph records, and often a deep sense of futility. Many of them took a job like Furry's, and also like him, not playing much or even keeping their instruments. The country blues, however, is a creative musical style that doesn't depend on instrumental virtuosity or vocal technique. A gifted blues singer has an emotional sensitivity and imagination that doesn't depend on technical display. As the singers grow older their music often achieves a new expressiveness.

The next afternoon I rented a guitar, a big Epiphone, from a pawn shop on Beale Street, and took it over to Furry's room. He had gotten off work early and he was sitting out on the porch waiting for me. He carried the guitar inside, sat down and strummed the strings to make sure it was in tune, then looked up and asked me, 'What would you like to hear?'

I was surprised that he didn't want to try out the guitar a little first, but I managed to think of 'John Henry,' one of his finest early recordings. Without a moment's hesitation Furry reached in his pocket for his pocket knife, put it between the third and fourth fingers of his left hand to slide along the strings, and sang 'John Henry' almost the way he had recorded it thirty years before. His fingers weren't as fast as they had been, but there was a new emotional subtlety and assurance to his singing. At fifty-eight years old he was still as exciting as he had been when he was twenty-eight years old. When he finished he leaned back, looked at me, and asked, 'How was that?'

He knew how it was. He was just making conversation.

When I returned to Memphis with Ann in the fall, Furry was waiting for me. He and his wife had settled their differences and he was back in their ornate room in a tree-shaded frame house on Leath Street. He still didn't have a guitar, but he had spent most of the afternoon sawing the neck off a Royal Crown Cola bottle to use as a slide on his little finger. It was easier to slide along the strings than his clumsy pocket knife. I remembered that Gus Cannon, the banjo player who led Cannon's Jug Stompers for Victor Records in the late twenties, had an old guitar in a case under his bed. Cannon worked as a yard man for a young family in a white residential neighborhood who knew about his early recording career and were pleased to be able to help him. In exchange for very minimal duties he had a room over the garage at the back of their large yard and he added to his small income by working for a nearby church, raking leaves and trimming the grass. Ann and I drove out to his room and rented his guitar, a serviceable Spanish-style instrument of uncertain origin with a red ribbon tied around the neck, and brought it back to the room on Leath Street for an afternoon session with Furry.

A number of friends had come to the house to listen to him sing, and his wife Stella was wearing her best dress – red lace with bright, jewelled accents. One of the young men who was also renting a room in the house, Willie Williamson, brought everybody something to drink; then Furry picked up the guitar, tuned it a little nervously and began to sing for us. He was a little self-conscious and stiff at first, but when he mentioned Stella's name in his first blues she started laughing noisily, everyone joined in, and his mood immediately changed. He sang with a pleased confidence for the rest of the afternoon. The small room, the group of friends, the quiet sounds from the street outside all fit the scale of the songs. He is not a strong, domineering performer. The music he recorded was a subtle mosaic of changing moods and emotions. His singing now had a sense of considered eloquence, of quiet maturity. When he finally put the guitar down on the floor late in the afternoon his friends sat for a moment in silence inside the room and out in the hallway, still caught up in the mood of the music.

As I spent quiet afternoons sitting and talking with Furry, or with Will Shade or Gus Cannon of the great Memphis jug bands, it was difficult to remember that the city was once a wide-open river town, with raucous saloons and seedy dance halls strung along the streets that led down to the banks of the river, and music of every style ringing out from the cabarets and cafes along Beale Street. Like New Orleans' Storyville and St. Louis's Market Street there was what Jelly Roll Morton, who played all along the river, described as 'Everything in the line of pleasure.' Memphis was home to jug bands, cafe entertainers, dance orchestras, and medicine show performers who spent their winters in the noisy clatter along Beale Street. Everything on Beale Street is closed now, and the clubs still operating around the city are tightly restricted as to what they can serve. The dance halls have been silent for many years, and the police even stop beggars from trying to earn a little money by singing on street corners. Memphis, like Atlanta, has a city government controlled by strict religious groups, and both cities have given up their celebrated night life. Late one night I tried to find a club with music that would serve me, and what I found were closed doors at the tops of narrow stairways – after hours bars, with expressionless, bulky guards at the doors who demanded that I show some proof of membership in the 'club' that was operating the bar that night.

One evening, as I was walking with Furry to the bus stop to get

Memphis Willie B., Furry Lewis and Gus Cannon, 1964
(Photo: Ann Charters)

back to my unprepossessing hotel south of the business district he
began talking about the old days.

'There used to be a lot more going on in this town than there is
now. Oh yes, you wouldn't believe all the things that there was to do
and the music there was to listen to.'

When Furry made his first recordings in the spring of 1927 he was
spending his summers and the fall harvest season working on the little
improvised stages of the travelling medicine shows. He was part of a jug
band led by the older singer Jim Jackson that worked the small towns
and crossroads of northern Mississippi with Dr. Willie Lewis's 'Jack
Rabbit Salve' show. He and Jackson travelled to Chicago together and
auditioned for Jack Kapp at Brunswick–Vocalion Records singing Jim's
popular number 'Goin' To Kansas City.' Kapp decided to record them
separately, and Jackson's piece, which he performed alone, went on to
sell hundreds of thousands of copies. Furry's singles didn't do as well,
but he continued to record for both Vocalion and Victor Records until
the fall of 1929 when both the first months of the coming Depression
and the changing taste of the blues audience began to limit sales.
Among the pieces he recorded were the well-known 'John Henry' and
'Kassie Jones', 'I Will Turn Your Money Green', with an intricate, lilting
finger picked accompaniment, and his 'Stackerlee', originally titled
'Billy Lyons and Stock O'Lee'.

Both the 'Kassie Jones' and 'Billy Lyons and Stock O'Lee' were
recorded for the travelling Victor Records unit, which was set up in
Memphis under the direction of Ralph Peer, who had been an A&R
director working with 'Race' artists at OKeh Records. He was also
gathering copyright material for what would become the music
publishing empire Southern Music. The unusual spelling of Furry's
versions of the familiar 'Casey Jones' and 'Stackolee' probably were
ways for Peer to claim a copyright for public domain material.
Another of the Memphis artists, Gus Cannon, also recorded for Peer
at the same time with his Cannon's Jug Stompers, and when a lawsuit
arose in the early 1960s over the copyright claim of one of Gus's songs
it was found that Peer had signed an 'artist-for-hire' contract with him,
claiming that the song had been written while Gus was an employee
of Southern Music. Gus had duly signed the form contract with an 'X.'
No royalties are paid on a work for hire, and although Gus's song was
the bestselling record in the United States it was necessary to bring

legal action against Southern Music to reach some kind of settlement. Furry doesn't recall that he received any royalties for his Victor sessions, so he probably was also classified as one of Peer's 'employees.' His version of 'Kassie Jones' included a fresh portrayal of the situation with a wealth of humorous anecdotal details that must have made it a success as a medicine show number. It was so unique that Peer released it on two sides of a 78rpm single.

When Furry took his job with the City of Memphis's Department of Streets, at about the time he was doing his recordings for Vocalion and Victor, he left his itinerant life as a medicine show entertainer behind and settled down in north Memphis. For some years he continued to play at little house parties, then he finally sold his guitar and it is only recently that he has been encouraged to begin singing again. A woman in the neighborhood who does most of his cooking for him now remembers listening to him play when she was still a girl. He would bring his guitar over and sit on the edge of her back porch while people danced to his playing and singing. She still enjoys listening to him sing, remarking thoughtfully, 'You don't hear any kind of music like that these days and times. Of course, it is quiet here now, not like it used to be.'

It is still an exciting event around Furry's neighborhood when he is going to play for someone. Friends stop by and people sit on the porch or out in the hallway to listen. He doesn't have a phonograph, so when the Folkways album we did together came out he had to take it to someone else's house to listen to it, but nobody minded. When I came to the house to take him to the Sun Studio to record again a year and a half later there were a number of people outside their houses, sitting on shady porches and enjoying the light breeze. He stopped by the car and turned to call over to them,

'Well, I'll see all of you. I'm going to make some records.'

A man waved lazily and called back, 'It's just like the old days.'

Furry nodded, waved grandly with the guitar; then got into the car with a pleased smile.

'It sure seems just like old days.'

(1960–1961)

Willie Boerum
Introducing Memphis Willie B.

Will Shade, the leader of the old Memphis Jug Band, still lives in a room in a ramshackle house behind Beale Street, and most of the older musicians in town drop around to see him and talk for a moment when they're down on Beale Street shopping. Usually I stop by Will's whenever I'm in Memphis, and over the years he's led me to other singers like Gus Cannon, Charlie Burse and Furry Lewis. He was in poor health when I stopped by in April 1961, recovering from a serious operation, but after we'd talked for a few moments he mentioned that one of the blues singers he'd known in the 1930s had stopped by his place a few weeks before.

'His name's Willie B. I don't know what all his name is, but that's what we call him. Willie B. He's one of those real hard blues singers like you're always asking about.'

Will sat on his rumpled bed fumbling with the papers jammed into his wallet. He was in his usual sagging undershirt and rumpled pants, his seamed, dark face shadowed with a stubble of beard and concentration.

'I put his number down here somewhere.'

Finally, Will's wife, Jennie Mae Clayton, who had sung with the jug band on the old recordings, still girlishly slight and still with a concern for the musicians they had known over the years, found the piece of paper with Willie B.'s number on it folded into one of the wallet flaps. Will held it out.

'He'll sing the real old hard blues for you.'

I called Willie B. over the weekend and asked him if he could come around to Shade's on the following Monday night. Some people were coming over to sing for a very loose audition, and I wanted to hear Willie B.'s blues. Will Shade had been raised by a grandmother, Annie Brimmer, so all of the Memphis musicians knew him as 'Son Brimmer'. I was probably the only person in Memphis who called him Will. When I spoke to Willie B. – who sounded surprised, but excited over the phone – I asked him to come over to 'Son's.'

It was already noisy when I got there. The room was crowded and heavy with smoke. Jennie was sitting on one of the room's skinny beds with two women friends, talking between themselves. Will had borrowed a few battered wooden chairs from other rooms on his floor.

Charlie Burse, a thin, snappily dressed man with a narrow mustache, who had recorded with Will as a member of the jug band and then done a session in the 1930s as 'Charlie Burse and his Memphis Mudcats,' was sitting on the other bed trying to tune his four-string tenor guitar to the new Hohner Marine Band harmonica I'd bought for Will. Charlie was bent close to Will's face, trying to hear the harmonica over the noise of the shouted arguments, the heavy dancing, and shrill singing. There was a sodden smell of cheap red wine permeating the crowded space.

The tuning more or less done to everyone's satisfaction, Charlie, Will and Willie B. began playing a fast jam blues. At first I just sat back in one of the unsteady chairs, trying to pick out the instruments over the noise. Willie B. was hunched over his guitar, playing with intent concentration. He had a strong, decisive face, with eyes that shifted quickly from one side of the room to the other. His large, expressive mouth was pursed in concentration as his fingers shaped the chords. Unlike most of the other men in the room he was wearing neat trousers, a striped dress shirt and a light windbreaker. He had clearly played often with Son and Charlie. He was filling out their rhythm with sudden runs, or emphasising the beat with sharp, percussive notes on the lower strings of the guitar. I could feel an unmistakable presence in his playing.

After three or four numbers Charlie broke a string and Will began arguing with a man who lived in the room next to his about a note he was making on the harmonica. I leaned over and asked Willie B. to sing a blues. He picked up his guitar again and began singing in a low voice. Even with the noise around him I could sense a little of the intensity of his singing. It was, as Will Shade had said, the '...real, old hard blues.' I realized we'd have to go somewhere else so I could hear a little more of his style. Across the room I was suddenly conscious of a rising noise of voices tangling. I glanced over to see that a tall, thin younger man had pushed his way into the room, despite Jennie Mae's protests, and he was facing off with one of the men standing close to the window. I looked back at Willie, who was watching the confrontation with a practiced wariness. In a low voice I asked him if we could go outside. He nodded, and with a wave toward Will Shade, who was at the back of the crowd, we made our way out of the door.

Will and Jennie's room was in a dark, looming house on an alley back of Beale Street, and there wasn't anywhere Willie B. knew of that we could find some place quiet enough for him to play. We finally settled for the front seat of his jeep, which was parked in the shadows alongside the house. He pushed the driver's seat back so he had room for the guitar, and began to sing one of the old blues that had been part of the Memphis repertoire more than thirty years before, 'If you're goin' to Brownsville, take that right hand road.' It took only a handful of choruses before I decided that it was important to record him.

Willie B.'s voice had a distinctive tone. It was hard and tightly focused, and although his playing was similar to the style of other Memphis guitarists that I'd heard, he infused a distinctive muscularity into his playing. The only question would be how many songs he knew, since he hadn't been playing steadily, and for an album there had to be more than the four or five blues that had been enough for one of the old sessions for blues singles. But I had heard enough and with a deep breath that expressed his relief he agreed to do a session, smiling broadly for the first time. He drove me back to the small hotel south of the business section where I was staying, we shook hands, and he drove off into the darkness still smiling broadly, waving out of the window as the jeep turned the corner.

Although Willie B. was born in Memphis, on November 4th, 1911, and raised in the city, his roots were in the blues traditions of the rural South. His father had come from Pocahontas, Tennessee, and he was still playing the guitar in the old bottle neck style as Willie B. was growing up. Willie B. (the family name is Boerum) learned some of his father's guitar tunings, some of his old songs, and much of his feeling for the blues. He began playing the harmonica in the early thirties, and his first teacher was the great Memphis harmonica player Noah Lewis. Lewis had been a member of Gus Cannon's Jug Stompers for a series of historic recordings, and he was working regularly and recording with Sleepy John Estes. Willie B. still sang some of his old repertory. After his first musical apprenticeship with Lewis he met the original Sonny Boy Williamson, one of the most exciting harmonica blues artists of the 1930s, who was a popular recording artist for the Bluebird blues catalog. The two of them toured Arkansas with small blues groups working out of Memphis.

Willie B. picked up some of Sonny Boy's singing style, and there is still a lot of Williamson's shouted exuberance in Willie's harmonica playing. Memphis was still a busy city with a widespread community of

Memphis Willie B., Memphis, 1962
(Photo: Samuel Charters)

singers and musicians, and someone like Willie was soon part of the loosely assembled groups. He worked with other singers around Memphis, and even played with the Memphis Jug Band, when Will Shade would put a little group together to play for a society function. Willie also worked with the older Victor and Paramount recording artist Frank Stokes, one of the legends of the blues in Memphis. Frank took Willie with him when he travelled to Mississippi to visit his family.

About 1937 Willie decided he'd have more chance as a musician if he learned to play the guitar, and he continued to play both guitar and harmonica for many years. During this period blues releases on 78rpm discs had become a small but consistent component in the mix of commercial recordings that were produced for the record bins in country general stores or small town variety stores, or through mail order everywhere in the South. The recordings were merchandised with such closely scheduled regularity that sometimes it seems that anyone who could play a blues instrument or knew a few blues verses recorded during this period. Willie B. recorded for the first time a year or so after he'd picked up the guitar. He and another guitarist named Alan Shaw travelled to New York with the Memphis singer Hattie Hart, and they accompanied her for a session for the American Recording Corporation. Neither of them sang on the session, however, and Willie had to wait almost thirty years before he went into a recording studio again.

The second World War interrupted Willie's musical career, as it interrupted the careers and the lives of so many millions of people everywhere in the world. He went into the service in January 1942. Eleven months later, in December 1942, he took part in the first North African invasion, then went on to the later landings in Sicily and Italy. At the war's end he was serving with a Quartermaster unit in the Italian mountains. In 1946 he returned to Memphis and took a job with the Buckeye Soya Bean Oil Company. Except for a three year interval from 1950 to 1953, when he studied radio and television repair on the G. I. Bill, he has stayed at the same job for many years. He married in the early 1960s and moved into a pleasant new home that he and his brother built on the outskirts of Memphis, working his day job during the week, and doing repair work on the weekends.

Willie B.'s life didn't fit any of the conventional patterns of the blues – he wasn't an irresponsible drifter, he was happily married, and he worked a steady job. Although he had made the decision to give up music as a career he never stopped playing the blues. Even while he was still in the Army he was given an assignment as a Colonel's driver for his last year of service, so he could spend some of his duty time singing for parties. When he returned to Memphis he was still considered one of the group of musicians who could be counted on for a job playing for a picnic or a dance, occasionally in the local clubs, usually with three or four piece blues bands.

Willie B. played less often after he was married, but he continued to work on new blues for himself, and he always sang at his family's parties. Sometimes his father would join in, playing one of his bottleneck blues. During the afternoons that we worked together in the repair shop attached to his house, picking the songs for his first album for the Prestige Bluesville series, neighbors would often stop by to listen to his new numbers. They'd find a place to sit in the middle of the usual repair shop clutter, then after a minute they'd turn to me and nod in agreement, 'He really can sing them old blues.'

Like nearly every singer I worked with during these years he had his own explanation for his songs, which he expressed during a break in the session we did a few days later. 'A blues is about something that's real. It's about what a man feels when his wife leaves him, or about some disappointment that happens to him that he can't do anything about. That's why none of these young boys can really sing the blues. They don't know about the things that go into the blues.' Although his life had settled down when I met him, he was still singing blues that were a window into the casual musician's life he'd led before he went into the Army. I could feel Sonny Boy Williamson's influence on some of them, and Willie had taught himself to play with a harmonica rack so he could counter his blues lines with a fierce response in Sonny Boy's style on the harmonica. He had also written one of the best of the pieces he sang, 'Overseas Blues', one of a surprisingly small handful of blues that were a direct expression of the military service that affected so many of the younger singers. He wrote it in the summer of 1945, when there was a rumor that the troops in Italy, among them his Quartermaster unit, would be shipped to the Far East to finish the war against Japan. His blues were his unhappy comment on the situation, the verses ending with the refrain, 'No, no, I don't want to go.'

The studio I used for the session – and for the sessions with Furry

Lewis, who was recording two albums for the Prestige Bluesville series the same week – was the now famed Sun Studio run by Sam Phillips, who had used the studio to record Elvis Presley, Johnny Cash, Carl Perkins and Jerry Lee Lewis. For me it was mostly an expedient space to do some uncomplicated sessions. I had a recording budget, and it would stretch to a studio, which meant I didn't have to use my portable machine and hold the microphone out for the singer, as I'd been doing for several years – but it wasn't the kind of budget that would take me into a more elaborate set-up. Sun was like most of the other studios I used outside of New York City or Chicago – a middle sized room, a piano that had been played more than it should have been, a control board that worked well enough if the engineer was used to it. The Sun engineer then was the guitarist Scotty Moore, who had been in the trio that accompanied Elvis for the legendary 'That's Alright, Mama' session. He subbed at the studio between his jobs with Elvis when there was a film in production. Scotty was much more interested in Furry, and his repertoire of Mississippi guitar tunings, but he also responded with a wry shake of his head at the raw intensity of Willie's blues.

After three or four hours of recording I was sitting on a stool in the studio, listening with Willie to a playback, and I suddenly noticed his fingers. He hadn't been playing regularly, and the steel strings had first worn blisters on the tips of his fingers, then the blisters had broken. I looked at him in some confusion, didn't he want to stop? No, he insisted, it was alright. We could go ahead. He wasn't feeling a thing. What I realised was that he had waited almost thirty years to record his songs, and not even the pain of his streaming fingers was going to stop him.

Once I'd decided that we'd go ahead, and since he was unwilling to stop, for me, with my continual interest in the older blues styles, the strongest of his performances were two songs he played in his father's old guitar tuning. I had only known 'Brownsville Blues' from the first recording of the song by Sleepy John Estes in the late 1920s, but as Willie sang it, with a hard voice and a drumming ostinato pattern in the guitar accompaniment, I realized that it was one of the 'core' songs that defined the blues of Memphis and Western Tennessee. To emphasize his roots in this tradition he sang another blues in the same mode and guitar tuning, 'Worried Man Blues,' and to show convincingly that he had also come out of the looser Memphis jug band style he did an uptempo number, 'The Stuff is Here', with a ringing harmonica introduction, and a loose, shuffling rhythm that he'd probably picked up in his occasional jobs with Will Shade.

As I sat out in the studio with Willie and listened to the playbacks I realized again that his generation of commercial blues artists had been – along with their role as musicians continuing the blues tradition and their emphasis on the elements of African American culture that had shaped the early blues – skilled, professional musicians. His playing was on a consistent level of technical virtuosity. He was a brilliant instrumentalist on either the guitar or the harmonica, and when he used the two of them together the excitement was even more intense. He had taught himself to alter the tone of the harmonica with the 'choking' and slurring when he was using the neck rack and playing the guitar at the same time. For most of the country harmonica players it took two hands to create the effects he could do with his mouth and lips. He was an exciting, emotionally moving singer in the classic traditions of the Memphis-style blues.

Even Willie B. was surprised at the sound of his performances when he listened to the first playbacks. Finally, after waiting for the opportunity most of his life, he had made a record. He shook his head. 'I was kind of nervous, you know, but that's really the blues. That's the blues just like we were talking about.'

Later in the year, I was in Memphis again and we made a second album, again in the casual atmosphere of Sun Studios. What Willie showed me in his new songs was the kind of creative stimulus that is part of any creative process, whether the artist is creating a blues or the plans for a skyscraper. When I stopped by his house on a close oppressive morning in August he was sitting in the workshop beside the house, his guitar on the couch beside him, leaning back in a tired slump. During the summer months the soya bean oil plant where he had his day job worked on double shift, hiring back the men that had been laid off during the spring, putting on some extra crews, and giving everybody a chance to get in a little extra overtime. Willie smiled wanly and shook his head.

'I've been working a little extra time, you know, going in the afternoon and working until we get everything in at night. We didn't get done until two-thirty this morning. After a while, working like that for a week or so, you begin to get a little tired.'

There were some sheets of paper scattered on the couch underneath the guitar, and a notebook left open on a work table in the center of the room. It was a hot sticky morning. The air in the small, crowded space was slack and unmoving. Willie got up to turn on a noisy fan at one end of the room and there was a flurry of loose papers from the couch. The pages of the notebook fluttered across the table. As we picked them up, putting them under the weight of the guitar, I noticed that they were blues. I asked Willie about them.

'They're just some blues I been working on.'

'How do you have time to write anything when you're working?' I asked, in some surprise.

Willie smiled and held up his hands. 'It's working that gives me my ideas. I walk around the plant at night, when it's quiet, you know, and I can hear men talking. Some of them is crying that their wife has left them or that she isn't doing them right, and somebody else is saying that his girl's took up with somebody else. I hear all that and that's what I put in my blues. I come back here and write down the things, rhymed up of course. I make the verses and things right when I'm still there walking around at the job.'

It was the most direct description any singer had even given me about the way they found the material for their blues, and I could feel the immediacy of his eavesdropping in lines like,

> *In my sleep, I could hear her call my name*
> *Lord when I feel over beside me, I couldn't feel a doggone thing*

or

> *Everytime I see you, I catch you in your gown*
> *Your hair all mussed up, your window shade pulled down.*

It was this blunt directness that so many singers had meant when they told me, 'The blues is the truth,' and in his songs I had come close to the hard reality that had fired the blues experience. As Willie B. said as he listened back to what he recorded, 'That's really the blues!'

(1961–1962)

Billie and Dee Dee Pierce

Anyone who listens to the blues today comes to a musical style that's dominated by the acoustic guitar for what still survives of the old country blues, or the newer electric blues sound out of Chicago, with its electric guitars. For any of us who came earlier to the blues, what we mostly heard first was women singers with majestic voices accompanied by pianists. By the 1950s the electric guitars – loud and cheap – had made it possible for most small clubs to give up their pianos – which cost money to buy, took up a lot of space, and were hard to keep in tune. It was the jazz clubs that still had pianos on the bandstand for their groups. Some of the most important jazz soloists of the era – Earl Garner, Thelonius Monk, Bud Powell, Oscar Peterson, Dave Brubeck, Mose Allison, Billy Taylor – were pianists and many of the clubs had excellent instruments, but their audiences didn't want to hear the blues, unless it was lounge blues by one of the artists whose style blended the blues with contemporary jazz – Jimmy Witherspoon or Kansas City's Big Joe Williams. The only place any of us knew about then that still had a piano and a small band playing the old blues anywhere was Luthjen's, a run-down neighborhood bar in New Orleans that had a dark, crumbling dance hall in a back room. In the dimly lit space was a much worn dance floor surrounded with battered tables, and at one end of the room was a small enclosure for the band, a rectangular space surrounded with a wooden fence and a railing. Sideways to the dancers at one end of the cramped space was a large, much used, clangy piano. There were two wooden kitchen chairs for the trumpeter and the trombonist set beside it, and behind the horn players, against the dark wooden wall, was room for a drum set.

Luthjen's had hired most of the veteran musicians in New Orleans at one time or other, but in all the years I was living in the French Quarter in the 1950s the band that worked there every Friday, Saturday, and Sunday night was the rough, exciting quartet led by the affectionate couple, pianist and singer Billie Pierce, and her husband, trumpeter Dee Dee Pierce. If Luthjen's could afford an extra musician you'd sometimes find clarinetist Emile Barnes also squeezed into the tight space, but the other horn player was usually a trombone player, Harrison Brazlee, and the drummer for much of the time was a veteran of the 1920s named George Henderson. Billie had come out of that blues era of the 1920s, and at a show in Mobile she had even accompanied Bessie Smith. For those of us who managed to get to Luthjen's at least once a week, and lingered over a battered table with a 25 cent beer, our eyes fixed on the bandstand so we wouldn't miss a note, Billie was the blues. My life as a record producer began with a duet session that I set up and recorded with Billie and Dee Dee in the spring of 1954. We used a dispirited apartment on Toulouse Street in the French Quarter that was even more run-down than Luthjen's.

The material from the session was released by Folkways Records as part of the series I recorded and compiled with some tracks done by other field collectors in the city titled *The Music of New Orleans*. Billie and Dee Dee were included in Volume Three of the series, *Music of the Dance Halls*, which also included tracks with Emile Barnes, Charlie Love, Albert Burbank, and Kid Clayton that had been recorded in 1951 by Dave Wycoff, Alden Ashforth, and Jim McGarrell. At the time I was writing many different pieces relating to New Orleans music, and these notes were to be included in an expanded version of the booklet that was released with the album in 1958.

From *Every Woman's Blues* (1958)

It isn't far to walk to Luthjen's corner bar if you live in the French Quarter in New Orleans. You walk away from Canal Street and away from the river, back into a neighborhood of old frame houses, most of them needing a coat of paint, but all of them with the patina of faded legend that still clings to so much of New Orleans, even with the newer suburbs spreading along the other side of the Mississippi and the quieter middle class neighborhoods filling in the lowlands out to Lake Ponchartrain. Luthjen's, at the corner of Marais and Almonaster, isn't different from a lot of shabby corner bars in the city, even with its rough dance floor in a big room behind the bar and its fenced-in bandstand up against the wall. If you're interested in the old New Orleans jazz styles there are still a dozen places to hear bands, even if most of them don't have music every weekend, and you never know who's going to play unless one of the musicians calls you. What we knew about Luthjen's was that every night on the weekends Billie Pierce would be

Luthjen's Dance Hall, New Orleans, 1954
(Photo: Samuel Charters)

sitting on the bench of the place's much battered piano and singing the blues, and her husband Dee Dee Pierce would be sitting on an old kitchen chair beside her, adding the lyric trumpet fills that are an indispensable musical complement to the classic blues style.

Billie and Dee Dee have played in Luthjen's for so many years that you don't really pay attention to the horn player beside them, unless it's someone who is also a jazz legend themselves. In the early 1960s the clarinetist Emile Barnes sometimes filled the kitchen chair that was next to Dee Dee's, behind the wooden fence that closes in the band. Most of the nights when I go now the second horn is a trombone player named Harrison Brazlee. Brazlee's determined playing is as breathy and fixed in its melodic phrases as Dee Dee's playing is freely rhythmic and eloquent. Brazlee is a friendly man in his late sixties who smiles often, but he is thin and worn and he doesn't have many teeth, and the trombone is a heavy instrument to hold up all night, so he rests the slide on the wooden railing in front of him. He has now worn a groove in the wood with his growling accompaniments. When the English cornetist Ken Colyer made it to New Orleans after jumping his merchant ship in the harbor in 1951 he did a pick-up session which included Brazlee on trombone. One of the tunes they played was the pop favorite 'Walking In A Winter Wonderland'. Harrison began playing it one night at Luthjen's and Billie turned around to ask what tune they were playing. Dee Dee shrugged, 'Some tune of Harrison's.'

The drummer is usually the pleasant, friendly George Henderson, but sometimes other friends, Albert Jiles or Cie Frasier, play with the usual New Orleans lightness on the snare, marking the rhythm with the soft press roll that sets the city's jazz drummers apart, and encouraging the dancers with thumping beats on the large bass drum.

Dancing is what Luthjen's is about, though most of us who are interested in New Orleans' jazz roots sit at a table all night, nurse one or two twenty-five cent bottles of beer and listen to Billie and Dee Dee play the blues. Most of us were self-conscious adolescents who didn't dance very well in high school, and we haven't gotten much better at it since then. Even if we could, though, we usually don't bring anyone to dance with, since most of the young women we know who live in the Quarter are working day jobs, and they don't have the energy to spend a night in the booming little dance hall. Across the shadowy dance floor from the two or three tables where we usually sit is a row of tables with middle aged women from the neighborhood who have come to *dance* – and if there's a crowd they'll be up on their feet for nearly every number. They are large women, with comfortably thick bodies, their hair carefully set, and their faces in make-up that might have suited someone a few years younger. They wear dark printed dresses and easy shoes. Each of them has her own decided dance style, and the men who come over to their tables to ask for a dance know what to expect.

Sometimes when someone new comes into town to listen to jazz and doesn't know about Luthjen's they take a chance on the first dance and go across the dance floor to ask one of the women if they want to dance. Whichever woman he asks stands up, folds him in her muscular arms, and gives him five minutes of the most relentless bump and grind he has ever experienced in his life. There is a startling contrast in the women's faces – which are set and expressionless – and the rest of their bodies, which rub relentlessly and efficiently against the stomach of their partner for the entire dance. Usually one dance is all one of the novices from our side of the room can handle, but the men from the neighborhood have come for the ride, and they usually manage to last for the night.

Billie and Dee Dee play almost anything, though Billie sometimes has to feel her way through the chords of new songs that are requested. They have their specialities, which for Billie is the blues, in a multitude of styles, and for Dee Dee is his vocal and trumpet rendition of the old Louis Armstrong warhorse, 'The Peanut Vendor', and the Creole favorite 'Big Mamou'. The much played and often protesting upright piano is set against the far left side of the bandstand fence, filling the space. It is set at a right angle to the dance floor so Billie can sing without having to turn her whole body toward the dancers. Some nights it feels like she is spending her entire life looking over her left shoulder toward the heaving crowd, glancing out of the corner of her eye at her left hand as it pumps out the chords. Dee Dee's chair is just to the right of her piano bench.

I don't think any of us who feel such affection for Billie would say that she is pretty. She must have been when she was younger, but now she is heavy and her body doesn't have much shape. Her kind, round face is lined and furrowed and she doesn't have the money to take care of her hair. She wears the same kind of formless print dresses as the women waiting to dance, and they get more and more rumpled as the evening goes on, but her arms have a muscular heft from the hours she spends at the piano. Her style is a rolling, persistent left hand rhythm, with a melody or a set of chords played with spread fingers in her right hand. She grew up as Billie Gootson in Pensacola, and began playing as a girl. When she was sixteen, Bessie Smith's pianist was too sick to play for a theater engagement in Mobile, and Billie filled in. When the blues legend from the 1920s Ida Cox did her last southern tour Billie was her accompanist. Since at Luthjen's she has to fill in for the missing bass and guitar her playing is relentless, crowding, and often electrifying. David Wycoff and Alden Ashforth, with a friend, Jim McGarrell, in their invaluable recordings done in the early 1950s, recorded Billie with a band that included several dance hall veterans, including a bass player, Albert Glenny, who had played with Buddy Bolden's Orchestra at the turn of the century. Their 'Shake It and Break It', with Billie sparking

BILLIE AND DEE DEE PIERCE
PHOTO BY CHARLES MC NETT JR.

Billie and Dee Dee Pierce, New Orleans, 1954
(Photo: Charles McNett Jr.)

the rhythm and shouting the vocal, is one of the classic performances of the New Orleans revival period.

Dee Dee, in contrast, is physically smaller and shorter. He is a slight, trim man, nervous and excitable, in shirts and trousers that, like hers, are much washed. His hair is graying and his face, with its long jaw, has its own lines and marks of wear. He played with most of the city's brass bands, finally parading most regularly with the Young Tuxedo. He had a day job as a brick layer, which meant he didn't have to find some kind of playing job every night. Billie and Dee Dee are in their fifties, and as you sit listening to the easy glide of their dance beat and the infectious pleasure in their vocals it feels like they've spent their lives in the New Orleans dance halls.

At the same time, all of us who come to hear them find something else in the relationship between Billie and Dee Dee that goes beyond their long musical partnership with the blues. When I first came to New Orleans searching for the older musicians earlier in the 1950s I saw Dee Dee playing for a parade with the Young Excelsior Brass Band. Even when he was marching along the street with the band's other two trumpet players there was still an exuberant lift to his playing, and on the stops, when there were often impromptu street corner jam sessions, Dee Dee's horn rang out over the noisy crowds. But now, since a job at Luthjen's doesn't leave time for breaks, when he has to leave the bandstand to use the toilet Billie turns to help him out of his chair, and the drummer, George, reaches out to take his arm. Dee Dee has become blind, and the glaucoma that has taken away his sight is continually painful for him.

What all of us who know them learn from Billie and Dee Dee is that love can work between two people. Even when she has been playing and singing for hours, and she has had too much to drink and her hair has come loose and her dress is ringed with sweat, it is her tenderness and her care that makes it possible for him to sing and clown beside her on the bandstand. When I recorded them, with a New York friend Bertram Stanleigh, in an unused apartment at the loosely managed old apartment building at 912 Toulouse Street, and Billie turned to him and said the usual things, 'Play it for me, baby,' or 'You know you can play little Dee Dee,' it was impossible not to hear the genuine emotion hidden behind the cliches. The music they played was the classic blues of the 1920s – even some of the repertoire was familiar – Bessie Smith's version of 'Careless Love', or the well worn 'Married Man Blues', but Billie's rhythm was the Luthjen's dance beat, and not the slow, stately tempos of the old recordings. Dee Dee's trumpet responses were freely phrased, lyric interludes that lifted and encouraged her rough voice. It almost seemed as though their blues hadn't come from old recordings or stage shows – their music had been on a parallel track, and in New Orleans, this is the way the blues sounded.

When some of us take a bus out to their small frame house in the Galvez district we have this same sense of a house that is bright with love, even if the rooms need new paper on the walls and paint on the woodwork, and the furniture had seen better days in some long ago decade. A cake that was carried on the bus for a birthday party by a staunch friend, Tulane student and amateur drummer Charley McNett, brought tears to Dee Dee's eyes, while Billie stood by, her face wreathed in a smile at her pleasure in his happiness. Then while we were clustered around the table, the candles still burning on the cake, Dee Dee insisted on bringing out his trumpet and playing softly for us; a lyric, intricate, whispering blues.

The New Orleans pianist and entertainer Jelly Roll Morton always said that there should be a different kind of song that wasn't just a blues – it should be called a 'joy,' since life had its good moments along with all the bad ones. Jelly Roll even composed one that became a band standard, 'Milenberg Joys', named after a section of the New Orleans lake front. When a group of us comes over from our stuffy, run-down French Quarter apartments and crowds into the dark little dance hall in the back of Luthjen's we've come to hear the blues – but with Billie and Dee Dee it's as much the 'joys' that linger when we come outside into the darkness many hours later, and that we take with us as we walk back through the silent New Orleans streets.

(1958)

Jesse Fuller

When the new blues audience of the early 1960s began to look around them at the musical scene they'd just entered, they found, somewhat to their surprise, that there were already some blues singers there. The artists had simply been hidden behind the tag 'folk singers.' Their blues had been mingled with songs like 'Frankie and Albert,' 'John Henry,' or even 'On Top of Old Smoky.' What they presented was the kind of songs they would have done for a country picnic in Alabama – with about the same blend of blues and jookin' songs and old favorites from the medicine show days. One of the most widely known of the country performers to emerge from the musical shadow of the folk music coffee houses was the watchful, guarded figure of Jesse Fuller, who had been found working on the streets in Oakland, California, and who had gone on to a long and productive career in music long after his street laboring days were over.

Before A&R producer Paul Rothchild left Prestige Records to go on to Elektra Records in the summer of 1963 he had signed a contract with Jesse to record two albums for the company's Folklore series. When I followed Paul in the job at Prestige, he had done only one of the albums, *San Francisco Bay Blues*, released the year before. Jesse was appearing in Boston, so after I managed to find where he was staying we agreed to do the second album at the recording facility that Steven Fasset had set up in his living room in an historic colonial building on Beacon Hill. Fasset was a careful and sympathetic recording technician who did many of the best albums of the Boston folk movement, but to keep his elegant living room from being cluttered with equipment he only had his microphones in the room, set up unobtrusively on his antique oriental carpets, close to the ivy framed windows. His small control room was on another floor, and he communicated with the performers through a small loud speaker. Jesse, as always, set up his equipment without assistance, and when I had to run up and down the stairs between takes to adjust microphones or change the position of one of his instruments he quietly settled into one of the large wing chairs in the corner and waited patiently for me to finish. The notes were written for the album in January 1965.

Jesse Fuller's Favourites

With the rediscovery of the blues in the 1960s we found ourselves continually dealing with the new excitement of finding so many of the legendary singers of the 1920s still alive and still interested in performing. At the same time it was as obvious as a fingerprint on fresh paint that we would have to think again about the occasional blues individualists that we'd usually considered 'folk' artists. For a period that had been a useful way of describing what they did, since it would help them find work in any of the era's folk clubs and coffee houses. Now the blues songs they did took on a new dimension. One of the most colorful and distinctive of the 'folk singers' of the blues was the sinew-tough, laconic singer from Oakland, Jesse Fuller, who played enough different kinds of songs that he didn't fit easily into the blues mould, but who was just as obviously an important blues artist.

With Fuller, along with two or three other singers who also came out of a rural southern setting, we had to define for ourselves what we thought of the role of the blues singer. Jesse was in reality what all of the early blues singers had been before they were configured into the world of commercial music by the record companies – Jesse was a *songster*. In the world of the rural South there had never been enough jobs for anybody who just played for Saturday night dances or sang lonely blues on a back porch. Everybody who played music or sang songs had a grab-bag repertoire of material that anyone might ask them to sing, from children's play party songs to what the singers could manage of the newest pop hits, to the Sunday morning gospel hymns. The record companies who came through the South looking for material had learned through trial and error that although they could sell almost any kind of blues, they couldn't sell the other kinds of secular songs that they auditioned. So everyone they recorded became a blues singer, even if the term to describe them would have much more accurately been *songster*, a performer who could sing everything. With few exceptions the only part of their rich repertoire that they were able to record was the blues.

Jesse, I know, would never have considered himself as an example of anything, but he was one of a handful of songsters who still were performing into the '60s. The territory had been generally laid out by Leadbelly, the songster from the Louisiana prisons who had been discovered by John and Alan Lomax, and who had gone on to a long recording career that took him from the prison farm to appearances in New York night clubs. Like Jesse, and like Pink Anderson, another songster who had worked for years in the touring medicine shows that trekked across the South and who was still living in Spartanburg, South

Carolina in the 1960s, each of the songsters was a unique figure who carried with him an indelible musical memory of a specific place and a distinct moment in African American cultural history.

In an interview Jesse did in the late 1950s with Lester Koenig, a record company owner who had produced an early album of his songs, he talked, not so much about his music, but about his abrupt decision to leave his job as a laborer in Oakland, and to try to make a living as a singer and entertainer.

'I decided I'd get into it and make me some money. I didn't know, I thought I might get lucky enough to get something out of it. If I didn't I'd just be the same old Jesse. I wouldn't cry about it.'

Jesse was a proud man. A tough man. It's hard to think of him crying about anything. He was nearly sixty when he decided to change his life and become a full time singer. At that point he was a weathered, thin, wary man with little to show for his long, hard years of laboring except the calluses on his hands from operating a jack hammer on the Oakland streets. He'd been living in Oakland since 1929, and he had a settled life there with a wife and family, but he always seemed ready to move on. He was aloof and self-contained, like most men who spent their early lives travelling. Like Jesse they always seem to keep something of themselves separate from their surroundings, so that if life should go badly for them and they find themselves drifting on down the road, they still keep the essential parts of themselves together.

Jesse had spent his early years wandering, and he had come out of the same emotional insecurities that shaped so many other singers. He was born in Jonesboro, Georgia on March 12th, 1896, but he never knew his father. His mother was too poor to raise him so she left him with a family named Wilson who had a farm outside of Macedonia, Georgia. What Jesse remembered most about them was their cruelty towards him. He began his travelling early, working the kinds of jobs that were there in the country for drifters like him, playing enough music that he didn't want to give it up when he finally settled. His wanderings finally stopped in Oakland. He travelled so much of his road alone that it was always to himself that he turned whenever he had to face a problem or a decision in his life.

Even in Oakland in the early 1950s, when young folk enthusiasts had discovered this street jackhammer operator who played a twelve-string guitar and sang old songs, he already seemed to be ready to move on. There were jobs at parties and at the small clubs that were opening up around the Bay area. A number of people were trying to help him move up to better paying music jobs, and he was appreciative of what they were doing for him, but he kept a stubborn distance between himself and their efforts to draw him into close friendships. He would show up an hour or so before he was booked to appear so he could get everything set up, then he would sit in a backroom until it was time to go on. Occasionally people misunderstood his attitude. They felt it had to be something he'd brought along with him after his years in the South. But Jesse just preferred to be alone, and he continued to depend on himself when he had begun to travel everywhere in the country and to most of Europe. He made only perfunctory efforts to meet the audiences who had become interested in his music, and turned down the usual invitations to socialize. He hadn't painted the sign 'The Lone Cat' on his 'fotdella' yet, but he thought of himself as a loner, and when he had finished one of his local jobs he would get his things back into his car, pick up his money, and drive off without stopping for the parties or the long sessions of music that were part of the East Bay scene in those years.

Jesse's famed fotdella was also an expression of his lone cat attitude. When he'd first come out to Oakland he was keen to keep playing the kind of music he'd started with back in Georgia, with the kind of small country bands that played everything for whatever audiences they could find. Jesse sometimes found musicians in California he could work with, but he couldn't depend on them, and there weren't enough who knew his Georgia blues and dance songs. What he did was turn himself into a country blues band. He used a kazoo and a harmonica on a rack so he could play the melodies along with the twelve-string guitar that was part of the Georgia style, but he missed the sound of a bass. To add the sound he was looking for, he built a heavy, rough wood frame with foot pedals that struck a row of bass strings. The strings were about two feet long, and they were strung from the top to the bottom of the frame. One of the reasons he had to show up early for his jobs was the time it took to tune the fotdella to the guitar and the harmonica. When he was sitting behind the fotdella's ominous looking frame, the kazoo and the harmonica in their rack covering a lot of his face, and the big guitar against his chest like a shield, he was the lone cat he'd always wanted to be.

With all of the things he brought with him to his jobs during that period he was still working with less equipment than he carried with him later, when he was touring outside the United States. He added a washboard that he played with his other foot, and then replaced the washboard with a standard sock cymbal. Also, since the little coffee houses were so small he didn't need to bring his amplifiers. Sometimes, though, there was still a problem getting even the fotdella onto tiny stages set up for a folk singer's skinny stool. Two Berkeley enthusiasts, Joe Glickman and Rolf Cahn, sometimes hired him for their little club on San Pablo Avenue, The Blind Lemon, but once they got Jesse and his instruments set up there wasn't much room left for customers, so he wasn't one of the club's regulars, despite his local popularity.

It was during this period that he did his first recording, and it was his albums that helped spread his reputation. In the casual populism of the folk era it was often committed individuals who took the first steps in establishing a new artist, and Jesse's first recording was produced by a young Berkeley couple named Margaret and Irwin Goldsmith for their World Folk Song label. For many of us in the East Bay – I was a student at Berkeley during some of these years – it was our first chance to hear Jesse sing. He was already a semi-legendary figure, but he was performing so infrequently that it was hard to get a chance to hear him in person. Jesse's musical personality was as strongly defined then as it was when he became more widely known, and the album had an unmistakable presence and authority. He was clearly an important discovery, however we defined what he was doing. One of the songs, a track-lining work gang song with only the fotdella as accompaniment, is still among my favorite performances on all of Jesse's recordings. With the help of people like Rolf Cahn and his wife Barbara Dane, both busy performers themselves, and a San Francisco record shop owner named Norman Pierce who for some time acted as his local manager, and with a growing audience that was beginning to find his recordings, it was only a matter of time before Jesse had established himself in the bustling festival, coffee house and concert world of the folk music boom.

What Jesse or any of the people around him couldn't have anticipated was that, with all his independence and his conscious aloofness from the world he found himself in, he would write a hit song. His raggy 'San Francisco Bay Blues' – 'Walkin' with my baby down by San Francisco Bay' – became one of the new folk song standards, and it was picked up and recorded by dozens of other artists. Jesse could have changed his lifestyle, but there was no outer sign that the song's success had changed him in any way. He was still as lean and decisive, his face still as watchful and his expression guarded, his clothes the same slacks and flannel shirts and sweaters he'd worn all his life. The only concession he made to his audiences when he performed was that even though his choice of songs was usually unplanned, he always sang 'San Francisco Bay Blues' somewhere in the set.

By the beginning of the 1960s Jesse was travelling steadily, and it seemed to suit him. He was still as ready to move on as he had been in those years in Oakland. In the United States he loaded the instruments into a new station wagon, travelling alone, making his own travel arrangements and schedules. Friends of mine who sometimes followed his station wagon to find their way to an out of the way job often came back shaking their heads in wonder. 'He never drives over thirty-five miles an hour! He says he doesn't want to wear out his new car!' But even with his steady travelling I saw him more often than I did when he was living in Oakland and taking time off from his laborer's job to sing at a party for an Elk's Lodge or a benefit at one of the clubs. He was now appearing regularly at nearly every folk festival in the country, as well as at every coffee house that featured 'authentic folk music.'

In all his travels and in his meetings with his new audiences he was still the aloof 'lone cat,' despite the efforts of his fans to help make his life easier. I remember him one night setting up the fotdella, the cymbal, and his amplifier in a cellar jazz club on Oxford Street in London in 1961. He insisted on doing everything himself, without the help of the young British fans who were trying to give him advice. Among other things, they were trying to tell him that English electric current is 200 volts, instead of the American 110. Jesse went on with what he was doing, assuring them in his laconic asides that he had worked it out. He finally turned on his amplifier and the entire collection of instruments short-circuited with an emphatic, noisy jolt. He just shrugged and went on with his set, even though it was impossible to hear him beyond the first few rows of fans sitting on the floor in front of the stage. When he finished, they cheered him anyway; then there was a general rush to get to the nearest pubs before they closed. As the crowd trickled back, Jesse found that a dozen of them had managed to get past the door with a pint of bitter for him.

I remember him, too, at the Swarthmore Folk Festival, in the suburbs outside of Philadephia. Jesse had shared the final Saturday night concert with folk blues artist Dave Van Ronk. Jesse did the first half of the concert, and, as always, brought down the house with his 'Buckdancer's Choice,' doing an old fashioned buck and wing minstrel show dance in his stockinged feet – he had to take his shoes off to play the fotdella and the cymbal – and accompanying himself with the guitar. I went behind the stage curtains during the last half of the concert to look for some notes the I'd left there during the afternoon, and there was Jesse, stretched out on five hard, wooden chairs that he'd lined up and pushed together to make an improvised couch. He was asleep, waiting for the concert to end so he could get paid, get his things off the stage, and begin the long drive to his next engagement. It felt just like the back rooms of all the little coffee houses in Berkeley: Jesse alone, waiting for something to begin, or for something to end, so that he could get on with the business of his life.

(1956)

5. The St. Louis Blues

The cities of the South were the first step away from the unending labor of the cotton fields and the crude exploitation of share cropping for many of the early blues singers. The cities weren't always safe – one of the nation's bloodiest race riots shook St. Louis after the First World War – but there was a sense that there was a little protection in the African American communities that grew up in each of the cities. During the war years it was Chicago and Detroit, cities at the end of the railroad lines, that had the biggest influx out of the South, but in the earlier period it had been the Mississippi River and its colorful port cities that had become a winding lifeline out of the countryside. New Orleans, at the Mississippi's mouth; Memphis, almost halfway to the Mississippi's meeting place with the Ohio River that created the river's imperious flood; and St. Louis, just below the mouth of the Missouri, which opened the river to the northwest. The three cities grew up on the river banks with a casual disdain for most of the rules that hemmed in life in the countryside. Throughout the 19th century they flourished as centers for the drifters, the river workers, the traders, and the ragtag groups trailing after them who clustered in their 'districts'. Storyville in New Orleans, Beale Street in Memphis, and Market Street in St. Louis. Jazz itself was shaped in the orchestras of the great steamers that carried passengers from New Orleans to St. Louis. The blues was just as alive, though the singers who moved out of Mississippi and Alabama went north, instead of further south, and New Orleans never had a strong vocal blues contingent.

All of the major record companies had agents and scouts in the cities, and in St. Louis the agent for OKeh Records, one of the first major 'race' labels, was a music store owner named Jessie Stone, who brought one of the bestselling blues artists of the 1920s and 1930s to the company, Lonnie Johnson. Many of the St. Louis singers eventually moved on, but a small group hung on in the poorer neighborhoods in the north of the city, among them two Mississippians, Big Joe Williams and his cousin J. D. Short.

I first visited St. Louis on the long research trip for *The Country Blues* in January 1959, and Ann and I were in the city again early the next year, though this time we were visiting the very enthusiastic researchers who were tracing the city's role in the development of ragtime, among them Trebor Tichenor and Russ Cassidy. We were in the city again for two recording trips, the first in May of 1961, and the second, to film J. D. Short for the documentary film *The Blues*, in the summer of 1962. Two of the albums, by Henry Townsend and Barrelhouse Buck, were released at the time of the recording. One album, with J. D. Short, was released as part of the Legacy of the Blues series in 1973, and the other albums were released by Folkways in 1984. The notes were written at the time the albums were released.

Daddy Hotcakes

Even after so many years have passed I still have a vivid memory of the first time I met George Montgomery, a ragged, cheerful man who called himself – when he sang the blues – 'Daddy Hotcakes.' A St. Louis policemen named Charles O'Brien, who had spent two or three years tracking down the city's scattered, lost older generation of blues artists, had been given his name by '…a fellow named Dave Mangurian.' When Ann and I came into St. Louis looking for singers to record, Charley suggested we try George Montgomery, who was living in a shabby apartment in one of the city's edgier neighborhoods. When Charley and I climbed up the stairs the next day and stood in front of George's door, Charley, who was a lieutenant on the vice squad, without thinking about what he was doing knocked on the battered door the same way he had knocked on hundreds of doors like it. He had a key in his hand, and he knocked half with the key and half with his fist.

After the sharp, clattering knock, Charley, who was in trim shape, sprang to one side, to be out of the way if something unexpected should come through the doorway. When he heard a shifting inside the room he called out, 'Open up in there!' with a tone that could have been in the accent of any one of several races – Charley was white – but was unmistakably a policeman's. There was a silence, then with a resignation that was as much without special thought as Charley's precautions, George opened the door and waited for us to say something, his dark face as expressionless as the faded, indecipherable writings on the wall of the corridor behind him.

I am still also as surprised – when I listen to what we recorded in his room over the next two or three days – at the complete, natural spontaneity of his blues. I never recorded anyone who was quite like him. Certainly there is a great deal of variety in the blues, but most singers develop a few ideas, usually concerned with the difficulties between men and women, and these verses and phrases turn up over and over again in their blues lyrics. With George, however, everything was material for the blues, and since there was so much material to select from, he never bothered to select anything in particular before he started singing. Using his imagination and a store of familiar blues phrases to help him through occasional hesitations he simply made up the songs as he went along. I had some of the same experience when I recorded Lightnin' Hopkins and Robert Pete Williams, but even as loose and free as they were with their blues I still could anticipate most of what they were going to do. Usually if there was a problem with a take we could try doing the song over again. With George, however, I never could be sure what might come next if I asked him to repeat anything.

George was a tall, bulky man, and I always saw him dressed in the rough clothes that he wore for his work as a watchman in the building where he had his apartment, and also for some of the neighboring buildings. If I had seen him on the street I wouldn't have noticed him. He had large, clumsy hands, but when he handled his much used guitar there was a careful gentleness to his movements. His face, the first time I saw him, was resigned and tired, his skin rubbed and worn with years of the grime from his job, but he talked easily to us without any suggestion that he had been defeated by his life. Later, when I looked at the photos Ann took of him what I saw was not his worn shirt or the scratched wood of his guitar, what I saw was the gentleness of his expression and kindness in his eyes. One of the pictures she took was later used as the cover illustration for the *The Bluesmen* and for the collection of her blues portraits *Blues Faces*.

The first day George sang for Charley and myself he did three or four quiet blues, with a melancholy feeling of loneliness that suited the drab day. It was a kind of informal audition, since neither of us had ever heard him sing. The next afternoon, however, when Ann and I went back with Charley to record George's songs, the mood had changed completely. This time he wasn't alone. There was a washboard player, a boy from the shoe shine stand on the corner who played harmonica,

'Daddy Hotcakes', St. Louis, 1961
(Photo: Ann Charters)

and two unemployed musicians who had dropped by to see what was going on. Instead of the restrained mood of the day before there was a mood of exhilaration and comedy as he and the washboard player shouted back and forth to each other in broad swatches of country humor. The harmonica player, still wearing his shoeshine apron, threw in a note whenever he felt there was an opening.

After a few numbers the little group had lost whatever sense of organization they had started with, and we decided to continue with George singing by himself. After the others had straggled out I asked him about some of the quieter blues he'd sung the day before. He looked confused. I'd written down the opening lines of two or three of them, and I read one back to him. He brightened, picked up the guitar, and sang a blues that sounded completely different, though I could hear that at some complicated level he was constructing the new song around the theme of the opening line I'd given him.

The next day when we came back, George was alone in his small front room. The other musicians had also returned, but they'd moved out into the kitchen and they were reading magazines. This time, to my surprise, he began with a piece that was more familiar. He retuned the guitar to the old 'Spanish' tuning and sang a version of 'Corrine Corrina' which stayed fairly close to the song's familiar outlines. But as soon as he'd finished it he thought for a moment and said, 'That makes me think about going to Hawaii.' Then he immediately began a new piece that he named – later – 'Hawaiian Dream Blues'. About half way through his rendition I realized that he'd gotten the idea from the guitar tuning, which was similar to the sound of the Hawaiian steel guitar style.

The rest of the afternoon continued with this completely unpredictable flow of ideas, images and responses. It felt a little like we were picking up a box, the way you do as a child, and we were shaking it without any idea of what might fall out. A question about his early travels led to a freely imaginative lyric 'Well, I've Been Down To Memphis', and a little rhythmic figure he picked out on the guitar led to a piece he decided should be called 'I Ride My Horses Anywhere'. He began to sing it without any warning, and I had to stop him so I could turn the recording machine on. In the few seconds that passed while he waited for the tape to begin rolling, the song changed key, rhythm and the idea he'd started with. Only the horses still were left, and if it had taken me a little longer to start the machine, I was sure that the horses themselves would have disappeared down one of the uncharted trails of George's imagination.

When later I went through all the songs, and spent some time with his spontaneous starts and half finished opening lines I realized that he thought of the blues the way a free jazz soloist approaches an improvisation. All of the elements of his songs were there in his fingers, and it was the impulse of the moment that determined how he put them together. Sometimes, when the mood led him to create something like a brooding song that he titled 'Strange Woman Blues', with its almost story-like description of a late night walk and a meeting with a prostitute, I found myself wishing that I could have found some way to move his mood to more songs with this sustained introspection.

Much of what George Montgomery had learned about the blues had come from his wanderings back and forth across the South. He was born in Rehovat, Georgia on May 15th, 1894, which meant he was just two days away from his sixty-seventh birthday when I met him. He grew up on a farm, but when he was still a boy he left and worked whatever jobs he could find – hod carrier, railroad laborer, and saw mill hand. He was working in Helena, Arkansas about 1918 when he decided to move up to St. Louis. As he recalled, he had begun singing the blues when he was very young, and he worked in the twenties as an entertainer, which meant he performed every kind of song. For several years he travelled with the Royal American Shows as a fire eater, and for a brief time in 1937 he was one of the singers on a daily radio program in St. Louis. He used the name 'Papa' or 'Daddy Hotcakes'. About this time the local blues artist, Charlie Jordan, who was recording his own blues and also working as a talent scout and had a rehearsal hall for the singers around town, offered to take George on one of his New York recording trips to the ARC – America Record Company – label, but there was some confusion about dates and times and George missed the trip.

The songs that George recorded in his room – as far as I know these were his only recordings – made me conscious again of the haphazard circumstances that had left their mark on what we knew of the blues. How many singers were there like George, who missed a recording trip because they didn't get the times right? How many were there who never were heard by anyone who knew where to send them to get their songs on record? Since the blues was a medium that only lived on through the records that were made, the only blues history we have is what – by chance or accident – made it on to records. If in some stack of discarded 78s in a Salvation Army Thrift Store in the 1950s we'd found a worn copy of an ARC single of 'Hawaiian Dream Blues' by 'Daddy Hotcakes,' George Montgomery would have become one of those elusive figures who were sought by dozens of blues researchers everywhere in the South. I often found myself wondering what an old version of the song might have sounded like.

In 1942, during the confusion and dislocations of the early war years, George left the travelling show and scraped together a living entertaining people on the streets. On the old fashioned streetcars that still rattled through the St. Louis streets there was room for somebody to play the guitar in the rear seat – in what was then the segregated section for 'Negro' seating. He spent his days riding the streetcars with a washboard player or a harmonica player, passing his hat for contributions. If he got tired of riding the streetcars he could usually find a church party or a neighborhood gathering in somebody's back yard. He still sang a lot of gospel pieces, and they usually had the familiar melody and the expected verses. His free creativity was confined to the blues. In 1961, when we met him, he had his job as a watchman, but he hadn't given up playing for occasional parties.

When George listened back to some of the blues he recorded he didn't seem surprised at the richness of his material. When I asked him about it he just smiled and said, 'I got remembrance of things.'

(1981)

Henry Townsend

I don't remember who it was that gave me Henry Townsend's address, but it it could have been Charley O'Brien, the lieutenant on the St. Louis Police Department's vice squad who helped me so much with the recordings that I did with my wife Ann's enthusiastic assistance on a trip to St. Louis in the spring of 1961. What I do remember is feeling a little surprised when I met Henry, who had been a name on a handful of startlingly original blues recordings done in the 1920s. He turned out to be a pleasant, well-dressed man in his early fifties who had sensibly decided to give up the blues when he found he couldn't make a living as a musician. When I met him he had been working for many years as an insurance collector, and lived with his family in a pleasant, modern apartment. So many of the veteran singers I was meeting at this time were poor and confused, some of them alcoholic, many of them sick and resentful, but Townsend had managed to avoid all of this, and he still played enough on weekends to keep his old feeling for the blues. The first night I talked with him, someone in the room – it was a neighbor in the apartment building in the new complex where he lived – asked me why I was bothering to record somebody like Henry, who was more a part of the past than he was of the 1960s music scene. While I was trying to think of something to say, it was Henry who answered quietly for me, 'To preserve the tradition.'

I was also surprised to find that Henry was so young. Most of us who were searching out the blues artists who had recorded in the first period of interest in the blues as a commercial product were young enough to think of anyone over forty as old, but some of the musicians we met and worked with really *weren't* very old. Henry had begun recording at the end of the twenties – in the middle of November 1929, in fact, which was about as close to the end of the twenties as you could come – and when he did his first session in Chicago he was only two weeks past his twentieth birthday. Between his first two releases – for the legendary Columbia Records 14000 'race' music series – and his two releases for the Bluebird blues series in 1937, he also managed to record two songs for the other legendary blues series of the twenties, the Paramount Records 13000 series, and a single for Bluebird in 1935. With the 1937 session his first recording career was finished and he was just twenty-eight years old. In 1961, when I met him, he was fifty-two, he still was playing for dancing in one of the local clubs on weekends, he had a new guitar, and it seemed perfectly reasonable to think of recording him again. He didn't expect that there would be much chance of anything he might do now selling very well, but as he had said, he also felt a concern about preserving his blues traditions, and he was interested in giving it another chance.

One of the things that was most intriguing for me about working with Henry was that this was the first time I'd ever recorded anyone playing an electric guitar. Somehow all of the music I'd recorded before out in the southern countryside or in New Orleans dance halls had been acoustic. He also asked if he could bring another musician to the studio, since he was used to working in a group now. When I met him for an informal rehearsal there was not only his electric guitar and its amplifier, there was also an electric bass guitar and its amplifier. A young musician, Tommy Bankhead, from the Mississippi delta, had worked occasionally with him in one of the bands that played in a neighborhood club, and Tommy was excited by the challenge of working out bass patterns that would fill in for what were to them the missing piano and drums. He had gigged around with a number of well-known bands, including Elmore James, and even knowing as little as I did about what kinds of bass lines he was looking for it was clear that he was a skilled and sensitive musician. The first blues they ran down together wiped out any lingering prejudices I had against electric instruments. It wasn't electric guitars that had changed the blues. It was the life in the African American ghettos, the new society, experiences of the people who created the blues that had changed, and it was the new instruments and their changed sound that expressed the new conditions of their lives.

Still, I couldn't stop looking for roots and sources, and I asked Henry if he knew any older numbers. As he worked his way through the songs he wanted to record, serious faced, putting on his glasses to look at the notes he'd made for lyrics and titles, he thought a moment, then began playing a piece in a style I'd never heard before. They'd been working through pieces for a couple of hours, and he was beginning to remember songs he hadn't thought of in a long time. What he had begun playing and singing had a distinctive double-time rhythm, a kind of lazy, rolling feel that flowed as much through the melody as it did through the accompaniment. The words were about Cairo, Illinois, a small, rundown city at the southern tip of Illinois, where the Ohio River flows into the Mississippi, and the piece had some of the rolling quality of Cairo's rivers. Then I realized that I had heard the piece before. It was a song that had been recorded by another St. Louis singer, Henry Spaulding, in the late spring of 1929, a few months before Henry had done his first recording.

Surprised, I called across the room to him. 'Wasn't that Henry Spaulding's tune?'

Townsend smiled and nodded, 'Henry and I was together at the Golden Lily on Market Street for a long time.' Of all the songs that he and Tommy recorded, when we went into one of the small, informal studios that were set up in St. Louis at that time, it was the 'Cairo Blues' – or 'Cairo Is My Baby's Home' as we called it finally – that stayed in

Henry Townsend, St. Louis, 1962
(Photo: Ann Charters)

my mind the longest, with its gentle nostalgia for a moment that was almost lost to memory.

With my wife Ann, I met Henry again the next summer, in 1962, when we filmed him performing a sequence for the documentary film *The Blues* that we were producing. We had brought a bottle of bourbon to celebrate the Prestige Records release of the album he and Tommy had recorded together, but since he was still out collecting the payments from his insurance clients his wife served us vanilla ice cream while we waited, talking cheerfully with four or five neighbors who had dropped in. As he came in the door Henry studied the ice cream and the bourbon with ice that we had poured for every one. He shook his head. 'Now ice cream and whiskey together – that's something I never heard of before.' Neither had we, but somehow it seemed to suit the moment.

For the rest of the evening we sat in the apartment listening to his new album while neighbors who had gathered in the kitchen kept calling out encouragement at the songs and the gentle arrangements. After a while he got out his guitar and tried out some of his latest songs. We made arrangements to come back the next night with the lights and the microphones and the cameras to film him playing. Although none of us could predict what might happen next it seemed reasonable to expect that a new musical career was beginning for him there. Within a short time he was playing, recording, and finally touring again. In the 1970s he even got as far as Europe on a blues tour, and he continued performing regularly until he began having problems with his health. As a final statement he worked with blues writer and photographer Bill Greensmith on a modest, insightful autobiography titled *A Blues Life*, which was published in 1999.

It was a disappointment for us that the sequence we filmed in his apartment didn't make its way past the final editing into the released version of *The Blues*, but in a way it wasn't necessary for Henry to be there. So much had already happened that he never could have expected, and the songs that he recorded for me in 1961, so many years before, were the beginning of a new career, rather than the ending of the career that had begun for him when he was so young and then he had half forgotten. As Henry said when we finished the recording, and we sat listening to the playbacks, 'Well, we'll see if something comes of it.'

(1981)

In those early years when the blues was a new experience for us, there were the continual disjointed moments when our old perceptions of what the blues *looked* like, had very little relationship to what they *sounded* like. We had never really considered the idea that at the beginning, the recorded blues was part of the commercial recording industry. But why wouldn't anyone just want to make a record? – not with the thought of stating some deeply considered attitude about the difficulties of contact across the boundaries of race, or to confront the economic inequities of the plantation system – but just to hear themselves on record, perhaps attract a little attention, and in a general way simply be part of the excitement. Often this was a chance for wives or girlfriends to take their turn in front of a microphone, and – if the studio mood was relaxed and there was decent accompaniment – some of these casual sessions are among the unexpected pleasures of the first blues era. This note was written for another of the volumes of *The Blues in St. Louis* which Folkways released in 1984. The recordings were originally done in St. Louis in May, 1961.

Edith Johnson and Henry Brown
A Nickel's Worth of Liver

I still find that even if I don't read a new book about the blues all the way through – the story, by now, has become a little familiar – I still leaf through the pages all the way to the end to look at the pictures. I'm still as curious about what the singers look like as I was in the 1950s, when all we had for a history of the blues were the listings of old records mixed in with the other records in the crammed pages of the jazz discographies. Who was Mildred Fernandez, I would ask myself, when I read that she had made a record of a blues song in 1921, what did she look like? Who was Laughing Charlie? What did Snitcher Roberts look like? What kind of costumes did Bobby Leecan's Need More band wear? What was the 'Turpentine Tree-O'?

Now that we know more about the blues these kinds of questions don't seem that unreasonable. 'Mildred Fernandez,' it turned out, was a pseudonym for Lillian Brown, whose picture turned up in Sheldon Harris's massive and invaluable compilation *Blues Who's Who*. She was very svelte, very beautiful and she looked fine in a silk top hat. I know what she looks like now, even if I have no idea what she sounds like. Often, late at night, I spend an hour with a book like Harris's, just looking at people's faces.

In that May of 1961, when I was doing my first sessions in St. Louis – Ann and I came back the next summer and we filmed parts of the documentary *The Blues* there – I kept having the experience of finally seeing someone who had been only a name on a record or in a discography listing. Henry Brown, an earthy barrelhouse and boogie style piano player from the 1920s, was one of these names, and he turned out to look about the way I expected. He was tall and rumpled, his face – like that of many bar-room pianists – without much expression, and his shoulders a little rounded from all the hours he'd spent hunched over a piano. He wasn't doing very well, and his clothes weren't new, but he was keeping himself going with a day job, and there were many people in St. Louis who still knew about his early career. I knew his name from some burly piano instrumentals, and the marvellous blues duets he'd recorded with the eccentric trombonist Ike Rodgers, and somehow he looked like the name on the records.

On the other hand I couldn't in any way relate the Edith North Johnson I met in her tastefully decorated, sunlit apartment with the girlish voice I'd heard on a single from the 1920s singing 'Gimme a nickel's worth of liver, gimme a dime's worth of stew, and I can feed everybody on Lucas Avenue.' Part of the effect of the record was the accompaniment, and as far as blues collectors were concerned, it was Ike's trombone, as much as her voice, that made the single so unique. Rodgers sometimes seemed to maneuver his way through an entire chorus of a blues with just varied, growling versions of a single note. His tone sounded like he had hung a piece of wire screening over the bell of his trombone – and one of the instrumentals was titled 'Screenin' the Blues' – but if it was some kind of screen he was using, it was a very rusty metal screen. Edith's clear voice hovered like a hope of sunlight over the darkness that Ike and Henry created as her accompaniment.

In the spring of 1961 Edith was a stylishly dressed, cheerfully competent woman who seemed to know everybody in St. Louis, and for most of her life she had been a successful business owner. That spring I seem to remember that she was managing a taxi company, and before that for many years she had run her own restaurant. When we all gathered in the recording studio that Bob Oswald, a local blues and jazz fan, had set up in his basement, the mood didn't feel like one of the classic blues sessions. Edith, in an attractive blouse and skirt, was sitting with Bob Oswald's wife. Vivian, an old friend, and they were gossiping about people in the St. Louis music world. Henry, in a rumpled shirt, was sitting awkwardly on the other side of the room, waiting uncomfortably for the microphones to be set up so we could begin.

When the microphones were ready, however, and Henry went over to try out the piano, it was clear that this was something he and Edith knew about. I could see in their faces that everything else about their lives was different, but at that moment they were sharing their feelings about the blues. Edith had brought three old songs that she'd written during her early recording career, but never had a chance to use, and I wanted her to record 'Nickle's Worth of Liver' again. When they tried it she stumbled over some of the verses, and she had to write some of the lines down so she would remember them. She decided to change the name of the street mentioned in the song from Lucas Avenue to Leonard Avenue, but once she and Henry had run over it three or four times she found the rhythm again. For the rest of the evening they had the feeling in the music that they had put together all those years before. She stood behind him as she sang, and Henry turned away from the keys, responding to the accents and the rhythmic shifts in her singing, underlining what she was doing with sudden flurries in the treble keys or a grumbling insistence in the bass. To give both of them a beat to work with he kicked rhythmically against the side of the piano's damper pedal.

If Edith Johnson didn't look like someone's idea of a blues singer in that spring of 1961, it was probably because her short career in the blues had also been untypical of the rough, tent show, down and out aura that surrounded some of the women blues singers of that time. She was married to Jessie Johnson, who was the local talent scout for OKeh Records, one of the major blues labels, and she worked behind the counter of their small record shop. She started singing along with the records they were selling, and finally convinced him that she should record herself. She began her recording career with a short session in New York, and then between September and the end of the same year she recorded four more times and did all of her best known performances. When the record industry collapsed with the beginning of the Depression she gave up singing, and I didn't have the feeling, talking to her between her business phone calls, that she'd thought much about it since. Perhaps because she hadn't been singing professionally during that time her style was still naively sincere and she still had a clear voice that nights of singing in noisy clubs would have coarsened, though the years had dropped the pitch of her voice down a few notes. She was living entirely in her 1961 St. Louis world, but her singing came out of another, and simpler, time.

Henry was a little older than Edith, and his involvement with music had been on a more professional level. He was born in Troy, Tennessee on July 25th, 1906, which made him just fifty-five when he recorded again. His first recordings, like Edith's, had been done in sessions in 1929. Brunswick Records had been having considerable success with barrelhouse and boogie, and their first release of his playing was the wonderfully descriptive solo 'Stomp 'Em On Down To The Bricks.' Then there were the instrumental sessions with Ike Rodgers, and Henry's last solo session included some of his classic performances, titles like 'Deep Morgan Blues' and 'Eastern Chimes Blues.' The solos he recorded in 1961 had much of the same feeling of the pieces he'd done thirty years earlier, even if his fingers had lost some of their ease. His instrumentals had the same careless, exuberant flavor of the old barrelhouse blues, and most of the time the propulsive rhythmic force came from a direct, no-nonsense boogie bass. The solos were all improvisations. He would try out a few ideas to see if they fit together, then he'd nod to Bob Oswald, and he would build the solo around the ideas he'd loosely sketched in his first run-through.

Edith's last blues was 'Drive My Baby Slow,' and as she sang they both became more and more involved with the sombre theme of the text. Henry echoed her last verses with an almost dirge-like tolling in the lower keys of the piano. When they'd finished there was a moment of silence; then, to end on a more cheerful note, Henry ran through a cheerful, raggy, stride version of 'Honeysuckle Rose.' As they laughed together afterwards, finishing a last drink and listening through some of what they had gotten on to tape, it felt somehow as though for the last thirty years time had stood still.

(1984)

6. The Blues as Poetry

One day in 1962 when I was in the Folkways Records office in Manhattan, Moses Asch asked me if I could produce a record for him that would document the poetry of the country blues lyrics. Although it might not have seemed a reasonable assumption that either of us was interested in the poetic qualities of blues lyrics, Moe had already had a long commitment to Spoken Word recordings of African American poetry. He had released 78rpm singles of readings by Langston Hughes on his early Asch and Disc labels, and the Folkways catalog included readings by, among others, Sterling Brown, Claude McKay, and Countee Cullen. I had published some poetry, but what was more immediately useful for him was that I had begun to produce a literature series for the company; editing the materials, and rehearsing and recording young New York actors in readings from the writings of Stephen Crane, Ralph Waldo Emerson, Herman Melville, and Emily Dickinson, among others. During this period, in an effort to correct what was perceived as a gap in the educational opportunities for students in the United States and the Soviet Union, the U.S. government was subsidizing school purchases of educational materials. Moe spent much of his time sitting in the Folkways booth at a year-round series of conventions for educators, and the Folkways catalog rapidly expanded to include a great many albums designed for classroom use. I remember for some months the company's bestselling LP was a selection of readings in classical Latin.

I put the album of blues poetry together for Moe, assembling a wide range of verses from recordings which I thought would illustrate the poetic range of the blues lyric. Since Ann and I were also travelling in the South that summer, spending time with the blues singers who would appear in our documentary film *The Blues*, I asked them to define the blues for me, planning to include whatever they told me in the notes to the album. When I listened to the tape I had put together, however, I found that even with my reasonable familiarity with southern blues I couldn't make out more than occasional words and phrases from the rumble of some of the rougher Mississippi accents. I couldn't imagine that a student in a classroom would have any more success in making out the words that a blues man like Charlie Patton or Frank Stokes was singing than I did.

Moe, however, had recently launched a small publishing subsidiary called Oak Books, and I went to him with the problem. Why didn't I present the blues poetry as a book, instead of a record compilation? He needed only a moment to decide I should try, and in the next few weeks I reworked the material I had assembled into the book *The Poetry of the Blues*, which he published in the spring of 1963. The book was an immediate success, reaching a much broader audience than either of us had anticipated. After a number of printings as an Oak book it was issued again as a trade paperback by Avon Books in 1964, and it was one of the alternative book titles that became part of the new culture of the 1960s. When the paperback edition was no longer available a few years later I decided not to offer the book to another publisher, and it has been out of print since that time.

From *The Poetry of the Blues* (1963)

With the lines and verses of the blues the African American society in the United States has fashioned its own popular song. Although it has been several decades since the blues played its role as the dominant black popular style, a residue of the blues has continued to shape many of the attitudes and the language of a broad swath of the black song that has followed. The blues functioned, in its beginning, simply as a reflection of the concerns and the emotional storms of every day black life in America, but there was never a moment in which the blues was the only expression of these moods. African American society has always had more varieties of popular song – ballads, love songs, comedy songs, vocal novelties – but the blues has continued to occupy a special niche simply by being so close to the heart of the long experience of being black in America. Since any popular song style in any culture functions as an expression for the anxieties of its young people many of its themes will be love and sexuality, their concerns, tribulations and small triumphs. The blues contained or hinted at other themes – the insecurity and the emotional toll that centuries of discrimination and segregation had taken on the black community, the dislocation and loneliness that joblessness forced on generations of so many of the men and women whose lives were mirrored in the struggles of many of the singers themselves – but for most of the blues artists it was the sexual game that was most often played out. It was generally taken as a given that the blues were for the man or the woman who was 'a fool for love.' As the Mississippi singer J. D. Short expressed it, 'Well, the blues first came from people being low in spirit and worried about their loved ones.'

Just being about love, however, doesn't lift a song lyric to the level of poetry. Poetry is, by definition, a language that is distinctive for the power of its expression, for the richness of its imagery, for the freshness of its themes and attitudes. Popular music has both the strength and the weakness of its position in any society. Its strength is that its themes can have an immediate resonance within its audience, its weakness is that it is usually too closely woven into the social textures of the group to break through the group's prejudices or limitations. Popular song in the United States after the Second World War was hemmed in by social conventions that insisted on a sexual and physical repression that became less and less realistic as social attitudes began to change. By the 1950s the disparity had become so obvious that there was a flight to alternate musical styles – like folk music – that offered at least some relief from the banalities offered by the commercial recording industry. The blues, drawing on a vein of imagery and language that was rooted in a different cultural background, had made the break many decades before.

The differences of opinion as to the commitment to social change in the music has been a complex issue for everyone who has written on the blues. The differences in attitudes has stretched from the assertion of one group of writers that the entire body of the blues is a 'coded' expression of anger at racial oppression, to other writers who simply accept the explanations of the singers themselves for the content of their lyrics, who don't insist that they are employing a language of *symbolic* protest in the songs. What everyone generally agrees on is that *overt* protest is only a small thread in the blues. At the same time the blues is a specific reflection of the differences between the two groups, white and black. If there had not been color lines, visible or invisible, drawn through the streets and the neighborhoods of the American cities there would never have been a distinct blues language.

It is also misleading to describe the blues as simply the language of the African American society. It is a society that is moulded by its deeply held religious beliefs, and for the fervent churchgoers who fill

America's black churches on Sunday morning there is often little tolerance for the songs that reflect the dissipation of Saturday night. Even during the 1920s, when the sales of blues records were the strongest in the black community, the sales of gospel records quickly assumed a significant counterbalance, and with the proliferation of recordings by the popular gospel quartets and the sermons by well known ministers, the sales of gospel records had already passed blues sales by the beginning of the 1930s. For most of the black audience it was jazz and the popular songs that formed the bulk of the new releases that dominated their radio listening and their record purchases.

At the same time, the blues was a kind of substrata, a geologic ground for so much that drew from it. The attitudes that the blues singers expressed still mirrored many of the attitudes of the larger black community. It is in some ways disquieting to regard the blues simply as an expression of 'differentness,' since it is the differences between white and black life in America – created by the pervasive presence of discrimination and prejudice – that often were used to justify the exclusions that prevented African Americans from taking their place in the larger American society. The reality, however, is that their long history of interaction has given each group, white and black, their own measure of distinctiveness. The differences that are mirrored in the blues are the differences that lie at the heart of the American social divide. The final measure of a democratic society, however, is not conformity, but diversity, and there must be a merging of the two separate societies, not necessarily into a group without differences, but into a single group that accepts these differences. The blues as poetry, the lyrics of the blues, at that moment can take their place as a force in the shaping of this new society, since the blues still are a reservoir of the attitudes and social responses that for the new African American society hold a long shadow of racial memory and a reflection of a developing social history.

Since the blues is so much a reflection of the life in segregated slums or on the isolated farms at the end of lonely dirt roads where most African Americans were forced to live until the breakdown of legal segregation in the 1960s, is it possible for someone who isn't black to understand the language of the blues? The widespread excitement over the blues everywhere in the world is obviously a reflection of a basic universality in so much of the blues language. Phrases, lines of blues verses, blues imagery have all made their journey to the language of popular music in every society, even if the songs that are titled 'blues' in a country like Sweden or Japan don't correspond very closely to what would be considered the American blues forms. There is no difficulty for anyone in understanding a verse with such universal meaning as,

> *Did you ever wake up, find your man had gone?*
> *Did you ever wake up, find your man had gone?*
> *You wring your hands, you cry the whole day long.*

It is just as obvious, however, that within any society there is a repertoire of song that is so embedded in the group's unique history that it is difficult for any outsider to fully sense the social implications. Probably no one who hasn't lived in the rural black community in the American South can intuit the emotional response to a verse like

> *My black woman, her face shinin' like the sun,*
> *Now my black woman, face shinin' like the sun.*
> *You know powder and makeup sure can't help her none.*

The blues sometimes seemed to have travelled a long road before the earliest recording helped settle it down. The trip, however, hasn't been such a long one. The phrases and the images of the blues grew from the work songs and the lonely 'hollers' of southern rural life, but the blues as a formal style, with an existence outside this loose collection of haphazard materials, seem to have developed around the turn of the previous century. It was by the period of the First World War that there was a consciousness that there was a musical style that was different enough to be given another name, *blues*. It was the intensity and the directness of the blues, when it had untangled itself from the first commercial bowdlerization of the style, that lent it a travelled feel. It had been many generations since European and American popular song had the emotional immediacy of the blues. Long back in the shadows of the European traditions were the ballads and fresh, pained lyrics that had grown from the rural life of the peasantry. With social change had come an increasing 'refinement' of the song materials until they had lost anything more than a symbolic connection to the emotions they described. In the blues, however, there was still a new, fresh vitality.

In the 1950s and 1960s many of the older musicians who had grown up with the earliest blues styles were still living, and many of them were still singing. They lived on back streets in southern cities like Memphis or St. Louis, on rundown farms, in smaller towns like Spartanburg or Macon. Some had settled in the ghettos of Chicago, Detroit, or New York. The most restless had even found their way to Los Angeles or Oakland. Some of them had day jobs, a few had become businessmen, somehow finding a footing in the shifting patterns of southern racial discrimination; others lived on welfare checks. Many of them who had grown up on poor sharecrop farms were badly educated, often broken physically by long years of hard, menial work, or by the drain of equally long years of steady dissipation. With strangers they often had difficulty expressing themselves in conversation, but they shared one subject on which all of them had definite and carefully weighed feelings: the blues.

Few of them travelled as much as they had done when they were younger; when a 'travellin' mood' would set them drifting from town to town until they settled down for a while with a new job or a new woman. The didn't see each other as much, and they didn't have as much chance to exchange songs and new instrumental licks, but their attitudes toward the blues had a marked similarity. Their bench mark for the effectiveness of a blues was its *sincerity*. For them the blues was a response to the difficulties and the disappointments of the life they saw around them in the streets and the tenement apartment where they lived. For the St. Louis singer Henry Townsend the heart of the blues was 'the true feeling.' Furry Lewis, in his Memphis kitchen, insisted, 'all the blues, you can say, are true.' As J. D. Short expressed it:

What I think about that makes the blues really good is when a fellow writes a blues and then writes it with a feeling, with great harmony, and there's so many true words in the blues, of things that have happened to so many people, and that's why it makes the feeling in the blues.

Many of them, in their concern for the truth of their songs, felt that not only did a blues have to have a 'true feeling,' but that it was the singers themselves who had to have been through the emotional experience that the blues expressed. Memphis Willie B. stated:

A blues is about something that's real. It's about what a man feels

J. D. Short, 1962
(Photo: Ann Charters)

when his wife leaves him, or about some disappointment that happens to him that he can't do anything about. That's why none of these young boys can really sing the blues. They don't know about the things that go into a blues.

When he was asked what the quality was that made a good blues singer, Henry Townsend simply laughed.

Trouble…that's right. That's the one word solution. Trouble. You know you can only express a true feeling if you're sincere about it. You can only express what happened to you.

Baby Tate, in Spartanburg, South Carolina, felt that it was '…difficulties. I don't put it all on drinking or nothing like that. I put it on troubles in your home.' Furry Lewis didn't even think of the writing of a blues as something that was separated from the emotions of the blues.

Well, one thing, when you write the blues and what you be thinking about, you be blue and you ain't got nothing hardly to think about. You just already blue, and you just go on and write.

From the immediate response to their emotions have come the dominant themes of the blues: love, disappointment and anger. In the blues, also, can come some release from the emotions. As Baby Tate put it:

I'll tell you what gives me the blues. When my wife makes me mad. Make me angry otherwise. A dog go mad. But if she makes me angry. I didn't do all I can do or something like that, and she wants me to do something else. She gets me angry. Well, the first thing I do I'll grab my guitar and walk out of the house to keep from having a fight…

J. D. Short nodded when he was asked if singing helped him to get through periods of emotional stress,

Yes, it actual do. It's a lot of times we can get very worried and dissatisfied, and if we can get to singing the blues and if we can play music and play the blues we may play the blues for a while until we get kind of pacified. That cuts off a lot of worry.

And, as he went on to say, there is also an emotional release for the person listening to the blues.

> Sometimes the people that's listening at you have actual been through some of the same things that I have been through and automatically that takes effect on them and that causes their attention to come.

Henry Townsend described his own feelings about the blues, saying,

> When you express yourself, how you felt, how you been mistreated, and the things that happened to you in life, that's the only thing you can say. If you sing anything else then you're singing something somebody else has felt.

Then he went on to explain how, as a blues artist, he can reach the emotions of his audience with something that someone else has written.

> Now some writer might walk up and tell you, 'Here's a song I want you to sing. Play it cheap, if you want, but it's the truth.' He wants you to sing it because he's not able to and he'd like it to be done, and if you're sincere enough about taking sympathy with the fellow you can do the song for him.

For the men and the women who created the emotional world of their songs, the language of the blues had the directness and the sincerity of their own experience. Even the dominant theme of the blues, the tangled disappointments of love, reflect this immediate response to their lives. For Furry Lewis,

> ...the blues come from a woman wanting to see her man, and a man wanting to see his woman.

And as Henry Townsend said with a shrug,

> You know, that's the major thing in life. Please believe me. What you love best is what can hurt you the most...

It is this immediacy of the emotions that gives the blues its terseness, an unadorned honesty that feels like someone is sitting you down and whispering in your ear. A blues often has no more than a dozen lines, but within this confined area the emotional statement is still strong and direct. Much of the power of the blues expression is in the relationship between the stanzas, but the stanzas, or verses, as most singers would call them, have a completeness of thought within themselves. The verse, rather than a single line or a rhymed couplet, is the brick out of which the structure of a blues is built. The variety of the early blues forms, before the influence of recordings imposed the familiar three line, twelve bar form, leaves the impression that there were a number of song styles that contributed to the earliest blues. One of the early influences, as the formal structure of what we came to call the blues took shape, was certainly the shouted work songs of the fields and the prison yards. The basic form, as a work song, was a call and response. The lead singer would call,

Well, you know I left my woman

and the gang would respond with a rhythmic phrase that emphasized the movements of their work. Some of the answering calls popular throughout the South were 'Great God A'mighty,' 'My hammer ring!' or 'Here, rattler, here.' The lead singer could either repeat the line, or finish the phrase with a line like,

Left her cold in hand!

and the sweating line of workers would add, 'My hammer ring!' A complete phrase would become something like,

Well, you know I left my woman,
My hammer ring!
Left her cold in hand!
My hammer ring!

It was a casual, freely improvised form, and accounts of slave songs before the Civil War include many examples of the inventiveness of the lead singers. Many of the leaders also developed some skill with rhyme, and there were common phrases like,

> *You ought to heard what that letter read,*
> *Here, rattler, here!*
> *Says my mother's just 'bout dead,*
> *Here, rattler, here!*

If the caller were to sing it by himself it would be a crude blues verse.

> *You ought to heard what that letter read,*
> *Says my mother's just 'bout dead.*

Among early blues recordings were a number which still used the two line verse. Typical would be lines like,

> *Tossin' and turnin' in my bed at night,*
> *Woman I love sure don't treat me right.*

or,

> *Woman I love, she don't want me to clown,*
> *She's a high brown lady, ain't no hand me down.*

Sometimes the verses were strung together without concern for lines that rhymed, but for most of the blues artists the use of rhyme was an essential part of the blues language. As Furry Lewis put it,

> The time when you get a blues, what you call the blues, you just haven't come out like you s'posed to and it don't be right. You have to go all over it again until you rhyme it up if you call yourself being with the blues. If it ain't rhymed up it don't sound good to me or nobody else.

Blues singers, however, weren't so fussy about the rhymes they used. Words that *sounded* close were good enough, just as formal poetry in the English and American traditions often uses rhymes that suggest the sounds. In the blues there was as much of what is called 'near' or 'slant' rhyme as there was of what is termed 'perfect' rhyme – words like red/dead, clown/down, or night/right. Some of the common near rhymes that helped singers put together their blues were combinations like man/hand, ground/down, or dime/mine, and with gerundive expressions, 'going,' 'grieving,' 'crying,' the final 'ing' usually worked as a rhyme by itself. Other rhymes were more loosely connected; Ride/by, town/now, deep/week. Country pronunciations also helped with some of the rhymes. If the word 'before' was pronounced with a casual southern softness to the terminal sound – 'befo'' – then it could rhyme with 'go' or 'slow.' The language of a great majority of blues songs makes it clear that most singers would agree with Furry Lewis, 'If it ain't rhymed up it don't sound good to me or nobody else,' but sometimes a rhyme that only loosely fit the definition would do as well.

It was when a singer first stumbled on the idea of repeating the first line of a new verse that the blues as we know the form today finally took its distinctive shape. The name of the singer will probably never be known. W. C. Handy, who heard the blues in the 1890s in Mississippi, encountered a man singing in what he recognised was something new. The great early blues artist 'Ma' Rainey first heard what she realized was a blues in Mississippi a decade later, and the singer she heard was a woman. There is some precedent for the repeated line – some of the Trinidadian *oratorical* calypso songs from an earlier period repeated their opening line, and the Caribbean was a much travelled entry to the southern states for many of the musical styles for the islands. The repeated first line, however, could have naturally emerged from the local country environment. It could possibly have been first used by a singer improvising his songs at a country dance, playing in the flickering light of a kerosene lantern as the couples danced in the shadows. As the night ground on and the singer got tired, if he was running out of songs he could begin singing old phrases from hollers and work gang chants. A woman artist would have lines from her own memory of field songs or the play party rhymes that were part of the memory of all southern children. She still had to put together lines that rhymed, and the creative moment that came to define the blues could have occurred when she repeated the opening line to give herself a minute to think of something that would give her the rhyme.

The first time a line was repeated it might have been sung with a halting emphasis, the repetition little more than a half-sung imitation of the first line, but the repeated line is the simple device that gives the blues its distinctive form, and the artists began lingering over it, lending their verses a new depth. The thought is still complete in the two rhyming lines, the first and the third,

Times is so tough, can't even get a dime,
Times don't get better I'm going to lose my mind.

but with the repetition of the first line the verse grows from a simple couplet to a more expressive stanza and it takes on a new emphasis. Usually the line was repeated with an alteration in the phrasing.

Times is so tough, can't even get a dime,
Yes, time's is so tough, can't even get me a dime,

Then the singer – as well as the listener – could conclude the thought with the rhyming line,

Times don't get better, I'm going to lose my mind.

The repetition of the opening line also adds suspense to the resolution of the verse, even if the effect is only momentary. To heighten the sense of delay the singers took the harmony a step further and repeated the second line in a different harmony – in what usually was a subdominant chord that resolved back to the basic tonic harmony, before moving to a dominant chord that introduced the final line. In its compressed form the fully conceived stanza had a remarkable symmetry. Three lines – three different harmonies. For someone who is used to harmonic shorthand and hasn't met the blues before, a twelve bar stanza in the most often used form can be noted as:

I – I – IV – I
IV – IV – I – I
V – V – I – I

Each of the numerals within the dashes is one measure in 4/4, or common time, counted with four slow beats. A common refinement is to treat the final measure of the first line as a transition to the subdominant harmony of the next measure – and the measure adds the seventh tone – two beats of the basic tonic, then two beats of the tonic

7th. This is indicated as I/I7. Like the poetic device of the repeated first line, the harmonic pattern is also effective in distinguishing the blues because it is simple, immediately recognizable, and flexible enough to work musically for every style of vocal and instrumental blues, from a Mississippi song verse by Charlie Patton or an intricate, freely shaped blues instrumental solo by bebop altoist Charlie Parker.

The richest strains of blues poetry have developed from within the small confines of the distinctive stanza form.

Although it is the three line rhymed stanza that is most characteristic of the commercial blues idiom, there are many variants that singers have exploited since the beginnings of the blues. Sometimes, instead of the usual three line stanza, the form had a two–line rhymed couplet in place of the more conventional first line and its repetition. In this form the two lines are broken musically into four shorter phrases, and the verse changes from,

> *I was standing on the corner with my hat in my hand,*
> *Looking for a woman didn't have no man.*

to,

> *I was standing on the corner,*
> *Had my hat in my hand.*
> *Just looking for a woman,*
> *Didn't have no man.*

Almost invariably a stanza beginning with this group of shorter lines resolves into the longer line of the usual stanza form. The two lines following these shorter lines could be,

> *I want to know, I want to know why did my baby go.*
> *I love that woman, love her 'til it hurts me so.*

Often in a blues which uses this mixed stanza the two longer last lines are repeated at the end of every stanza, until they become a kind of refrain. Champion Jack Dupree's 'Let It Be' is a complex song which comes into a broadly defined area between the blues and religious sentiments. It uses the hints of the song's themes in the opening two lines as a source of the allusions that follow in other verses, tying the threads of the song into a refrain–like pattern of stanzas.

Oh Lord, how long it'll be how long will it be,
Oh Lord, will it be
When the time comes, when the time comes for me,
Will it be there, will it be pain, will it be misery,
or will it be pain?
Oh Lord, how long it'll be,
Oh Lord, how will it be?

I have suffered all my life,
And I been misery, heart ache, and pain,
I been everything in the world,
I've been every, every thing but a human being,
There is no more, no more sorrow,
And no more tears and pain,
Oh Lord, don't let me be,
Oh Lord, be in no pain…

God will take care of you, no matter what you do,
I know, I know,
He will, he will, he will take care of you.
May the good Lord in heaven, hope he will remember me,
Will it be, Will it be,
Oh Lord, will it be?

In J. D. Short's 'Slidin' Delta', a blues which seems to suggest a melodic form from an older type of country song, it is the second line in a four line stanza that is repeated as a refrain.

Oh, early this mornin', creepin' through my door,
Now, don't you hear me a-cryin', pretty mama,
Early this mornin, cryin' through my door.
Well I hear that whistle blow and she won't blow here
no mo'.

Oh, slow down train now, bring my baby back home,
Now, don't you a-hear me cryin', pretty mama,

Slow down train, bring my baby back home.
Well, she been gone so long, ooah, make my poor
heart burn.

One thing now I don't understand,
Now, don't you a-hear me cryin', pretty mama,
One thing now I don't understand.
I been nice to my baby, ooah, she gone with
another man...

Although the poetic meter of the blues lines seems sometimes to be casually conceived, the usual way a blues line should be measured is not *syllabic* – that is, with a strict count of loud and soft stressed syllables within the words – but with *accentual stress*. The singers create their lines in what is a suggestion of a basic line of five stressed accents, the stressed syllables counted, however, by stressed words or parts of words, which can be noted as,

I want to <u>know</u>, I want to <u>know</u>, <u>why</u> did my <u>ba</u>-by <u>go</u>?

The standard blues line has five accents, and the shorter line has two,

I was <u>stand</u>-ing on the <u>cor</u>-ner

Often a blues line will fall into a natural iambic pentameter rhythm, as,

I <u>won</u>-der <u>does</u> my <u>ba</u>-by <u>call</u> my <u>name</u>?

but the singers have always been comfortable mixing multiple types of poetic meter.

In his conversations about the blues Furry Lewis talked about the way the stanzas – verses – in a blues relate to each other:

The first verse could be the last. You know, just any old verse that I wanted I could make that the first, then go right on from there and just rhyme up from it and make them all kind of match, you know.

By making them 'match' he meant relating them by theme or idea.

Just like I was to rhyme something, if I was to have a song now, and say, '*Bye, bye, I got no more to say.*' Well that could be the first verse, and then the next verse I could say, '*I'm sorry, baby, you treat me this'a way.*' That'd be in a different verse altogether, and the next would go on, you know, just like that. You want all the verses to be talking about the same thing.

As Furry emphasised, most blues are constructed from a sequence of verses that are related in their mood or their response to the same emotional situation. What began the train of thought, 'Bye, bye, I got no more to say,' could have led to the line suggesting the final implications of the incident, 'I'm sorry, baby, you treat me this'a way.' As Furry's comments about the order of the verses also emphasize, a blues usually isn't a narrative. The blues generally don't tell stories. Within the African American traditions there is a rich vein of story telling, but with only a handful of exceptions the blues have expressed an emotional situation, not a specific occurrence. Most singers – in fact most Americans who have grown up as members of groups like the Girl Scouts or the Boy Scouts – know some of the verses to songs like 'John Henry' or 'Frankie and Johnny,' which relate to the black experience. There were certainly occasional blues in the 1920s that described a larger social event, but there was little use of the 78rpm blues single to tell the detailed story of a local murder or a mining disaster or a death on the highway that could compare to the balladry of white 'country' recordings of the same period.

The catastrophic Mississippi River floods of 1927 were described in several blues of the period, among them Bessie Smith's majestic 'Back Water Blues', and Charlie Patton's carefully detailed and emotional 'High Water Everywhere', but even in these songs there is an element of generalized response. Bessie Smith's song, with its famous opening line, 'Well it rained five days, and the sky turned dark as night,' had been written the year before and what she was singing about was an Ohio River flood outside of Cincinnati. Its release coincidentally came just in time for it to be picked up as the unforgettable description of the Mississippi flood. The most descriptive group of blues are the songs recorded by country artists like Patton, Son House, or Sleepy John Estes which evoked local sheriffs or auto mechanics, like Patton's 'Dry Well Blues', which narrates the effect of the drought of 1930 on his

Mississippi town of Lula. Estes sang about several people in his small town of Brownsville, northeast of Memphis, including Vassie Williams, who repaired his car, the local mortician, Al Rawls, and his grocer, Pat Mann. In a line about the hazards of riding a freight through town he named the two men who would probably be enforcing the law: 'Mr. Will will get you and Mr. Guy Ware will wear you out.' Perhaps the closest any rural blues artist came to the kind of detailed narrative of their white country neighbors is Estes' brilliantly evocative 'Floating Bridge', which describes his near drowning when a car he was riding in slid off a pontoon bridge, 'Tell me five minutes time in the water I was hid.'

What the blues achieves, in its use of verses that develop emotional situations through juxtaposition and association, is a larger suggestion of the world of African America. When social change comes to the United States, as it certainly will, if the blues simply mirrored only a hidden protest at the injustices of the current era they would finally have little more than an historical interest, like the songs of the Suffragettes or the Grange Movement. Instead, as the emerging black society in America struggled to find a fully realized life on the other side of the racial line, the men and women who created the blues turned to their music as the expression of their own immediate and personal experience, which had larger dimensions than the daily buffeting of discrimination. In their concern with what they called the 'true feeling' the singers of the blues have given us a human reality which includes all of the multiple facets of their day. In the honesty of their emotion is an insistent reminder that on either side of the racial divide live only other men and women, who find the same moments of pain and joy in the experience of their lives.

(1963)

Although many of us had used the term 'poetry' to describe blues lyrics there were only a handful of singers who seemed to bring a conscious literary sense to the words they sang. Of all the 'poets' of the older style blues none was more active, or more successful, than Lonnie Johnson. From his first session in 1925, until his final recordings forty years later he continued to expand and develop his blues language. Moe Asch had

Samuel Charters recording Sleepy John Estes,
Brownsville, Tennessee, 1962
(Photo: Ann Charters)

recorded Lonnie for his old Asch and Disc labels in the 1940s, then in 1967 he was asked by Verve Records to do an audition session with him. Since there was no follow-up from Verve, the tapes were put on a shelf and Moe simply forgot about them. When he found them again in the early 1980s he asked me to edit them and to write the notes for the two albums of material. I had written about Lonnie in *The Country Blues*, and I was pleased at the opportunity to write again about an artist I greatly admired.

Lonnie Johnson
Mr Trouble and Tears Don't Fall No More

When Lonnie Johnson finished recording the songs for this informal session he talked for a while with Moses Asch of Folkways, who had done the recordings. Moe asked him if anyone was writing his biography, and he answered with his usual pleasantness, no, he didn't know why, but the writers always seemed to be looking for the wrong things from him. 'They look for me to mostly tell the hardships of my life, instead of the best part of my life…'

At that time – the session was done in 1967 – it did sometimes seem difficult to know just where to put Lonnie Johnson and his blues. Over his long and successful career he had not only sung and recorded hundreds of solo blues, he had recorded as a jazz guitar soloist with artists like Louis Armstrong and Duke Ellington, worked in the 1940s in nightclubs with swing groups, and in the last phase of his career become a sensitive and gifted performer of pop ballads. All of this was difficult to reconcile with the disconsolate, ragged, down-at-the-heels image of the blues singer that was wide-spread at the time. Certainly none of this confusion concerned Lonnie. He had experienced a hiatus in his career in the mid-1950s, following his final single releases by the Cincinnati R&B label King Records and a related tour of England in 1952, but he had become active again during the blues revival of the 1960s and he continued performing until he suffered a fatal stroke in his home in Philadelphia in 1970.

It is also clear from these recordings that Lonnie's genius was as clearly evident at the close of his career as it had been when he had made his first blues recording in 1925, more than forty years earlier. He was in superb form for the session; compellingly inventive and musical. His blues lyrics still had their unique, imaginative skill. He sketched in the emotional turmoil of his urban world with clear and telling strokes, accompanying himself with the brilliant repertoire of guitar figures that seemed to have become more supple and assured with the passing years. Perhaps it was just as well that the tapes were forgotten on a shelf in the Folkways storeroom. In 1967 the emphasis was still focused on the rural blues and its country singers. Now in 1982 it was possible to respond to an artist like Lonnie with more objectivity. The tapes showed again his artistic maturity and intelligence, as well as demonstrating as clearly what a dominating influence he was on other singers of his generation. As he reminded Moe Asch, it would be a mistake to look only at the 'hardships' of his life. In his own words, 'I had many a happy day…'

There was another mistake made about Lonnie in the first years of his rediscovery. In the book *The Country Blues* I included a long and sympathetic chapter about him, but his birthdate – which I'd found in a jazz directory – was given as 1889. He had actually been born in 1899, on February 8th, in New Orleans, so the book had added ten years to his age. The mistake was unfortunately continued in the generally useful *Blues Who's Who*. He didn't seem to have minded the mistake about his age, but he was never entirely comfortable about being included in a book about country blues singers. When he was asked about his own musical style he always answered with some firmness, 'Urban blues.'

Although Lonnie, looking back on his life, did think of himself as a fortunate man, his early life had been marked by a tragic event that did seem to leave its emotional traces on the mood of his early blues recordings. He was born into a large family; all of them, as he remembered, were musicians. In 1915, with the exception of Lonnie, an older brother, and his mother, the rest of the family – his father and nine brothers and sisters – died in an influenza epidemic in New Orleans. Out of this experience might have come some of the haunting loneliness that characterized so much of his music. One thing that tempered his memory of the experience, however, was the fact that his mother was still living when he talked with Moe Asch. She was then 94, they still were emotionally very close, and she had an affectionate relationship with Lonnie's daughter Brenda, her only grandchild. He finished the sentence that began 'I had many a happy day…' with a heartfelt '…and she's cause of it.'

Despite his memories of a long and fulfilled life, the blues he sang in 1967 still had their customary sting of cynicism and disillusionment. For Lonnie this was the essence of the blues, the expression of unhappiness and disappointment, of an anger that had a larger dimension than the physical details of poverty and decay that he saw in the neighborhoods where he performed and where he was forced to live for most of his life by the nation's racial politics. What he often seemed to be singing about was a poverty of the spirit in a world where even love itself had no meaning. These were standard blues themes, but in his repetitions, in his skilled mingling of these observations with the physical details of his verses, he lifted them into a larger emotional context. In a blues like 'Raise Your Window High' from these 1967 tapes he wrote opening lines to the verses that presented specific physical images,

Hang up your lantern, baby, raise your window high…

or

When I found that empty pillow I walked the floor and cried all night.

and he leaves the first and second verses unrhymed, as if he were choosing to emphasize the secondary theme of the verses, that the woman he is describing is 'evil'. The verse beginning '…raise your window *high*' ends with a rhyming phrase, but it is a rhyme that emphasizes an emotional crisis. It concludes, '…you so mean and evil, so many days you have to *cry*,' which exaggerates the rhymed dissonance of 'high' and 'cry.' In the second verse the phrase '…I couldn't get through to you' is set against a repetition of the closing line of the first verse, '…you have to cry.'

In another of the songs, 'I've Been A Fool Myself,' he reconsidered some of the standard blues themes, but suggested a personal identification with the familiar phrases.

He opened it with a line that was a direct contradiction of most of the sentiments that are characteristic of most popular song lyrics, 'Men, if you single, pray to God you stay that way.' In this blues, however, he used rhyme in the ultimate lines of each verse: '…stay that way' is rhymed with the conclusion that a woman is not interested in a 'good' man, but wants him only '…to pass the time away.' In a concluding verse he reiterates a sentiment that was a theme of many blues of this period, 'I know what I'm talkin' about, I been a fool myself,' and this time he ends the verse with a near rhyme in the final line, declaring that the woman he loved, in another of the standard blues sentiments, '…she belonged to somebody else.'

A mood of sour misogyny hangs over many of his recordings, and it was only in occasional verses that he dropped his tone of disappointment and sang about a relationship that was characterized by honesty and fulfilment. This doesn't mean that Lonnie's life was a series of unhappy love affairs. Despite everything that has been written about the 'honesty' of the blues singer, most of the 'honesty' is metaphoric – which means that that singer is in reality only expressing the emotions of his audience. As Chicago bluesman Otis Rush described it, 'If you're honest you can take on that other man's troubles.' At the height of his career, the moods of Lonnie's blues were a reflection of the unhappiness and insecurities of the thousands of people who were buying his records.

Since I began this introduction by saying that there had been some mistakes in the perception that many of the new blues audience had about Lonnie Johnson, I should also clarify another mistake that people often made about Lonnie in these later years. One thing that sometimes distressed his audiences in the 1960s was his penchant for singing popular songs. Sometimes they were formally included in one of his performances and recordings – there was even an album on Prestige titled *Blues and Ballads*, with Elmer Snowden, an old friend from the Duke Ellington years, joining him on a second guitar for the backgrounds. Pop ballads were included on the tapes he recorded for Moe Asch. More often he simply inserted one of his sentimental ballads into his shows, whether the audience was anticipating it or not. At a memorable concert in New York's Carnegie Hall, Lonnie was introduced as one of the living legends of the blues, and in what was perhaps a misguided moment of artistic integrity he looked out at his expectant audience and sang one of his lounge favorites, 'Red Sails in the Sunset.'

For Lonnie's new audiences who were listening to the blues as a refuge from what they felt were the banalities of their own 1950s pop culture, songs like 'Prisoner of Love' or 'My Mother's Eyes' presented a confusing challenge. Lonnie, for his part, loved popular ballads, and he was one of the most sensitive ballad singers around. Some of the successful singles in his last years as an artist for King Records had been ballads; his enthusiasm for songs like this went back many years. In the 1940s, when he was a lounge entertainer, he sang almost as many ballads as he did blues. So he sang them, and let the audiences do what they wanted with them. Listening to them now it is obvious that in the ballads he found an emotional counterbalance to the cynicism of the blues. In the ballad verses he found the sentimentality and tenderness he rejected in his blues verses. For Lonnie the ballads were just as much a part of his personal emotional canvas. He was, in the final consideration, a musician of such confidence and skill that everything became an expression of his genius.

There were many things that were surprising about the songs Lonnie Johnson recorded for Moe Asch in 1967. One of the surprises, certainly, was that the material existed at all. Moe had recorded Lonnie many years before for his own small Asch and Disc labels and he was asked by Verve Records – who had signed a licensing agreement with his Folkways label – to do a demonstration tape with Lonnie for consideration as a possible expanded Verve album session. Moe chose to do the recording himself, in the small studio that took up a corner of his crowded office, and he still had the veteran microphone that he'd built himself and used to record his classic sessions with Woody Guthrie, Leadbelly, and Pete Seeger. The arrangement with Verve proved to be more confining than Moe had anticipated, and he finally put the boxes of tape on a shelf in the back room of his office. His tape archives were packed and unpacked in a series of moves to different addresses in Manhattan, and he didn't think about the Lonnie Johnson tapes until fifteen years had gone by, when he found them again in one of his occasional efforts to sort through old material.

A second surprise with the tapes is the range and the depth of the material that Lonnie recorded. The sessions weren't his final recordings, but these have such a breadth of style and expression that they could stand as a summary statement of his artistry. A last surprise was that, after more than forty years of recording, and at the age of 68, he sounded as good as ever. His voice had the same suppleness, and the guitar playing had the freshness and the fluid imagination of his early blues accompaniments and jazz solos.

It is no surprise, however, to find that all of his old skill as a writer was undiminished. Lonnie had always been one of the true poets of the blues. He used most of the standard blues material, sometimes verses with the standard imagery, but his song texts had a clarity and a consistency that other singers' material often lacked. Of all the singers of his generation it was only Memphis Minnie who had some of the same depth and range and individuality in her blues texts. She had begun her career several years after Lonnie had already become established as the blues' most successful recording artist and his style was an important influence on her own writing. What she learned from him was his use of the telling detail, the touch of imagery or description that gave the best of his verses their vividness. Since he always thought of himself as an urban blues artist, rather than a country blues singer, it was the gritty life of the ghetto streets that found its expression in his finest performances.

It should also be admitted that Lonnie was much more concerned about the verses of his blues than he was about the melodies. He once remarked that during one period of his career he had copyrighted 148 songs, and all of them had the same melody.

Perhaps the characteristic that most distinguishes Lonnie's finest texts is his ability to sustain a metaphor over a number of verses. A blues is usually constructed with verses that are linked by a theme, but without a single, sustained image. Lonnie, however, often shaped his texts around a dominant symbol or idea. One of his effective devices is the *personification* of an element in the text. In his well-known 'Careless Love,' which he recorded in several versions, including one in this session with Asch, it is Careless Love itself that takes on the shape and the emotions of a human figure. He ends the song by blaming this personification of Careless Love for what has happened to his mother and father, and he declares that he is going to shoot this Careless Love figure and bury it deep in the earth. In the song there is no precise description of what he means by the image, but a concrete definition is implied in his text. As he narrates the story he cries that Careless Love '...worried my mother until she died' and pressured his father until he '...lost his mind,' and he decides that the only answer for him is to shoot this figure of Careless Love, shoot it '...four or five times' and then stand waiting until he is certain that it is dead. To complete his act of revenge he intends to bury the body of Careless Love, digging the grave with a silver spade and leaving the body in the earth where its story will never be told.

One of the most arresting of Lonnie's personifications is the figure of 'Mr. Trouble,' which he included in this selection of songs. He is clearly describing a figure related to his old nemesis Careless Love – and certainly as a poetic concept Mr. Trouble has many similarities with the generalized figure of the blues, or 'Mister Blues,' that he and many other singers presented in other songs. Here, however, the imagery is particularly vivid, with its description of Mr. Trouble 'strolling' down a dark night street, stopping at one door after another. Another unexpected twist to the text is its happy resolution. The usual anticipation of a blues lyric is some variant of despair, but for this song, one of Lonnie's finest, the emotional range has been extended to include the possibility of happiness.

In the first verse he describes a town '...fast asleep' when 'Mr. Trouble makes his rounds/ And every time he knocks on someone's door you can hear a mournful sound.' As Mr. Trouble is making his rounds,

> *Some poor woman cries out, 'My man is gone, Lord, what am I goin' to do?...*
> *I never knew how much I need him until the day he say we were through.'*

Mr. Trouble continues his walk to the next house.

> *Mr. Trouble strolls on down, stops at the house next door...*
> *A poor man cries out, 'My woman's gone, baby won't be back no more.'*
> *Says, 'I lost the only woman I love, listenin' to what my friends had to say...*
> *And every since my baby's been gone I've been dyin' slowly day by day.'*

The lyric's positive resolution comes at the end of the walk that Mr. Trouble has taken along the darkened street.

> *Then Mr. Trouble walks on down, stops at the last house on the line...*
> *He knocks on the woman's front door, she's standin' in the back door cryin'*

She says, 'Mr. Trouble, I'm not cryin' 'cause I'm lonesome, I'm happy
as I can be.
I'm not cryin' 'cause I'm lonesome, I'm happy as I can be.
I thought I lost my good man, but he's headin' home to me.'

In the song's final verse it is the happy woman who has the last word.

'So Mr. Trouble, please go and let me alone.
Mr. Trouble, please go and let me alone
'Cause I haven't had a peace of mind since my good man been gone.'

In his conversations with Moe Asch, Lonnie was at his ease talking about his work and his career, but unlike most performing artists he said very little about his personal life. He made it clear at the beginning that there were things about his life that were private, and there was no need to go into them. It was also clear from his relaxed tone that he was comfortable with himself and with his memories. He was vague about the dates of various moments in his career, but he was also unconcerned about them. He did, however, remember the details of his first recording correctly. It was 'Falling Rain Blues', which he had recorded again for Moe Asch. The first version was released in the fall of 1925, on the other side of the release, 'Mr. Johnson's Blues,' which the company advertised more heavily. The titles had been recorded in St. Louis where, as Lonnie remembered, he had won a blues contest a few months earlier. The contest was held in the Booker T. Washington Theatre, and one of the prizes was an opportunity to make a record. As he also remembered, he was living then in East St. Louis, working a job in a steel foundry.

It seems fitting, somehow, that this group of songs, one of his last, should include a blues from his first session. Lonnie Johnson's blues were part of a long, continuing story. These careful performances he recorded for Moe Asch served to tie to together a life and a career that was one of the most productive and successful in the history of the blues.

(1982)

The Mississippi Delta

7. The Blues' Angry Voice

Although there is widespread acceptance and appreciation of the texts of the blues as a vital modern poetic form, for many years there has been a continuing controversy as to whether, within the blues lyrics themselves, there was a coded protest against the social conditions that produced the songs. One of the writers most insistent on this 'encoding' was author Paul Garon in his 1975 study *Blues and the Poetic Spirit*. In the book he is dismissive of the hundreds of interviews which have been done with blues artists over the last half century, in which the singers have almost invariably described the blues as some variant on 'what a man feels about a woman, and a woman feels about a man.' He cites instead a well-known example of singers discussing their situation from the perspective of racial discrimination. It is a conversation Alan Lomax recorded in 1947 with Big Bill Broonzy, Memphis Slim and Sonny Boy Williamson, which was released ten years later under the title 'Blues in the Mississippi Night.' When Lomax played the tapes back for the singers he remembered that '…they were terrified' that white southerners would hear what they had said, and when the material was released Lomax substituted pseudonymns for the names of the artists.

Although the three singers never presented a specific alternate language to be found in their own texts, they described the harsh realities of the American racial situation with undisguised anger and despair. Garon's criticism of writers like myself was very specific on this subject. 'Did they really expect black artists to speak to them honestly about their feelings for whites in general and for them in particular?' I can only respond by saying that I don't know how any of us sort out our very complex feelings about the social situation in which we find ourselves, and the literal texts of the songs that I recorded conformed closely to the verbal context which the singers themselves had described to me. Many of their comments are included in the chapter from *The Poetry of the Blues* that is excerpted in this book. For myself, it was with considerable excitement and relief that I witnessed rap finally emerging in the ghetto communities in the 1970s and 1980s, with its vehement, emotional expression of the rage that everyone had sensed was just beneath the surface of the African

American consciousness. There could be no disagreement about rap as a vehicle for political protest.

For some time the controversy has simply been a side issue in blues scholarship, since there has been so much else that took precedence. There was, however, an early song collection which – if Garon or myself had had an opportunity to look at it – would certainly have had an affect on our attitudes toward the texts of the blues as they were presented on commercial recordings. Garon mentions the collection in his book, but without specific details. A copy of it appeared only recently on a list of African American literature and art from a New York City auction house, and when I discussed it with Garon he said, also, that he hadn't seen a copy before he wrote his own study, though as a book dealer he finally encountered a copy a few years ago. The collection – Lawrence Gellert's *Negro Songs of Protest*, published in 1936 – is a fascinating though troubling volume published in the midst of the American Depression and which seems to answer some of the questions – but raises almost as many more. This article on Gellert's collection was written in 2004.

Lawrence Gellert and *Negro Songs of Protest*

I am aware that for many years I was only one of many people who sought in the blues some explicit protest against the rigid system of apartheid that controlled the lives of African Americans, not only in the South, but in the North as well. There was no way I could not be conscious of the housing restrictions, the job discrimination, of the de-facto segregation of every American city. I was also acutely aware of the degrading role that African Americans were forced to play in entertainment and literature, of the continuing insult of American popular culture, and the always present danger of violence that hung oppressively in the background. I kept listening for overt hints in everything I recorded or heard that would express this angry consciousness, but I could never say that I had found something that made the open statement of protest I hoped to find. Occasionally a songster would offer one of the handful of verses that had become such a conventional expression of the complicated southern racial situation that they could be sung in front of white audiences without fear of retaliation. A common example was the verse I heard in many uptempo dance numbers:

Nigger and the white man
Playin' seven-up.
Nigger win the money,
But he's afraid to pick it up.

Another set of verses I often encountered were some variation on the lines that contrasted the social situation of blacks and whites, usually with a knowing nod toward the black man's assumed abilities to make the best of the situation. The verses had such widespread currency in the South that I sometimes wondered if they could have been part of a southern black minstrel tradition.

White man sleeps on a feather bed,
His lady she does the same.
Nigger sleeps on shucks and straw,
But he's sleepin' just the same.

The singers usually went on to describe the same situation with Cadillac cars and T-Model Fords, and whatever other comparisons came to mind at that moment. These verses were much more closely tied to the songster repertoire than they were to the blues, and the songs in which they appeared were usually intended to be comically entertaining. In contrast, it was difficult to find more than a handful of lines in hundreds of commercial blues recordings that expressed any *explicit* protest. It was possible to make sociological constructs that would interpret a line in the blues about 'Goin' to Chicago, don't you want to come?' as a protest about the conditions of agricultural labor on the cotton plantations of northern Mississippi, but the line was still simply, 'Goin' to Chicago, don't you want to come?' and I was distrustful of my own interpretations.

So now I open the pages of a slim, staple bound songbook from the Depression years and at the close of the introduction I read:

...these songs, reflecting as they do the contemporary environment – the daily round of life in the Black Belt – aside

Along a Mississippi Roadside, 1973
(Photo: Samuel Charters)

from their musical and literary worth, are human documents. They embody the living voice of the otherwise inarticulate resentment against injustice – a part of the unrest that is stirring the South. They speak now mildly, now sarcastically, now angrily – but always in a firm and earnest manner.

And they will be heard!

The title of the collection is forthright – *Negro Songs of Protest*. The name of Lawrence Gellert is printed on the cover as the collector of the songs. It was published in 1936, in the depths of the Depression. If everything about the collection were as clear as it seems, it would perhaps have continued to have a wide circulation, and it would certainly have been reprinted at some point. It is with other paragraphs in the introduction that it becomes more difficult to interpret the collection. The introduction opens:

'"Niggers!" I was told, on my first visit South many years ago, "are a happy and contented lot. Find me one that ain't and I'll give you a ten-dollar bill, suh. Worth it to string up the biggity black so and so…"'

'And that's the official dictum of the South.'

'For more than a dozen years I lived alternately in Tryon, N. C., and Greenville, S. C. I enjoyed the friendship and protection of influential whites. And with impunity I haunted the Negro quarters. Long and painstakingly I cultivated and cemented confidences with individual Negroes without which any attempt to get to the core of the living folklore is foredoomed to failure…'

'I slept on dirty floor pallets in miserable ghetto hovels or ramshackles half disappeared in malarial swamps. I fared on the usual Black Belt coffee "bitter as gall," 'taters, cow peas, perhaps augmented by sow belly or a "piece o' lean" – often neither the best nor the worst but all in the larder. And always there would be a brother or sister or friend to "git lookin' up" – a new contact somewhere along the lonesome red-clay road ahead'

Even with an initial sympathy for the paragraphs, I find something about the tone that sounds forced. Who was the collector of the songs, Lawrence Gellert? Or who was Hugo Gellert, who did the heroic drawing on the title page of a sweating black laborer with a pick, wearing a ball and chain? I didn't even notice the title in the crowded pages of the Swann Gallery catalog, a New York City auction house that has a once-yearly sale of books, art, posters, and musical manuscripts relating to the African American experience. I wasn't expecting a collection titled *Negro Songs of Protest*. My wife Ann noticed it, however. She was initially drawn to the listing by the name of the previous owner. Inside the cover was pasted the bookplate of Eleanor Roosevelt, with a small tag identifying it as having been part of her personal library. Lawrence Gellert had signed the title page.

What I did recognize about the book was the name of the publisher, 'American Music League.' It was one of several fronts which had as their ultimate source the American Communist Party. In this period the Communist Party, for what ultimately proved to be their own purposes, had turned to the black community and its plight. The sympathy was genuine – the emotions expressed a deep abhorrence for the American social dilemma – and at that moment in the national consciousness there was virtually no one else willing to fight openly for black freedom. The other names connected with the material, Elie Siegmeister, who did the transcriptions of Gellert's original field recordings and wrote the piano arrangements, and Wallingford Riegger, who wrote the forward, were also active in Music Front causes. It was a time when many intellectuals were drawn to the Party, whether or not they became active members, and among black writers who were allied with the Party for some part of their careers were Langston Hughes, Richard Wright and Ralph Ellison. In a poem from this period Hughes wrote:

> *Goodbye,*
> *Christ Jesus Lord God Jehova*
> *Beat it away from here now.*
> *Make way for a new guy with no religion at all –*
> *A real guy named*
> *Marx Communist Lenin Peasant Stalin Worker ME –*
>
> *I said, ME!*

So, as I held the collection and carefully turned its pages, I found myself asking, 'Can I trust it?' 'What can I say about the songs?'

Gellert himself proved to be no mystery. He was a young New York Greenwich Village Communist with a Hungarian background. Because of ill-health he had to find a more moderate climate, and he moved to Tryon, North Carolina in 1923, dividing his life between Tryon and Greenville, S. C. He edited a local newspaper, but he was in an uneasy situation because he had begun a relationship with an African American woman. It was through her, however, that he gained an insight into the black life around him. He began collecting work songs – 'work reels', as he termed them – shortly after his arrival in the South, and over a period of several years, travelling with a primitive recording machine and aluminum discs or working with singers he met in the communities where he lived, he recorded more than 300 songs. Although he had left New York, he continued to be associated with the best known of the Left periodicals, *New Masses*, and contributed some of the songs for reprinting in its pages, introducing them under the heading that became the title of the collection, *Negro Songs of Protest*. After the publication of the collection in 1936 there was little else that was added to his list of book titles – another song collection three years later, in 1939, then in the 1940s an introduction to a volume of 'lost' early plays of Eugene O'Neill.

In a recent book, *When We Were Good*, a study of the New York folk revival, author Robert Cantwell discusses Gellert briefly and says of his activities, 'He collected chain gang, work, and other African-American songs, many of them unnervingly candid in their expression of racial antipathy, regularly forwarded them for serialization in the magazine [*New Masses*] and later published them under Mike Gold's title as *Negro Songs of Protest*.' Cantwell adds, writing about the 'Composer's Collective,' another front organization, 'In 1934 Composer Collective member Lan Adomian proposed an expansion of the workers' chorus repertories to include Gellert's "*Negro Songs of Protest*," railroad songs, cowboy and hillbilly songs, virtually duplicating the categories developing in the Lomax collections in order "to root our work in the traditions of American music." '

Knowing all of this, I found myself asking again, 'What can I say about these songs?'

Once I turned to the songs themselves, I found that although sometimes the protest is told 'slant' – in Emily Dickinson's term – it is certainly there. No one had ever collected such a range of African American material from the rural South which expresses so openly these feelings of black anger. In *New Masses*, the songs Gellert was collecting were presented as, in Cantwell's term, 'politicized spirituals and folk songs.' 'Politicized' is too detached a term for what were cries of rage.

To deal with the collection it is first necessary to do some selective editing, as it is with all of the collections of the period, from the popular songbooks by Carl Sandburg to the collections put together by the Lomaxes. The piano accompaniments for the 24 songs in the American Music League collection were intended, as Riegger wrote in his short introduction, '...(to provide) practical and interesting accompaniments for informal singing, around the piano as well as for concert performance.' It is probably only in the tormented 1930s that someone could envision standing informally around a piano and singing, 'You take mah labor an' steal mah time, Give me ol' dish pan An' a lousy dime, 'Cause I'm a nigger, dat's why...' Also, although Siegmeister was a conscientious and gifted musician, the struggle to accomodate the melodies of songs that were sung in nearly pure five and six tone vernacular melodies to European concert scales was as uneasily and clumsily unsuccessful as these efforts generally are. The piano accompaniments are skilled and sophisticated, but for 'informal' singing it would have been more helpful simply for anyone who wanted to try the songs to work with Siegmeister's accompaniments and the lyrics, and then make up melodies that would fit. The Lomaxes had dealt with the same problem in their book *Negro Folk Songs As Sung By Leadbelly*, from the same period, and their solution had been to put a plus or a minus over tones that didn't correspond to a tone in the European scale. This would probably have helped Siegmeister, but it would have defeated the purpose of the volume as a weapon in the struggle against racial discrimination.

Some of the songs also have more of the feel of a political meeting than they do of a backroad cabin. It is difficult to imagine a song like 'Scottsboro' – about the infamous trial of the group of African American boys accused of the rape of a vagrant white woman in a railroad car – with lines like, 'Seven nappy heads wit' big shiny eye, All boun' in jail an' framed to die,' or 'White folks an' nigger in great Co't [court] house like cat down cellar wit' no hole mouse' – was actually created by the folk process.

At the same time, however, with some of these reservations, it is still clear that there are verses and images in the collection that understandably did not make their way into the pages of the other gatherings of songs from the same time. Dr. Robert Stephens, Professor of World Music at the University of Connecticut, grew up in the South, and his voice rose when he saw the first song in the book. "'I Went to Atlanta!" That was a song we used to sing when I was growing up in Savannah. It's just the way we sang it!' The song was widespread throughout the southern states:

> I went to Atlanta, Never been dere afo'.
> White folks eat de apple, Nigger wait fo' co.' [core]

In subsequent verses the city named becomes Charleston or Raleigh, and often the final verse names Heaven as the ultimate destination. As the song progresses the White folks sleep on 'feather bed, Nigger on de flo', the White folks wear 'de fancy suit, Nigger overo' (overalls), and in Heaven the White folks sit in 'Lawd's place, chase Nigger down below.' The theme of the song was similar to the verses I had recorded about feather beds and T-Model Fords, but without the suggestion of the ability of the black man to deal with the situation.

There are songs of every style in the pages, and the theme of white injustice is taken up again and again. In the song 'Out In De Rain' there is an allusion to the work boss Captain Bob Russell, whose name became ubiquitous in prison work songs, and a line declares that Russell 'He kill a mule, go buy him another, kill a nigger, jes' hire his brother.' The song ends with an open threat: 'He better not come mess wit' me no mo', Ah's all ready dis time wit mah foh'ty fo'.' Several of the songs are a response to the southern system of arrest and imprisonment; one, 'Lice In Jail', expresses the mood of a half-humorous prison lament. Another song, 'Preacher's Belly', begins as a familiar attack on corrupt ministers, 'Religion is somethin' fo' de soul, but preacher's belly done git it all,' but verses at the end of the song are more stridently anti-religious, 'Two prayin' Niggers ninety nine years in jail, waitin' fo' Jesus to pay dere bail, waitin' fo' Jesus to pay dere bail, das a fac'. De Lawd make you po' an' lean, de sorries' sight ah eber seen.'

Despite the heavy dialect the more literary style of some of the verses suggests that even if Gellert had collected them from a black singer, the singer could have had some contact with the Party organization, or with the labor organizers who were struggling for union recognition in southern factories. The song 'Sistren an' Brethren' continues the theme of the futility of turning to organized religion, 'Stop feelin' wid pray. When black face lifted, Lord turnin' away,' but the final verses, like the lines from 'Scottsboro', are troubling in their self-conscious use of image and language. The song's image of a lynching and its open call for armed resistance has more of the feel of a political pamphlet.

> Yo' head 'tain no apple fo' danglin' from a tree, ['tain – ain't]
> Yo' head 'tain no apple fo' danglin' from a tree,
> Yo' body no carcass for barbacuin' on a spree.
>
> Stan' on yo' feet, club gripped 'tween yo' hands,
> Stan' on yo' feet, club gripped 'tween yo' hands,
> Spill dere blood too, show 'em yo's is a mans.

A verse from another song, 'Oh Ma Kitty Co Co', however, seems to be touching a more solid vein of folk poetry: 'Goin' some place white folks ain't inchin', Nigger's belly ain't allus pinchin', Oh mah Kitty Co Co.'

The forms of the songs are as varied as the themes, often with verse and chorus. The blues is a presence in several of the songs, even if there is also a chorus following a verse in the blues style. One of the songs, 'If You Catch Me Stealin'', is a classic blues with three line rhyming stanzas, but the first and the last stanzas are harsher than any blues that would be expected to make its way into the small town, general store record bins.

> If you catch me stealin', don't blame me none.
> If you catch me stealin', don't blame me none.
> You put a mark on my people, an' it must be carried on…
>
> I'm tellin' you, white folks, like de Chinaman tell de Jew.
> I'm tellin' you, white folks, like de Chinaman tell de Jew,
> If you don't care nothin' 'bout Nigger, cinch I care nothin' 'bout you.

What is clear, after some effort to approximate the melodies in a more realistic scale and to weed out verses and images that seem politically self-conscious, is that Gellert could somehow have tapped into a stream of black protest that was almost entirely silenced in other gatherings of material from African American life, including commercial recordings, and popular film and radio. It may be, as some writers have contended, that in the blues singles issued by the record

At Izzy Young's Folklore Center, MacDougal Street,
New York City, l-r Samuel Charters, Izzy Young, Memphis Willie B.,
Furry Lewis and Gus Cannon, 1964
(Photo: Ann Charters)

141

industry of the time there were veiled inferences of protest and rage within the lyrics of the songs. What seems more likely is that there could have been another layer of black song that constituted the angry cry we have been searching for. We were just never given the chance to hear it.

What is perhaps the most troubling aspect of the collection is that Gellert never identifies the sources of his recordings, and that although many of the discs have survived, some of the most inflammatory verses have not been included in the CD compilations that have been released and that include some of his material. It is also problematic that no one else during those years when so many people were working in the South collected any songs with corresponding lines and verses.

Gellert himself became a familiar figure in the Greenwich Village folk music scene in the 1960s. He became friends with Izzy Young, who owned the Folklore Center on Macdougal Street, and Izzy remembers that he was living in a bookstrewn apartment on Sullivan Street. He and Izzy sometimes went on trips to collect books in small bookstores that only Gellert seemed to know about.

'We'd go out to the end of the subway line and he'd take me to some little store he was the only one who knew how to find. Even to New Jersey. We'd take a bus.'

What kinds of books were they collecting?

'Larry had known all of the poets in New York in the twenties and thirties and that's what we looked for – poetry. Collections and books by people he knew.'

Izzy also remembers that Gellert at this time was following the example of Alan Lomax and copyrighting songs he had collected, listing himself as writer of both the melody and the lyrics. Once Izzy met him on the street and Larry rushed up to him in considerable excitement.

'Harry Belafonte's going to record my song "Look Over Yonder"! I'll make more money from that than I made from everything I've written all my life.'

Sometime later Gellert left the Village, and there is still no documentation for the sources of his material. The collection, however, with all the awkwardness of its sources and the possible reasons for its publication, is a remarkable document in the complex history of African American song.

(2004)

8. Chicago and the South Side Blues

If you're interested in the blues you end up, sooner or later, in Chicago. I first did interviews on the South Side and listened to the local bands in 1959, when I was doing research for *The Country Blues*. I did my first Chicago blues album in January 1964 with a band led by the veteran guitarist Homesick James, and set up a studio session with the young harmonica player Billy Boy Arnold and a band that included guitarist Mighty Joe Young and pianist Lafayette Leake. Then in March I did an album with Muddy Waters and his band, including James Cotton and Otis Spann, to help them pay for a New York hotel bill. The next year, with Ann, I worked in Chicago to record the three volume series *Chicago/The Blues/Today!* for Vanguard Records. There were extensive notes with the original albums, but for a three CD re-release package in 1999 I had the opportunity to write about the background of the sessions as well as the artists themselves. Although I produced a number of other albums with Chicago artists, as the sixties passed there was more emphasis on the artistic design of the albums, and less concern with the kind of lengthy introductions that had seemed necessary when the blues audience was first learning about what was on the records. As a contrast with the more serious writing from the initial series, I have included an impressionistic note I added to a Vanguard album with Junior Wells from 1966.

Chicago/The Blues/Today!
– Remembering the Sixties

Chicago in those years? The late fifties and the early sixties? If you think of the city then, you think of the South Side and the blues. I had been coming in and out of Chicago for a half dozen years, taking the El south to the little clubs and dingy bars where the bands played. Occasionally I climbed badly-lit stairways in run-down apartment buildings on South Michigan or South Indiana to talk to veteran blues artists like Tampa Red, who gave me a glimpse into the 'old days,' when

Chicago was a different kind of blues town. I came to Chicago for the first time in the winter of 1959, as part of the long research trip for the book *The Country Blues*, and I found my way down to the legendary Pepper's Lounge, Muddy Water's home club, to hear the band play. In the usual style of the neighborhood clubs, Muddy sat out the first set, sitting at a table beside the bandstand, greeting friends and signing occasional autographs, letting the band warm up the audience. With his broad shoulders and his majestic face, his presence dominated the crowded space. On the little stage his exciting band, led for the set by pianist Otis Spann, pounded out the blues, and they had been joined by another Mississippian, B. B. King, as guest vocalist.

For the next few years I was in and out of Chicago – and after so many nights down on the South Side listening to the bands, I was becoming more and more impatient to go into a recording studio to document some of the unforgettable music I was hearing. But the companies I was involved with – Folkways and Prestige – either didn't have the money for the sessions, or they weren't ready to record the electric blues. From 1963 to 1965 I worked for Prestige Records as an Artists & Repertoire director, which meant that alongside the new sessions I was producing, I spent a lot of time editing tapes and programming albums with material that was already on the company's shelves. When the company sent me to Chicago, it was to audition folk singers for its steadily growing Folklore Series. I had an opportunity to record albums with two of the South Side bands, Homesick James and Billy Boy Arnold, in January 1964, and I managed to slip a Muddy Waters album into the company's release lists two months later, but Muddy's session almost cost me my job.

Muddy and the band came into New York in March 1964 to appear in a concert in Carnegie Hall. I was doing the onstage introductions, and Muddy and I talked a little before he and the band did their set to end the first half of the concert. He woke me up the next morning with a phone call from the Albert Hotel on 10th Street, just at the northern edge of Greenwich Village, where a lot of the travelling bands stayed over. They had been paid so poorly for the concert that they didn't have enough money to get back to Chicago. It was Saturday morning and I couldn't reach Bob Weinstock, who owned Prestige Records, but I decided to go ahead with the session anyway. The problem, which Bob explained to me angrily the next week, was that because of Muddy's contract with Chess Records we couldn't use his

Pepper's Lounge, Chicago, 1964
(Photo: Samuel Charters)

Muddy Waters, New York, 1964
(Photo: Ann Charters)

name on the album, and in an effort to keep his presence hidden Muddy hadn't sung any of the solo numbers and he hadn't used his metal slide for any of the guitar solos. We would have to release the album under the name of the pianist Otis Spann, who had done most of the vocals, and the band's very exciting young harmonica player, Jimmy Cotton. Weinstock's anger at my decision to go ahead with the session without getting his permission almost led to him firing me on the spot, but it was in part the incredible experience of that afternoon working with Muddy and his band in a studio I found off a hotel lobby on 5th Avenue in Manhattan that led to the sessions that became *Chicago/The Blues/Today!* for Vanguard Records a year and a half later.

Nine months after I'd recorded Otis and Jimmy, with Muddy playing back-up guitar and singing on the choruses, I finally lost my Prestige job. I was fired for the usual reasons A&R people are fired. None of the artists I had signed and produced had sold enough records. But in the last few months that I was still with the company I had a chance to get back to Chicago, and I was able to record some blues again. I heard a University of Wisconsin student named Tracy Nelson sing the blues at a campus party, and I recorded her with a promising young white harmonica player I'd met named Charlie Musselwhite. It was the first recording for either of them. Charlie was working at the Jazz Record Mart, a shop owned by Bob Koester, who also owned the blues and jazz label Delmark Records. His little shop was the center for the blues in town, and you could usually find two or three local musicians leaning on the counter or sitting back in Bob's small office.

When he wasn't working, Charlie was spending all his free time hanging out on the South Side, and on my Chicago trips Charlie went along with me to some of the clubs and introduced me to the musicians he was meeting. The club visits led to the albums with Billie Boy Arnold and Homesick James, and they also contributed to the Vanguard sessions the next year. The sound on the Billy Boy Arnold album was boomy and the tracks were a little uncoordinated, but I was beginning to learn how to work with Chicago's electric blues sound.

One night a few months after Bob Weinstock fired me, I ran into Maynard Solomon in a New York folk club. As the president of Vanguard Records Maynard had turned the company into America's most significant and most successful folk label, and he'd done it by spending his nights in the folk clubs and listening to what the musicians he met told him. The world of folk and blues recordings was much smaller then than it is now, and we had often run into each other at concerts and at the downtown folk clubs. In 1963 I'd travelled with him to Memphis to help locate veteran jug band artist Gus Cannon and sign a copyright contract for his song 'Walk Right In', which one of Vanguard's groups had turned into the nation's bestselling single.

Maynard knew that I'd left Prestige, and he asked if I wanted to do a few weeks work for him editing the tapes from the previous summer's Newport Folk Festival. Vanguard's office was then in a tall building at the corner of 14th Street and 7th Avenue in Manhattan, and to get to the job I rode the subway down from our much lived-in student's apartment on W 109th Street. Ann was in the final year of work for her PhD in American Literature at Columbia University, and she had found us an apartment in the neighborhood close to the university so it would be easy for her to walk to the library. The summer days were hot and the apartment was small and stuffy, but the Vanguard editing studios were air conditioned and I spent most of my days there alone with the tapes. When I had finally worked out a program for all of the material, I stopped in Maynard's office to tell him I was finished. To my surprise he looked up at me and asked, 'What should we do next?' Without a moment of hesitation I smiled broadly and said a single word, 'Chicago!' I finally had the chance I wanted to record the music of the South Side.

It took only a few days to work out a contract with Maynard for any sessions I might be able to produce when I'd spent some time in Chicago. I wouldn't be employed by Vanguard, the project would be done on a freelance basis. I would produce the sessions, edit the tapes, and write the notes to the albums. There was a budget of a few thousand dollars for paying the musicians, for the studio costs, and for our travel expenses. Ann had been photographing the older blues singers in their segregated neighborhoods or in their isolated houses along lonely back country roads for the albums and the books I'd been producing since the late 1950s, and she would come along to add a visual document of what we hoped to do. She had to defend her PhD dissertation, however, which meant we couldn't leave New York until the middle of December.

Sometimes, when I was asked later about the albums, people asked why I didn't do whole albums with each artist. The most significant reason, for me, was that that wasn't what I was trying to do. What I dreamed of documenting was as much as I could of the music that was happening on the South Side. I hoped to capture some of the excitement and the wily strength of the blues traditions that were hanging on in the crowded, dimly lit little clubs scattered through the side streets. I could only show the rich variety and excitement of the music by recording several bands. Another reason, of course, was that whatever I might have wanted to do, I couldn't record many of the artists I was interested in if I asked for an entire album. Most of them had some kind of contract arrangement, however tenuous, with another record label, all of the musicians were very suspicious of someone they didn't know very well, and they'd never heard of Vanguard Records. What I suggested to Maynard was that I would do something like a union session with each group – four or five songs in a few hours – then ask the singer who was the leader for the date for an option to do an entire album within eighteen months following the release of the series.

When December finally came, and Ann had defended her dissertation, we filled our small Volkswagen with clothes and notes and our Irish setter and drove to Chicago. One of the first things we had to do was find some kind of kennel for our dog, since we couldn't leave her in the cramped room we found close to Division Street. The next thing we had to do was find the musicians.

I still had the names and the phone numbers of the South Side musicians I'd recorded the year before for Prestige, and I also knew how to get hold of Charlie Musselwhite, who had been spending a lot of time with the veteran harmonica player Big Walter Horton. Ann and I began with the list of numbers as a place to start, using the phone in our room. One of the most important groups I wanted to contact was the quartet Junior Wells was leading, with Buddy Guy as guitarist. They had done an album entitled *Hoodoo Man Blues* for Bob Koester's Delmark label, and their sound represented the mainstream of what was being played on the South Side. I found Junior at home at his mother's, and despite his misgivings, the idea of an abbreviated session for a New York label, whoever they were, that didn't ask him for any kind of exclusive artist's contract, and let him select the material he wanted to play, had a strong appeal for him.

Junior was in the same situation as the other South Side blues musicians. The Chicago blues style had lost much of its popularity with its own audience, and most of the bands were struggling. Muddy Waters hadn't had a record on the R&B sales chart since 1958. All of the bands were hungry. They were looking for anything that might give them exposure to a new audience, but wouldn't tie them to a restrictive contract, in case something that seemed more promising turned up. Both Koester, with Delmark, and Pete Welding, with his Testament label, were recording many of the club artists, but their labels still were handicapped by limited distribution. The heady days of the Tower Records chain, with its willingness to stock every kind of music, and Bruce Iglauer's Alligator Records, with its matchless documentation of the South Side scene, were still a decade in the future. Even if Vanguard

Junior Wells at Theresa's, Chicago, 1966
(Photo: Ann Charters)

didn't plan on releasing juke-box singles – which was the immediate question from everyone I reached on the phone – the sessions I was proposing fit what most of the bands were looking for.

We were fortunate in our phone calls to Otis Spann and Jimmy Cotton. Muddy's band had just gotten in from a road tour and would be in the city over the next weekend. We drove down to Muddy's house – immediately noticeable for its screen door with the words 'Muddy Waters' spelled out in metal letters – and said hello to everybody again. They were tired and just getting out of bed when we got there. All of them still had their hair wrapped, and they were in undershirts or wrinkled shirt sleeves. There wasn't much glamour in a Chicago blues musician's life in the 1960s. Muddy was uneasy about doing a session himself in Chicago, with his own label, Chess Records, there in the city; so this time he told Jimmy and Otis to go into the studio without him. Otis had a bad cold, which roughed up his voice, but the band was leaving town again the next week, so if we didn't record them while we had the chance they couldn't be part of the project.

I had tried talking with the harmonica player Little Walter Jacobs, who had played for several years with Muddy's band and had a major

Buddy Guy at Theresa's, Chicago, 1966
(Photo: Ann Charters)

hit with his own band, the 'Jukes.' It was a classic single that introduced Willie Dixon's song 'My Babe'. Walter, however, had problems with alcohol and with his contract situation at Chess Records. Probably the best of the harmonica players working the clubs was Walter Horton, who was usually called 'Big Walter' or 'Shaky Walter' by other musicians. He also had health problems, and he was unpredictable on the job, so he didn't play regularly with any of the bands. When we went to talk with him we found him living in a derelict apartment building in the heart of the South Side. I've never forgotten the assembly of broken locks and forced door frames on each apartment as we climbed up the creaking stairway to his door.

When we left his apartment after a discussion about the coming sessions, Walter painstakingly redid the skimpy padlocks that held his door closed, wrapped himself in his heavy hat and coat, and led us through the snow to a club under the tracks of the El. It was a long, low-ceilinged, dark bar called Turner's Blue Lounge, and at end of the room on a cluttered bandstand the slide guitarist J. B. Hutto was playing with his band, the Hawks. Hutto had learned to play a slide from listening to recordings by another South Side musician, Elmore James, and his steamy, storming beat was one of the styles of blues we had been looking for. The Blue Lounge was one of the blues clubs you heard about at Bob Koester's shop, but it was also a rough neighborhood bar, and it wasn't until we came out into the snowy darkness that we realized a police car had been parked across the street while we were inside, waiting to see that we came out without any trouble.

Most of the other musicians whose numbers I'd written down during the months I'd been in Chicago the year before were still in town when I called. Johnny Young, the Mississippi mandolin and guitar player, had also been recording for the local labels and he was always available for a session. Since I had arranged for the Prestige album with Homesick James there was also no problem contacting him again. The musicians were scattered across the South Side and the West Side, none of them living very close, but they ran into each other at their jobs and they had an informal system for getting in touch with each other if something came up.

We were also fortunate with the uniquely talented older musician Johnny Shines, just as we had been with Otis Spann and Jimmy Cotton from Muddy's band. Shines had only recently been rediscovered working as a night club photographer, and he was cheerfully willing to go back into the studio to re-record some of the songs he had done as 78rpm singles twenty years before. A few nights later I had a chance to talk with Johnny and Walter Horton over a bottle of whiskey in Johnny's apartment, and they reminisced about Robert Johnson. They were among the handful of musicians I had met who had known Johnson when he still was a 'ramblin" man.

Of all the bands we listened to in the clubs, the only one that caused us to hesitate was Otis Rush's five-piece group. They were playing on the West Side in a cavernous lounge called Curley's that was trying to be a little more upscale than the cramped places we were used to on the South Side. To blend with the room's ambitious decor Otis was slickly dressed, with an elaborate hairstyle, and he was playing mostly soul music. He and the band seemed to be putting as much distance as they could between themselves and the blues. When he joined us at the table I couldn't, for a few moments, decide what to tell him. It wasn't until he nervously asked me what I thought that I immediately answered that we certainly wanted to have him on the sessions.

I had already recorded in most of the small studios in Chicago, but for these sessions I wanted to use the big RCA studio building that was built on pilings over the lake. The sound in the main studio's big room was good, but just as important for me was the history lingering in the space. It was the studio that had been used for the Chicago blues recordings on the old Bluebird label. As I found also, another advantage to using the studio there was that everybody knew how to find it. Not only the musicians, but friends and hangers-on and an occasional girlfriend showed up to help with the atmosphere. The easy familiarity of the studio helped turn the sessions into a kind of spontaneous party. Some of the band men turned up early so they could listen or trade ideas; Sunnyland Slim dropped by to see if we could find time for him if he got a band together. During a break I looked over at the chairs pushed against the wall of the studio and overheard Willie Dixon trying to teach a new set of lyrics to Junior Wells so he could record a new Dixon composition. I realized that this had been moved outside the control room when the older generation of blues artists had gathered in the same studio.

In the studio we worked as simply as possible, with as little echo and equalization as I could get away with to counter the dead sound that had been built into the studio for modern, electric sessions with their high volume. Also, we didn't do any overdubbing. The vocals were recorded at the same time as the instrumental back-up. Since the microphones at that time were multi-directional, this sometimes presented a problem, with noises from enthusiastic drumming or loud piano chords that filtered into the vocal microphone. If we had gone back to overdubbing, however, we would have lost all the interplay between the singers and their back-up groups. I still listen to the taut, cohesive feel of the Junior Wells quartet's blues with a sense of wonder at the sensitivity of Buddy Guy's responses to Junior's vocal phrasing, and at the infinitely subtle shifts of Jack Meyers' bass lines as he feels the mood changing in the tone of the voice or the guitar. In all the recording that Junior, Buddy and I did together later we never caught the same intensity of that afternoon in the old lakeside studio. I also needn't have worried about Otis Rush. It was his startling guitar virtuosity that lifted the excitement of his five tracks. The blues he did echoed B. B. King, but there was a bright professionalism to everything the group recorded, and 'Sax' Crowder's alto saxophone contributed a different solo texture to the sessions.

While I was working in the studio Ann came and went. She was documenting the South Side at the same time as she was photographing the musicians inside the studio, then asking them to pose outside against the building's weathered brick walls and loading docks. The days were cold and the streets were heaped with snow, but she found her way around the neighborhoods along the El tracks and then came back to the studio when she thought I'd need her for one of the musician's portraits. I wondered sometimes, when there was a pause in one of the sessions, if she was all right, wandering the streets with her camera, but she never had any problems. One of the shots she took on a platform of the El, on a dismal, snowy, late afternoon, was used as a cover for the albums.

Sometimes, when I see that bleak image again, I find myself thinking of a dark, blustery winter morning close to the end of the sessions. On that morning, we woke late, and we were walking through swirling snow when we left the run-down guest house where we'd found the cramped room. We were heading toward a cafeteria two or three blocks away where we'd been eating breakfast. When we opened the door and went inside, we studied the menu hanging on the wall, then stopped to stare around us. Inside its white painted, shiny walled, neon lit space, the cafeteria was serving Christmas dinner! We had been so immersed in the recording sessions that we hadn't noticed it was Christmas. We looked at each other and began laughing helplessly. For breakfast we ate the steam table turkey, potatoes and cranberry sauce.

Some of the excitement and some of the complexities of the days in the studio concerned the overall concept I had conceived for the music on the albums. I had consciously chosen blues artists from a spectrum of styles – from the country-oriented sound of Johnny Young's mandolin, or the solid rhythm of Johnny Shine's forties era beat, to Otis Rush's contemporary flash. Against this I was also trying to create an overall design of sounds. Pulsing piano blues with Otis Spann, muscular slide guitar with J. B. Hutto, two different harmonica styles of Jimmy Cotton and Walter Horton, the almost breathless intensity of Junior Wells and Buddy Guy, the more gently lyrical slide blues of Homesick James.

When I put the music together on the albums I tried to capture this richness of the South Side blues world by emphasising the contrasts in mood and rhythm in the programming – from guitar to piano, from harmonica to elegant guitar, from modern to older modes of playing. When I was asked by Vanguard to go through the albums again for a re-issue package in 1999, I listened to all three of the albums again in their order, for the first time in nearly thirty-five years, and I found that what I had tried to capture was there on the series. The sounds of the South Side blues were still as exciting as they'd been when I first heard Muddy Waters' band in Johnny Pepper's crowded lounge forty years before.

I was finally so tired after the concentration of the sessions that I wasn't really sure what we'd recorded. Maynard remembers that when I brought the tapes back to the office on 14th Street I was half apologetic. 'I don't know what's here, but it's the best of what I could get,' I told him. What I meant was that I hadn't been able to go into the studio with any of the major Chicago blues artists, like Muddy Waters or Howlin' Wolf. They were tied to their contractual commitments. What we had was a portrait in sound of the everyday working blues musicians who were still part of the life of the South Side. What would people think of it?

I don't know who was more surprised by the sudden enthusiasm and interest that greeted the albums. It was Maynard who had suggested adding the word 'Today!', with its exclamation point, to the title of the series, and that had helped the new blues audience understand that this was music that was part of their own world. As the interest of this new audience shifted away from their enthusiasm for folk music, any signs pointing the way toward the next musical style were immediately picked up. I missed much of the excitement because I left the country as soon as the albums were edited and the notes were finished. I spent five months alone, travelling slowly from Europe to Turkey, India and Japan. It wasn't until the next summer that I dropped by the Vanguard office again. I'd spent the last two weeks of the long trip in the Bay area, just in time to hear the new psychedelic blues that were coming out of the San Francisco dance halls and Berkeley's public parks. This time when Maynard asked me what they should do next I smiled again and said, 'San Francisco!'

It seemed simpler for Vanguard at this point just to hire me, so I became the company's first outside A&R director, and almost immediately I was back in Chicago. I signed individual artist's contracts with Buddy Guy and Charlie Musselwhite and produced their first albums. There were solo albums with Junior Wells and – assisted by Michael Sunday – Otis Spann, making use of the option clauses in their contracts from the original sessions. I spent months trying to get Otis Rush back in the studio again, but he steadily found ways to put all of us off, and I wasn't able to do a solo album with him until 1977, when I had left the United States and was working for the company that distributed Vanguard Records in Sweden.

The reality was, however, that the excitement over the *Chicago/The Blues/Today!* largely focused on the albums themselves. None of the sessions I produced with Junior Wells or Buddy Guy later for Vanguard struck the same fire with the new blues audience, though I asked Junior for another option, and we did a second solo album, *Comin' At You*, and I still consider Buddy's first solo album, *A Man and the Blues*, one of the best Chicago recordings to come out of these years. Both Junior and Buddy were sourly disappointed with their experience as Vanguard artists, but when they moved on to other labels they had even less success. Buddy had to wait almost thirty years before he finally achieved serious recognition. Of all of the musicians I recorded for the series Jimmy Cotton used the sudden attention most successfully. He moved quickly to form his own group and he signed with another label in time to be part of the chaotic music scene that was centered around the Fillmore auditoriums in San Francisco and New York. Otis Spann perhaps could have duplicated some of his friend's success, but he died of a heart attack not long after the release of his Vanguard album. He was still in his early forties.

The sessions in the Chicago winter of 1965 were clearly something that framed a musical moment, but it wasn't a moment that anyone could have planned and the results were something no one could have anticipated. The moment was just there, and suddenly there was an audience ready for what we wanted to record. I still feel, after all these years, an almost breathless sense of surprise that I had the good fortune to be there.

(1999)

Chicago / The Blues / Today!
The 1965 Notes – Volume 1
The Junior Wells Chicago Blues Band
J. B. Hutto and his Hawks
Otis Spann's South Side Piano

To get down to the South Side you take the Elevated somewhere in the Loop, or walk down one of the entrances on State Street where it's still a subway. The 'El' lines fan out across the flattened hand that's Chicago like the veins close to the skin. Over the rooftops you see the trains, on their rusted metal trestles, rushing past above the streets. The buildings have been dredged out of the ground for twenty blocks south of the business district for an urban renewal project, but after the El gets south of this you begin to see the slums, one of Chicago's sprawling black ghettos. The backs of the buildings line the tracks, rows of wooden porches, spindly and weathered, painted a dull gray-blue. The patches of yard between the porches and the tracks are black with coal dust and littered with loose trash and garbage.

Toward the lake you can see the stone apartment buildings along South Parkway and Prairie Avenue. After a spring rain, or on a slow, darkening sunset afternoon there is a dim elegance to the South Side. The brick and stones have a soft warmth, and since the buildings are low you see the sky hanging above your head. When you get off the train and walk down the painted iron stairway to the street you see the worn paint of the window sills and doorways, the cracking pavement of the sidewalks, the worn ground in front of the buildings, which always means too many children and no place for them to play.

But you go down to the South Side for the blues, not for its dirty streets or shabby apartment buildings. The South Side is one of the last places left in the country where a living music is still played in local bars and neighborhood clubs. The music scene has some of the excitement New Orleans used to have in the 1930s, what Memphis and Beale Street had in the 1920s. In Chicago, on the South Side, it's still today for the blues.

You get off the El train after two or three stops if you want to find the music. Turner's Blue Lounge is just below the tracks at 40th and South Indiana, a one storey building with a few tables inside, a bar along one wall, a juke box, and a small bandstand. The music you find at Turner's is just like the place, rough and direct, and everybody's played there at one time or another. One night there was a noise around the neighborhood because there was a new musician just up from Mississippi, a young, intent singer who was playing an electrified slide guitar. He had to tune it two or three times for the crowd, and they watched his fingers while he played.

When I get to Chicago nowhere for me to go.
When I get to Chicago nowhere for me to go.
Left my home town, everyone I know…

If you get off at 43rd Street it's only a few blocks down the street to Pepper's Lounge. There's still a window mural painted on the outside of the club, a large drawing of one of the bluesmen, 'The Boss, Pepper's,' 'Otis Rush…The Great Muddy Waters…,' usually a sign over the door listing who's going to be playing for rest of the week. Beer's 35 cents a bottle, and there's usually a chair empty at a table near the bandstand, so you sit until the night's half over, listening to the blues.

It's only a block to Theresa's from the El stop at 47th Street – an old basement apartment in a brick building at the corner of 48th and Indiana. You go down a short flight of steps to get to the door, past a signboard fastened to a wire fence beside the steps. 'Beer to go at popular prices…featuring live music…free gifts to the ladies.' A tattered notice, 'Every Fri. Sat. & Sun. Jr. Wells'. A narrow, dark room, the bandstand at the far end with a little space left cleared between the tables for anybody who wants to use the concrete floor for dancing.

Theresa's Tavern, Chicago, 1966
(Photo: Ann Charters)

And from Theresa's it isn't too far down 47th Street to the J. and C. Lounge, with its painted strip of cartoons that slowly revolves above the bar and its suspicious doorman who holds the door shut with a length of chain until you can prove that you're old enough to drink. Inside it's crowded and the music clamors against the narrow walls over the heads of the dancers milling in front of the bandstand. The guitar player and the drummer stay on the stand, but a harp player from the neighborhood pulls the microphone cord as far as it will go and sits at a table beside his girl, blowing the blues for her over the din. You keep your coat on for a set or two; then you finish your bottle of beer and get back on to the street. The blues is still the South Side's music, and the stares get hostile if you stay too long, but the music stays with you as you ride the El back to the Loop, rubbing against your skin like a cat you picked up on the street.

It's difficult to place Junior Wells against the background at Theresa's, but he's been there off and on for the last ten years. It's a loose, casual club, and Junior and his music have a high professional polish. Junior is only 31 – he was born in Memphis on December 9th, 1934 – but he's been playing since he was fourteen, sneaking into the clubs when he was still too young to hold down a job. As he sings in his beautiful 'Tribute to Sonny Boy Williamson,' Sonny Boy '…was my teacher and he taught me well.' There were other teachers, Little Junior Parker, Big Walter Horton, Little Walter Jacobs, but he still feels closer to Sonny Boy – the second 'Sonny Boy Williamson,' Rice Miller, who died in 1965 after returning from a successful European concert tour. Junior and his quartet, led by the guitarist Buddy Guy, feel as though they're breathing together in their blues. All of them define the highest technical level of the contemporary Chicago style, and Buddy who records as an artist for Chess Records, is one of the greatest of the Chicago guitarists. Junior, as he plays and sings, becomes completely immersed in the music, standing in front of the microphone with his shoulders tensed and hunched, his hands acting out the emotions of the verse. At the tables in front of the bandstand at Theresa's people talk louder to hear themselves over the music, and the women along the bar stare at the rows of bottles, but for Junior playing the blues is enough. He shrugs, 'All I want to do is play the blues, and I hope the people like it.'

J. B. Hutto and his Hawks, at Turner's, have the rough directness of the club. J. B. is a small, intense man who learned his blues after he got

J. B Hutto at Taylor's Lounge, Chicago, 1965
(Photo: Ann Charters)

to Chicago, but plays with the raw emotionalism of the men he learned from. His music goes deep back into the Mississippi blues roots, even though he was born in Augusta, Georgia. His family moved to Chicago when he was ten and the blues in Chicago is Mississippi's music. His teacher was Elmore James, and J. B.'s one of the few younger bluesmen – he's 36 – who play with a metal slide. His music doesn't have the technical polish of Junior Wells', but it has the fierce insistence – the 'total expressiveness' of the best blues.

The best way to hear Otis Spann play is when he's working out a new piece for himself, or just relaxing with the drummer S. P. Leary, who's with him in the Muddy Waters band. As Muddy's pianist, Otis

161

usually stays in the background, though he's an unmistakable presence even when the band is at its loudest. Only 33 years old, Otis, without argument or qualification, is one of the greatest of the contemporary blues pianists. Inventive, sensitive, intensely rhythmic – since he came up to Chicago from Jackson, Mississippi, when he was 17, Otis has been one of the dominant instrumentalists of the South Side's vital blues style.

(1965)

Chicago/The Blues/Today!
The 1965 Notes – Volume 2
The Jimmy Cotton Blues Quartet
The Otis Rush Blues Band
Homesick James and his Dusters

'Sweet Home Chicago' – up from Meridian, Mississippi, up from Tuscaloosa, Alabama, from Jackson, from Selma, Memphis, Helena, Brownsville, Bessemer, Natchez…to a rooming house on S. Indiana, to a run-down hotel on West Roosevelt, to a folding bed in a sister's apartment on S. Lake Park. If you're black it's better in Chicago than it is in Mississippi – unless you're aggressive or talented or lucky, it's not much better, but enough so that you get on a Greyhound bus in Jackson or Tupelo with some food in a shoe box and your clothes in a paper suitcase, or you sit up for a gritty night in a railroad coach, or you get a ride with somebody who's got a battered car. Jobs? There aren't many, and what there are don't offer much more than you could have gotten back in the South. Some place to stay? The rooms are small and dirty and you live poor and cramped until you can get a steady job and move into something better.

Most of the time – if you've come up from a cotton farm, or from a slow back-country town – everything around you has changed. The buildings along Indiana or Prairie in the south 30s, or on the streets going east to the lake, have a heavy, imposing look. Stone and brick, with names carved into the top stone arch like 'Doris,' 'Paloma,' 'Windermere,' but the stones are black with soot and the names are grimy and weathered. In the entrance hallways a broken light bulb dangles from the ceiling, and the names are scrawled on the walls beside the battered mailboxes. Beside most of the names a note like, 'Third floor rear ring two times.' There isn't enough money to rent a whole apartment; so a five-room apartment becomes four rooms for four families, with a kitchen for everybody to share. Along the inside hallways the doors have been wearily dragged shut with wires and hooks and cheap padlocks, but on most of them are old scratches and broken hasps, the marks of thieves who hang around in the dark hallways and back entrances of the buildings. But some things haven't changed as much. Climbing up the stairs to somebody's apartment you can hear voices from the rooms around you. Children crying, women calling to each other, somebody singing, an abrupt argument…and you can hear music. Somebody's always playing a radio or a phonograph, and most of the time the music is the Chicago blues.

The blues is still the same expression of emotions that it is in Mississippi, but in Chicago, like a lot of other things, the blues has changed. It isn't only that the sound is different, that the clubs have to have three or four piece bands instead of one or two men with guitars. The instruments have all been electrified to be heard over the noise of the crowded barrooms where the musicians work. The old styles were less aggressive, less relentless, the songs were concerned with country towns and country roads and country cabins. It was 'country' blues. If you grew up out along one of the rivers of the delta, or back on a one lane dirt road, there was at least the sun and the afternoon wind and the streams to fish in and the fall mornings when you could hunt in the overgrown fields; so the music was gentler, sometimes with a warm sense of easy concern in its worries with love and loneliness. But there isn't much sun in the South Side streets, and the apartment houses are overcrowded, and the winters are bitter and the spring comes late; so the music is harder, with some of the city's mean ferocity.

Otis Rush, Jimmy Cotton, and Homesick James Williamson are all from Mississippi, and each of them has found a place for himself in Chicago through his music. If you're good, with a style of your own, there's a Chicago blues business waiting to pick you up. Otis Rush is one of the best of the young Chicago bluesmen. He works steadily, seven nights a week at a lounge on the West Side. The lounge, Curley's, doesn't get much of a crowd on week nights, so he lets somebody from the neighborhood work the first set, and he sits at a side table with two or three friends. It's dark in the large room and the band works on a high bandstand under dim red florescent lights. The crowd at Curley's is younger, and they've been away from the blues for a while, so Otis can stretch out into the area where the blues and jazz intermingle. 'I was born in Philadelphia, Mississippi, but I left when I was fifteen…' He plays left-handed, looking down at his fingers on a solo. 'It was winter when I first came up and it was cold, but I had a sister living here, so I stayed with her.' He's only 31 and he looks younger. 'As a kid I just liked the looks of the guitar, but I didn't play. I started after I got up here and got a little older and heard Muddy and Buddy Guy and T-Bone Walker…' Otis has always been an exciting singer, and he has matured into a brilliant, inventive guitar player. The rest of the band, except for the alto player, is even younger, and they move from the blues of Otis' 'I Can't Quit You Baby' to the hard-edged blues-jazz of 'Rock' with an easy familiarity. The alto sax player, 'Sax' Crowder, is a thin, quiet veteran musician from the 1939 Earl Hines Band. His jazz has always had a blues feel and his blues style has always felt like jazz. This is the new, young, 'tough,' Chicago blues – 'tough' the South Side term for the newest, the most exciting.

With Jimmy Cotton the sound comes closer to a country drawl. He's been Muddy Waters harp man since 1957, and Muddy doesn't stray far from the first band sound he developed in the mid-1940s. At Pepper's Lounge, where the band usually works when it's in town, you can get down close to the bandstand and hear Jimmy sing. In the usual night's work Muddy sits out the first set, like most of the leaders, and lets Jimmy or Otis Spann do most of the playing. The Chicago harmonica – 'harp' – style is one of the distinctive sounds of the Chicago blues, the instrument played differently than it was in the South. Jimmy, like Junior Wells and Little Walter Jacobs and Big Walter Horton, holds it against a cheap amplifier mike, cupping both the microphone and the harp in his hands. He's in his early thirties, and despite ten or so years away from the South there's still some of the easy country enthusiasm in his exuberant singing – and even some of the country concerns in his blues – about the outskirts of Helena, Arkansas, about bad cotton crops, and about new cars and ungrateful women.

Homesick James has been up from Mississippi longer, since 1947, but he has as much of the down home sound as Jimmy. His style comes partly from his cousin, Elmore James – Homesick worked with him on and off before Elmore's death in the mid-1950s – and partly from his own country background. The sound is as distinctive to Chicago as

Jimmy's harp. It's the electrified 'slide' style that Muddy and Elmore developed out of the Mississippi 'bottleneck' playing. You put a metal bearing ring or a piece of metal pipe on the little finger of your left hand and you can work the strings to get almost any kind of sound. Homesick works at most of the South Side clubs, but he's had a steady factory job ever since he got to Chicago, so he usually plays only on Friday and Saturday in one of the small clubs. The sound of the blues has changed on the South Side, but there's still some of the sound of the Mississippi blues around the corner in a neighborhood bar, or in a lounge near the El tracks – the loneliness and the insecurity of the southern country styles intensified, pushed to a new creative excitement, in the slums of the challenging northern city.

(1965)

Chicago / The Blues / Today!
The 1965 Notes – Volume 3
Johnny Young's South Side Blues Band
The Johnny Shines Blues Band
Big Walter Horton's Blues Harp Band with
Memphis Charlie

Johnny Shines and Walter Horton sit around a table in Johnny's apartment drinking a little from a fifth of Teacher's, and after the television set in the next room is shut off the talk goes back to their early years in the blues. 'Robert Johnson?' Shines laughs and shakes his head. 'I ran with Robert for two years when I was first starting to sing. He was only a year or so older than I was and I was seventeen at the time. When? It must have been 1933 – in Helena, Arkansas.' Walter interrupts. 'You couldn't run with Robert for long; he wouldn't stay in one place.' Johnny shrugs, 'He did run off after we got here to Chicago. We were staying someplace – I don't remember where it was – and he got up in the middle of the night and left. Just like that! I didn't see him for five months.' Walter has another drink. 'He was that kind of fellow. If anybody said to him "let's go" it didn't matter to him where it was they were going, he'd just take off and go. It didn't

165

matter, either, what time of day or night it was.'

Johnny Young leans against the bar where his band works on 47th Street, his broad, worried face perspiring from the last set. 'I grew up in Vicksburg so I heard all them guys. Even Charlie Patton. Of course he didn't come to see me, I was too young. He come to see other people, but I was there anyway. The mandolin? I was playing that back in Vicksburg, but I did hear Charlie McCoy play, too. He was a mandolin player living over in Jackson that made some records about that time.'

The poor, hard, city life in the Chicago slums has changed the blues styles of Mississippi, Alabama and Tennessee, but the ties between the old country music and the new city blues are still close. For the artists in their twenties and thirties, like Junior Wells, Otis Rush, Jimmy Cotton, Buddy Guy, it's less personal. The old country styles are something they've heard people talk about. But for the artists in their late forties and early fifties, like Johnny Shines, Walter Horton, Johnny Young, there's still a direct, vital connection. You sit at a crowded table trying to listen to Johnny Young over the noise of the people around you and the words of the blues he's singing could be from Tennessee in the 1930s. 'I asked sweet mama, let me be your kid...' He could have heard the verse on a Sleepy John Estes recording, but it's just as much like the other pieces he sings as it is like Estes. Johnny stands on the low bandstand, his tie knotted in place and his coat still buttoned, despite the hot, stale air of the club. 'I'm stealin' back to my same old used to be...'

In the early 1950s Johnny Shines came into a recording studio and did a piece called 'Ramblin'' that came closer to the emotionalism and the musical style of Robert Johnson than anything else he has done before or since. He took a moment to remember it, then nodded: 'Ramblin'' was really picked out of the sky. We got there to the studio and we didn't have enough time and we didn't have arrangements or anything, so I just started singing the first thing that came into my mind.' Without arrangements or much time, Johnny went back to the first blues style that he'd known, and today he still sometimes puts the guitar in an old Mississippi open tuning and begins to sing with some of Robert Johnson's inflection and phrasing, the style as natural to Johnny as it was to Robert.

The open tuning and the bottleneck go back even earlier for Johnny. 'I had an older brother, Willie Reed, who played, and I tried to learn from him, but I couldn't make all the chords that he could…' Johnny grew up in Frazier, Tennessee, just north of Memphis. There's a shopping center there now, but the rest of the town has become another Memphis suburb '…then one day I ran into Howlin' Wolf, who was young himself at that time, and I saw how he was playing with the open tuning and the slide. I said to myself, "If it's that easy I can do it too." Wolf went away and left his guitar there and when he came back I was playing the same thing that he had just played…' A young man at 51, Johnny's voice is one of the strongest and most exciting sounds in Chicago blues today, and his music is a complex intermingling of the country and the city – the delta melodic lines and the Chicago bass guitar and backbeat drumming – the South Side harmonic structure and the delta verses, 'Mister Boweevil, you done ate up all my cotton and corn…'

Johnny laughs, 'Walter? I've known him most of my life.' Walter nods, 'The reason Johnny and I know what each other is going to play is that we started together when we were kids in Memphis.' The casual, drifting life of the early blues artists kept them close to each other as they rambled in twos or threes from job to job. Shines and Walter Horton started playing together in Memphis and they stayed together through the ragged years of the Depression, working at occasional jobs and running into each other when they were in the same town. Then, in Chicago, living not far from each other and working with each other's bands kept the country roots of their music strong and vigorous. 'When Johnny did 'Ramblin'' and 'Brutal Hearted Woman' he was working in my band in a club on West Madison,' Walter remembers, nodding again with a grin. A tall, nervous man, his face worn and scarred, Walter now limits his playing to a few sets with the bands working near his apartment on Indiana Avenue. When he's feeling good he's one of the most challenging harp men on the South Side. His health now is poor, but when he's in the mood his playing is still magnificent, his thin body moving unsteadily across the bandstand, his face withdrawn and intent in the dim lights.

The blues backgrounds of Mississippi and Tennessee are woven into the fabric of the music that Johnny Shines and Walter Horton play. It's there in the shifting, restless sound of Johnny Young's mandolin and in the insistent push of Johnny's guitar accompaniments, in the verses of his blues and his singing style. The blues has changed in Chicago, but it's still close to the country background, and it's a music that has gone beyond the limits of its South Side neighborhoods. Memphis Charlie Musselwhite, who plays a harp duet with Walter, is in his early twenties, and he's white. He's from the South and he's grown up with the blues, so he's been able to cross over into the South Side blues world. He had already learned to play in Memphis, but Walter helped him when he got to Chicago, and when Charlie's working with Johnny Young's band, Walter tries to get down on a Saturday night to do a set with him.

This is the blues in Chicago today – the new virtuosity of musicians like Junior Wells and Otis Rush, the country sound of J. B. Hutto and Homesick James, the exuberance of Jimmy Cotton and Otis Spann, the deep blues involvement of Johnny Shines, Johnny Young, and Walter Horton, the young artists learning the style, like Memphis Charlie. A new music has emerged on the South Side, a living music that has kept its own audience, its own expressive voice, and its own truth. To hear it today all you have to do is take the El down to 40th or 47th Street…walk a few blocks through the empty streets…it's thirty-five cents for a bottle of beer and as you sit at a table as close as you can get to the band the music fills the club around you like a sweet, intense voice that won't stop singing…

(1965)

Since our new audiences now had some idea of the kinds of music they were buying, the notes on the albums I was producing with artists like Junior Wells and Buddy Guy became shorter and shorter, although for some time all of us still felt that there should be *something*. The style of writing became more impressionistic – the emphasis was more on mood than on dates of birth – but there was still a concern with bringing the listener somehow closer to the music. This 'introduction' to Junior's first solo album on Vanguard, *It's My Life Baby!*, was written in 1966.

Junior Wells and *It's My Life Baby!*

Half light south side club – Junior singing, Buddy with his guitar on the cramped stage behind him. Not enough room for them to move…but they move. Dim in the corners, yellow, red, blue lights from beer signs, whiskey signs, the light bulb over the cash register, faces in the lights, a girl in a black dress, a guitar player from another band standing against the bar. Whatever the blues is – whatever the blues has to say – it's here in the club with Junior. His hands around his harmonica, eyes closed, body bent over the microphone, Junior Wells doing his blues.

Long, long hours in the club – the first set Buddy on the guitar, Junior making phone calls, talking to girls, sitting at the bar and hustling up the next job – then on the stand until three in the morning, four on the weekends. Some of the blues are standards, some new pieces, sometimes somebody else's, sometimes Junior's. Sometimes a line that Buddy adds – 'Shake it baby and I'll buy you a pretty dress…' and they stand back against Fred Below's drums to work up the verses – young, hard, serious – artists in their world of the blues – Junior one of the finest of Chicago's young singers, Buddy the hardest guitar player on the south side, cool together, tough together. 'Shake it baby, I'll buy you a diamond ring…' As he sings Junior begins to change it. It's 'shake,' a woman's scene – then it's a dance, 'You walk and I'll walk…', then it's something to shout at Buddy, 'You scratch and I'll scratch…' It doesn't matter about the rhyme when you get into it. Just so it comes out and says something to the people. Noises and shouts when they finally end it. 'Now how are you going to remember what you did in that?' Buddy says. 'Thank you kindly, friends, thank you…now for our next…'

Does anybody listen, hear what they're saying? Over the bottles of beer, against the wall near the door, back along the bar, the crowd listens. They hear the blues from every singer working the club, but nothing says what they want to hear as strong as the blues. The long, slow blues at three o'clock in the morning, listening, hearing, getting it, until even the cash register is left to sit silent on its shelf behind the bar.

'It's so sad to be lonesome…' Junior sings it with his hands, his shoulders, his arms, filling in the phrases, the silences – Junior's language, the blues, his voice, his life, and his art – the blues, Junior Wells' letter to the world that never sent him one damn thing else, but this is all Junior has needed. 'You just start it baby, I'll take it from where you leave off…'

(1966)

West Africa, Gambia, Banjul

9. Roots, Finally

When I looked out of the plane window in the winter of 1974 and I saw the dry brown savannah of the African coast coming up to meet me I murmured to myself, 'Finally!' It had been twenty years since I had done my first blues recording in New Orleans in the spring of 1954, and I had decided that I had to mark the date by travelling – finally – to the Africa I had thought so much about for so many years to search for the African roots of the blues. On this trip, and on later journeys, I used portable equipment to record a wide range of music that was released with extensive notes on six LPs, three by Sonet Records in Europe and three by Folkways Records in the United States. Sonet released a double album which documented the first of the trips with the title *African Journey* in 1975, then in 1977 the company released an album of griot songs and narratives by Mandingo griot Jali Nyama Suso that I recorded in Gambia on a subsequent trip. I made a selection of the griot narratives for Folkways, which released the material as a double LP box in 1975 with a title of their choosing, *Ministers of the Spoken Word*, and Folkways three years later issued a selection of recordings of Fula and Serrehule flute music from Gambia. The book *The Roots of the Blues*, which was drawn from the experiences in West Africa, was published by Marion Boyars in 1981, and it won the Deems Taylor Award in 1983.

In the spring of 1964, on my first journey to Africa, I spent several weeks in the small city of Banjul, the capital of Gambia, living in a bare room in a primitive hotel with a balcony that looked over the Gambia River. Working with a young Fula named Musa Camara who was employed at Gambia's radio station, I quickly met several well-known traditional singers, who were called in their own languages 'jali,' for Mandingo singers, or 'halamkatt', for Wollof singers. The musicians also were comfortable with the generalized term 'griots' as a description of their skills, though they didn't all have the repertoire of historical narratives that are the griot's stock in trade. After some conversation they were willing to record for me, and soon there were also opportunities to record younger musicians. What I found in my journeys in West Africa was that music was still a vital part of African life, and although the older musical styles were changing, they still were an integral part of traditional African culture.

A kora is a twenty-one string lute like instrument, with a large body made from a dried calabash shell, a balafon is a handmade xylophone with wooden keys tied down to a rough frame. Alhaji Fabala Kanuteh was a Mandingo griot – one of two appointed as official griots to Gambia's President. He accompanied his complicated narratives on the balafon, and I had recorded him in his compound in the village of Brikama, close to Banjul. Nyama Suso, who played the kora, was a Mandingo jali who had a broad repertoire of traditional songs and praising songs for village ceremonies. I had recorded him in his compound in the village of Bakau, also just outside of the city.

From *The Roots of the Blues* (1981)
Chapter 6. Some Young Griots

In a town as small as Banjul word spreads rapidly if something unusual is happening, and other people began to notice that someone was interested in the griots and the jalis. In the market I began to see people I'd met at the jalis' houses. Two or three days after I'd been to Bakau Village and recorded Jali Nyama Suso there was a polite note waiting for me at the hotel, telling me that two young Mandingo jalis would be playing at a small party in one of the stucco buildings a few blocks from the river. It was after nine in the evening before I finally found my way to the house. It was quiet in the streets, and except for the gleam of lights at the corner cigarette stands it was still and dark. In some of the compounds there was the yellow glow of a lantern from the inside of a room, but most of the windows along the street were dark. I could see the curtains swaying softly in the light wind, but they moved without a sound, as if someone were continually slipping away from the window and then coming back to it when they thought I'd passed.

As I came close to the building and then stopped below it, I could hear the sound of music from a window in the second storey. The light, silvery sound of a kora blended against the delicate, dry tone of a balafon, and I could hear a voice singing softly in Mandingo. I walked slowly up the stairs, trying to feel my way in the darkness, listening to

Alhaji Fabala Kanuteh, Banjul, 1974
(Photo: Samuel Charters)

173

the voices and the sound of the instruments, hearing laughter and a low murmur of and the sound of the instruments, hearing laughter and a low murmour of conversation in darkened windows beside me as I felt my way along the coarse wall to the door of the room where the music was coming from.

Inside, half a dozen men were sitting on hard chairs, two or three in undershirts, the others in shirtsleeves. They were wiry, muscular men, used to hard work. There were two young women with them, in European dresses, but without makeup and their hair in traditional lines of plaits. The furniture was simple, some chairs, a bed, a cabinet, all of it of wood with a cheap veneer finish. A bare light-bulb was hanging in the center of the room. The only obvious difference between the scene in the room and a room like it in any other country was that no one was drinking alcohol. They were Moslems, and the bottles on the table were filled with soft drinks or juice. They looked up when I came inside the door, waved a greeting, three or four leaned over to shake hands, and then they went back to their conversations or to the music.

The two musicians were sitting on the floor, their instruments in front of them. They were in shirts and light trousers, their sandals put aside so they could curl their bare feet under them. The balafon player was about twenty, with short hair and a broad, friendly face. The kora player was thinner, and three or four years older, but they were from the same village and they had been playing together since they were boys. Like young musicians everywhere they let the instruments dominate the music. There wasn't the same care with the recitation that I'd heard with Alhaji Fabala Kanuteh, but the mallets hurried over the keys of the balafon, and the kora player's fingers flashed on the strings when they played the instrumental interludes.

The music had a light, staccato sound. Both of the instruments are delicate in tone, and when a balafon player is accompanying a kora player he handles the mallets very lightly so he won't cover the sound of the other instrument. The men and women in the room were tapping their feet, one man clanking a ring against his bottle. Often kora players have someone to tap the rhythm out on the body of the calabash while they play, so the clanging was as much a part of the tradition as the figures the balafon players used to end the phrases of a song. When the balafon player played a fast descending pattern, then ended it with a rattle up the wooden keys, there was murmuring and nods of appreciation in the room.

I found, however, without someone like Musa who spoke enough English to tell me about the songs, I didn't know what they were singing. Many of the songs they did were already familiar – the tales of kings and warriors I'd heard from Jali Nyama Suso – but often it was a melody that was unfamiliar, and since they were singing in Mandingo I could only make an attempt to understand what the song was about by glancing at the listening dark faces around me. I thought of it then as part of the excitement of the evening, as something that lent a little exoticism to the music, but it was to become a problem when I met the two jalis again.

I'd gotten to know another man who was familiar with the singers, a man in his fifties named Aliu Dabu. Aliu was a thin, graying, quiet man who had been a school teacher in the countryside – or the 'provinces' as he called the area upriver – before he moved into town. He was a Serrehule, but like most Africans he spoke two or three languages, in addition to his own Serrehule and English. His English was clear and soft, still retaining many of the speech patterns of the English colonial schools, even though it had been years since he was in the classroom. He and his wife had a room in a compound at the edge of Banjul, and most of the other people in the compound with them were related to them in some way or other. Their own room was crowded with two large beds covered with simple cloth spreads, home made chairs, a table, and a cabinet against one wall. The room was dark, and it was often stuffy from the small pan of live coals that his wife set in the middle of the floor to keep food warm, but it was large enough for me to sit comfortably on the floor with my legs stretched out in front of me.

Aliu Dabu was closely involved with the music of the griots. He had begun working with the national radio, reading the evening news program in Serrehule, but because of his interest in music he had become a producer for the radio, presenting Jali Nyama every Sunday for a fifteen minute program. Gambia is so small and so poor that Aliu's jobs paid him very little, but he and his wife could get by, and with land he had in his own village up the river he was able to add to the food supply of the compound. The government was trying to collect as much griot music as possible, despite their meagre resources, and he was one of the men who went into the countryside to make the recordings. His room was always filled with the sound of the kora and singing as his old tape recorder slowly wound its way through tapes he had collected.

175

The Young griots, Banjul, 1974
(Aliu Dabu is wearing a hat)
(Photo: Samuel Charters)

'I know from what my great-grandparents have said and what my
father has said to me, that griots begin with a man called Swahata,' was
a typical way for Aliu to begin an afternoon's talk about griots.
Sometimes I met singers at his compound, sometimes I just sat on the
floor with my back against one of the beds and listened to him talk. If
his wife had food ready she would come in quietly, her robes gathered
around her, and put a covered bowl and a spoon on the floor beside
me. Usually it was rice and cooked meat, but occasionally it was cooked
okra, always with pepper 'to give it some flavor.' Aliu was a devout
Moslem, and I sometimes interrupted him when he was praying. He
wouldn't look toward me, but I was uncomfortably aware that I had
come at the wrong time. I would stand outside his room, in the
shadowy gallery that ran the length of the compound building, waiting
until he had finished. The talk would pick up again where we'd left it.
For him the griots and their role were bound up with what he knew
of his own history and his religion. And from his description I could
understand how the griots had continued to be part of the new society,
despite the changes of the last decades. The 'Swahata' he had begun

telling me about, when I asked him about the first griots, was a follower of the Prophet Mohammed when Mohammed still lived in Mecca.

'He goes after the Prophet,' Aliu went on in his slow voice, 'and wherever the Prophet goes, Swahata would go out after him and call out to the people to come and meet the Prophet. So whatever gifts the Prophet got in those days, the best part of the gifts were given to Swahata. And some of the followers of the Prophet were jealous of this, so they grumbled and quarrelled about it until one time the Prophet decided to go without Swahata. So as he went about with his followers without Swahata, this time they got no gifts at all, because Swahata was not there to shout to the people that the Prophet has come, that he is a great man, that he is a messenger of Allah. Then the followers of the Prophet asked him, "We had a lot of gifts wherever we went in the past, but this time none. Why?" And the Prophet said to them, "This is the reason the best part of the gifts were given to Swahata. Now you realize that without Swahata we get nothing, and this is why Swahata was given the best part of whatever we had.'

Often when Aliu talked I had the feeling that I was hearing two voices at the same time. What he was telling me was from his African past, with its conceptions of caste and ceremony, but the language he used was English, with a vocabulary of idioms learned from an English school book. After his years as a teacher he now had me as another pupil. Occasionally he looked over as he talked, but usually he was stretched out on his bed, smoking a cigarette, looking drowsily up at the yellowed netting.

'This is why in most villages you find the Swahata name very common with the griots. Most of the griots believe that they have come from Swahata. Their profession still is to follow kings or follow the great men known as "marabouts". They follow people who are good, they talk about them, they talk about their ancestors, they talk about their great deeds. They are given money for this. This is how they earn their living, how they earn food for their families, and this is the way it has gone on up to the present day.'

Some people I met still thought of the griots as having magical powers. As an elderly man told me, 'The griots know all about what has happened. All. They don't be like natural men. They don't breathe when they talk. All those names they know! And some of it I think is true!'

Aliu, who knew them better, thought of them as clever. 'They're very clever, these griots. They know a little – sometimes more than a little – about every family name in the village. They can sing and talk about each name, even if they don't know so much. So wherever the griot goes, if he meets someone with the same family name as the name in his village, he begins to sing about this person's family. If you tell him you're a Jabi, straight away he begins to sing about the Jabis and the greatness of the Jabis. Then you are touched by what he is singing about you, and you give him money. They're very clever.'

Could they tell much in detail about a family's history?

'Oh no. They have only the persons' name back to the grandfather or perhaps his father, and it is only the names they have gotten from the family, and the family of the man's wife and of her relatives. But they can sing about that for a long time if they know all the relatives in the village.'

Could the griots make up verses about anything that happened in a family's life, if someone told them the details?

'Yes, they are very clever in that. If you tell them any story they can make it to be part of the name. They don't need much time to do it. If you can give them a day or two days they can have it ready.'

It was perhaps this cleverness that was one of the reasons the griots had once been so feared, and why, in some tribes, when they died their bodies were left out in the forest to rot.

Other singers came to the compound, but most of the musicians who sang in Aliu's room were Mandingo jali. They sat on a mat on the floor tuning the strings of their koras as they talked with him, pulling their robes out of the way so that the folds of their clothing wouldn't interfere with their playing. Sometimes their wives came with them to perform; once there was a young wife with a small baby, and she nursed the child as she sang. I found that their repertoire of historical songs was limited, and that most of them knew the same major pieces. The real interest for me was in their own interpretation of the familiar stories. Aliu still felt that there was a place in West African society for the griots, although the changes in the way of life would force the griots themselves to change.

'I think it's becoming harder and harder for them, taking it from one angle,' he said decidedly. 'Taking it from another angle, you might find it's becoming easier. That is, if they try to move with the times, try to make themselves modern, learn new things and new ways of playing, new ways of making money – then they may live happier. But if they want to live the old fashioned way, by going around singing for people and begging from them, I'm afraid there are quite a lot of people who would say no to the griots. I hear the young men say, "Why should I give money to a griot? He's strong enough to do something, he's healthy. Why doesn't he go work on the farm as I do and not go around begging?" Quite a lot of the children are beginning to say that. I hear it around me. So if the griots want to live in the village in the old way, they will find it difficult in time to come. But those who want to play in new ways, to make shows or make their instrument work for them, they will find it even easier.'

Most of the musicians I was listening to had found a way to live with the new conditions, but some of the less sophisticated singers hadn't found a way to deal with the changes. One afternoon as I walked to Aliu's compound, two young men waiting on top of a wall hurriedly looked at their watches as I turned the corner of the street and ran ahead of me to the compound's gate. They were in ordinary work clothes and street shoes, but piled against the wall beside the curtain to Aliu's room were instruments and a much wrinkled performer's robe. The men were jelefos, griots of the Fula tribe. One man had a large, worn calabash, and the other had a one-string fiddle called a riti. The music of the jelefos was not as highly developed as the songs of the jalis or the halamkatts, but it had its own rough hardness and personality. Aliu had never met these musicians, but he spoke Fula and he tried to find out how much they expected to be paid and how many songs they wanted to sing. He looked surprised, but as gently as always he turned to me and explained in his schoolbook English, 'They expect that they will be paid by the minute.' I said that would be alright. Everyone had been paid by the minute, since it was also the way the radio archives paid for their recordings and the musicians were used to it.

Aliu explained in an even lower voice, 'They are counting the minutes from the time they saw you.' I understood now why they had looked at their watches before hurrying to the gate. I also understood why they had been so pleased when Aliu wanted to take a little time to talk to them politely about their songs. They listened to him explain that they would only be paid for the minutes they played and sang, and their faces grew troubled. The riti player, a strong looking man in his early twenties, began talking in a loud voice. He started two or three times to go out through the curtain, then came back as Aliu went on talking in his patient voice. It was obviously a conversation Aliu had had many times before. Finally they talked between them. The younger one said something to Aliu and then they turned to stare at me, as Aliu translated what they'd said.

'They said they will sing very long songs.'

I replied that it would be alright, and they picked up their instruments to play. The riti was small and simply constructed. A skin head was stretched over an opening cut out of a small dried calabash, and a single string made of cotton was stretched from a wooden neck over a bridge mounted on the skin head to the bottom of the instrument. A curved wooden bow was strung with horsehair. The singer played a few figures on it, sounding a little like a country fiddler from the American south, except that here the Arabic influence was obvious. It was an instrument that had come from the North, over the desert with the Arab trading caravans, and the musical style had come with it. The other man was busy slipping broad silver rings on his fingers; then he lifted the large calabash, it's swollen, bowl-like belly as hard as a board. The way of playing it was again something that I'd seen in the southern states. It was the kind of rhythmic rattling and scraping that was used on the popular novelty instrument, the washboard.

I was a little uncertain when the musician with the calabash played his first few beats, but when they both started on a song together I had to shout loudly enough for them to hear me to make them stop. The two jelefos had no experience with any kind of recording, or even with microphones. I'd set up the recording machine on the floor against the bed where I could watch the dials as I sat beside it. I had placed the microphones at some distance from the two musicians, but it was impossible to create any kind of balance with what they were playing, and what they wanted to sing over it. The riti would play a few notes in its thin, sawing tone; then the other man would come crashing in with the calabash, the silver finger rings rattling on its hard, hollow belly. It was like trying to listen to a whisper as a train passed.

Every time I started the machine the clattering began again, with all the subtlety of someone throwing stones against the metal roof of Aliu's room. He looked thoughtful. The two musicians looked again at their wristwatches. There was more arguing when they understood that they wouldn't be paid for the two or three minutes of thundering confusion they'd played before I managed to stop them. Finally they agreed to try playing something without the calabash, and enough music emerged

Fula Griots, Banjul, 1974
(Photo: Samuel Charters)

for me to hear the rough simplicity of their style. The riti player repeated a small melodic figure over and over again, humming a drone tone at the same time. The other man sang the sparse chant of the narrative, using a single melody line that, like the drone figure, was repeated again and again. The song was like something hewn out of wood, and when they finished they were as winded as if they'd done the hewing with their bare hands. It was a music that hadn't begun to adapt itself to the new times.

It was not only the style of the griots from the other tribes that had given their music its professionalism, it was also that most of the musicians who had come to play for Aliu were experienced. One night he sent word to the hotel that the two young jalis I had heard 'entertaining' at the small Banjul party had come back to town from their village up the river, and that they would be willing to play for me if I was interested. I finished the bread and canned meat I'd been eating at the table in my bare room and hurried to his compound. The two young griots were friendly and relaxed, both of them related to Aliu, and even if I was a stranger, they'd seen me at the party. I didn't know how much of the jali repertoire they had learned, and I couldn't talk to them because of the difficulties with the languages. But with a smile they slid their instruments into the space between the sagging beds and sat down on the floor beside me. The three of us, along with the tape recorder and the microphones, took up all the floor's space. As they were going through the patient process of tuning the hand-made kora to the hand-made balafon, a third young man, also from their village upriver, came in and greeted us. He would sing and play with them, Aliu told me, looking at them with an almost paternal warmth, even though they were Mandingos and only distantly related to him through his wife's family.

It was when they began to play that the fact I couldn't understand what they were singing finally became a problem. They played some songs I knew, and then they discussed what they wanted to do to finish, playing a little of the melody for me. The melody and its accompaniment figures were simple and musical, touching in their directness. Aliu leaned toward me to say, 'It's a song called "Tutu Jara," about a woman who wants to have a child, but she can't have a child so she goes out in the forest and asks the snake to help her so that she will have a baby who will be a great king and do great deeds.'

I nodded, and they began to sing. It was a beautiful performance. The three each sang, trading verses, and sometimes singing in unison. After more than fifteen minutes of the music the recording tape was ready to run out, but I felt I had enough of the song. I was completely satisfied with what they'd sung for me. The next day, after they had gone back to their village, I sat with Aliu and listened to what they had recorded, asking him to tell me what the words meant. The first verse was,

> Great men come from great men,
> great men always succeed great men.
> You don't know, fathers are not the same,
> and sons are not the same.
> This is the time that calls for great men.
> Aliu Dabu!
> Who is descended from the great surname Dabo,
> the husband of a Mambouray woman.

The praising went on and on. It was beautifully, expressively sung, but there was nothing about a woman or a snake or a forest. The last verse they sang before I had asked them to stop was,

> I'm thinking about the great trader now,
> the great trader who is always kind to us.
> A man without shame is always free.
> I have stood in front of great men and they were
> always ready to welcome me.
> Who are they? (a shout from another singer)
> They are the people I met in Sefadu and Peyma,
> This is true! (another shout)

I began to say to Aliu how upset I was with myself for stopping them, when he interrupted gently. 'You must remember that these boys are only young griots.'

'What does that mean?'

'They must begin by learning the instruments, the kora and the balafon; then they must learn the melodies. After that comes the praising. They must be able to praise the people they sing before if they want to have any money for what they do.'

'But what about the words to the song?' I protested.

Aliu shrugged and looked down at the floor, his expression apologetic. 'They will perhaps learn the words next year. Then they can sing the song for you.'

(1981)

When I travelled to West Africa I was working as a record producer for Sonet Records in Stockholm, but I took a leave from the company for the journeys I was planning. I had no idea what music I might find, or if I would find anything at all that Sonet might be interested in releasing. I took the trips on my own, following whatever traces I could find of the blues roots that I was searching for. When I returned to Stockholm I met the company director I worked with the most closely, Dag Haeggqvist, at a company gathering and I showed him a photograph of one of the tribal brass bands I had recorded in Ghana. They were in their colorful traditional robes, and they were holding an assortment of dented instruments that looked like something that had been seized from a defeated British army band. Dag looked at the photograph, shook his head, and said he had to put the music out. If the band looked that interesting the music must be interesting too!

Three albums of the music from the trips were released on Sonet, but Dag also realized that I intended to hold some of what I'd gathered for Folkways Records, with its more scholarly approach to field recordings. Sonet had distributed Folkways in Sweden for many years, and Dag had a sincere respect for Folkways' efforts to document all of the world's music, and whatever could be documented of its oral expression. What I selected for Folkways from the tapes I brought back was a group of griot narratives, and I devoted one entire LP side to the long 'song' Toolongjong. I have always felt that this was one of the most important performances I had ever recorded, and it was particularly important for it to be released in the United States because it recounted the story of the first sale of slaves to the English colonies in North America by Dutch merchants early in the 17th Century.

The singer who performed the song was a Mandingo griot named Alhaji Fabala Kanuteh. He was a bluff, imposing man, who dressed in long, formal robes, a Mandingo who was one of the two official griots to the President of Gambia. He lived in a compound in the straggling village of Brikama, twenty miles south of Banjul. He accompanied himself on the balafon, resting his voice between verses with skilled flourishes of his sticks up and down the keys of the instrument. It was a dry, spare sound, its rhythms matching the thoughtful cadences of his narrative. When I asked him if he knew a story like this he looked at me with a half-smile and shrugged, 'I can tell you the history of everything, Africa, India, China, everything. But you must come when you have time to listen.'

I worked with a number of people in Gambia to translate what Kanuteh had sung, among them Aliu Dabo, and I made a synthesis of their different versions. There are many spellings of the names in the narrative. Perhaps the most important, which has many alternate spellings, is the name Sunyetta, the great ruler of the Mali empire, whose name is sometimes spelled Sunjata or Sundiata. The names of the places in the narrative are villages or small towns along the banks of the Gambia River or along its tributaries in Senegal. The text of the song first appeared in the book *The Roots of the Blues*.

The place called Jang Jang Bure in the narrative is a flat, brush covered island in the Gambia River called Georgetown by the British, who cleared it and used it as the site of a small trading station and warehouse. I travelled in an overloaded van on incredibly dusty roads to get to Georgetown, hoping to see what Alhaji Fabala had described as the 'slave house.' The later British colonial administrators had built a complex of offices and residences, but the only thing that was left of the trading station was the ruin of the old warehouse – the roof gone and nothing left standing except the old walls. No one in the village could confirm that it might once have been used as a slave pen. The building looked as though it had been built some time in the mid-1800s, and the British had ended the slave trade in Gambia a half century earlier. Although I had found nothing there that told me more about the slave trade, I set my 1983 novel *Mr. Jabi and Mr. Smythe* in what was still left of the old district administration buildings, and based the story on the imagined return of the last colonial administrator, nine years after Gambia had become independent.

TOOLONGJONG

Sung by Alhaji Fabala Kanuteh, with instrumental interludes, interludes of praising and music from the balafon.

Toolongjong is the song that was sung for Sunyetta,
the king of Fuda.
This same Toolongjong was also sung for the great soldiers of Sunyetta.
This Toolongjong was sung for Musa Molo, the king of Fuladu,
for Seneke Jammeh, this Toolongjong was sung for the Koree Danso,
for the Sang Kala Maran,
this Toolongjong was sung for Mansa Demba of Berending,
this Toolong jong was sung for Wals Mandiba.

Now I will tell you how slaves came to be sold to the Europeans.
How it came about is what I'm going to tell.
In that time Mansa Demba was the king of Nomi.
and Seneke Jambi was at Bakindi Ke.
There were two wharves, one at Jufreh Tenda and the other at Albreda Tenda,
and anyone who went there, to Youmi Mamsa, went to the king there,
that is the king Mansa Demba, and to the woman king called
Kodending.
If they got hold of any slaves they took them to Mansa Demba
and sold them to him.

At this time Han Sunyetta was the leader of the world,
he made another king for the village of Sillia,
and made another king at Salum,
and made another king at the village of Baul.
Another king Murujang and Gao.
Before that Satifa Jawara and Fakolly Kumba,
and Komfatta Keying and Nana Jibril, they were the strongest of
Sunyetta's soldiers.

Then the Europeans came from Europe,
and at that time the only Europeans were the Portuguese.

When the Portuguese came they brought their ship
to Sani Munko and they left the ship at Sani Munko
and raised their flag there.
Mansa Seneke Jammeh, a king, sent people to Sani Munko
to see them.
The messengers arrived at Sani Munko and they found the
Portuguese there and the Portuguese asked them questions.

*The first man they saw was Kambi Manneh and the Europeans
asked him what was the name of the place
and he told them 'My name is Kambi,' and they wrote
the name of the place down, Kambi.
And they came to this place and they found people cutting
these sticks called the bang and the Europeans asked them
'What are you cutting' and they said they were cutting the
sticks called bangjolo, and the Europeans wrote that down
for the name.
Then the Europeans said to Seneke Jammeh, 'We are looking
for something,'
and Seneke Jammeh asked them, 'What is it?'
And they told him, 'We are looking for slaves.'
Seneke then went to Tambana and fought with the people of
Tambana, then fought with the village of Baria,
and then fought with Jokadu Dasalami.
When he had these slaves he went
and sold these slaves to the Europeans.*

*Then he sold the slaves to the Europeans,
and the leader of the Europeans was called Wampiya,
and he took the slaves to the city of Salamki Joya.
He went with the slaves to the Walendaya,
that is to the people of Holland,
and he sold the slaves to the Walendaya,
then the Walendaya took the slaves to America.*

*Then Musa Molo, the king of Fuladu, took four slaves
and gave them to the men called Dikori and Dansa.
He told Dikori and Dansa to take the four slaves
to the place called Youmi Mansa, to Seneke Jammeh,
then the two messengers said to Seneke Jammeh
that we were sent by Musa Molo to bring these four slaves
to you and sell them to you, to sell them to you for
gunpowder and white cloth.
Seneke Jamme said, 'Well it's true we sell slaves
to the Portuguese,' then the Portuguese took the slaves
to the Walendaya, the people of Holland,
and the Walendaya took them to America.*

So then they took the four slaves and sold them to the
Portuguese and the Portuguese took them on their ship
and the Walendaya took them to America, and when they got
to America they sold the slaves there.
Then Dansa and Dikori returned to Musa Molo and told him
that they sold the slaves at Youni.
And Musa said, 'Is that so?'
Then he said, 'I would have taken my army to the people
of Youmi and fought them,'
Then Musa went with his people to Kunti Wata, to Mansa Burekamara.
Mansa Burekamara gave Musa Molo three hundred and three slaves,
and then Musa Molo left again.
He went to Almam Basise of Yani, who was together with
Bamba Esa Jamili,
and each of them gave Musa Molo three hundred and three slaves.

Then he went to Lyama Banta, to Ngari Sabally of Kachamb.
Ngari Sabally gave him one thousand slaves.
He then went to Jatta Sela at Toro Koto with those one thousand slaves
and when he came to Jatta Sela then Jatta Sela told him,
'I will give you four hundred slaves.'
And then they went to Samkarangmarong
and he, too, gave Musa three hundred slaves.

Then Musa crossed the river.
He left the Jokardu district,
he came to the village of Tambara,
and to the villages of Baria and Darselami,
and he sent a message on to the village of Bakindiki,
and the drum was beating there.
The drum was beating at a village called Berehkolong.
Another drum was beating at Berending and at Jinakibarra,
and another drum at Tubau Kolomb.

When they arrived they sent a message to the lady king
Musa Mansa Kodending and to Seneke Jammeh
and another message to Bumyadu
and another message to Berending
and another message to Sangako

and another message to Misseramding
and another message to Missiraba
and another message to Jinakibara
amd another message to Jinaki Kajatta,
and they said Musa Molo the king of the east has arrived
and come to visit the king of the west, Mansa Demba.
Then Mansa Demba said, 'I will send a message to Seneke Jammeh'
and they sent a message to Bakindi Ke.
When the message came to Bakindi Ke the people then
got ready, and they said,
'Musa, we know what you want,' and they gave him one hundred slaves.
One hundred young girls. One hundred women. One hundred young boys.
Money, one hundred. Gold, one hundred. Cows, one hundred.
Goats, one hundred. Sheep, one hundred.
Musa then said, 'If there is going to be a war you can see that
it is only because there is something we want to have.'
Then he said to the people of Bakindi Ke,
'There is no fight between us.'
He told the people, 'You have divided your land between the
two villages, Albadar and Jufering,
and these two villages took slaves and sold them
to Sanne Munkujoyeh. Since you have been doing this,'
Musa told them, 'I would like to meet the Walendaya themselves.'
And the people told him that it was the Portuguese who came,
and not the Walendaya himself
'But when the Portuguese come we will take you to the place,'
then they took the Portuguese to a river place,
the place they called Jang Jang Bure, and that is the name
of two brothers there.

Then when Musa Molo came he collected all the people
of Fuladu, from Ndorma up to Santangto Bubu Tabanding.
Up to Santangto Wuruma. Up to Chargel.
He collected them all and he told them,
'Let us build a house at the place of the brothers
Bure and Jang to put slaves in,
and then sell them to the Europeans.
If we build that slave house then we can
sell the slaves when the Portuguese come

with their ships to sell them to America.
Then the people said, 'Yes, we're going to do it.'
Then they built the house, and up to now
the house is still there,
the kind of house the Europeans used to call
'Slave House.'
The building is still at Jang Jang Bure.
At that time when they sold the slaves
the people who caught the slaves for Mansa Musa Molo
were Dikori, Dansa, Malam Buletema, Yungka Mandu,
Kemo Sarata, Funjungu Kemo,
and they were the people who got all the slaves,
and Dembo Dansa was also among them.

When the Europeans came,
when they brought their ship from Portugal,
the ship used to start its journey from Banjul,
then it went to Sanemunko Joyo to collect slaves there
in the presence of Seneke Jammeh, and Mansa Demba Sanko,
and Samkala Marong, and Wali Mandeba, and Jata Sela.
Anyone who had slaves they collected them altogether
and took them to the places called Aladabara and Jufure
to sell them to the Portuguese.
Then the Portuguese put them in their ship
and left there and went to Jang Jang Bure.
When they arrived there they went
right to the slave house to collect the slaves there,
and take them to the Walendaya.
Then the Walendaya collected them and sent them to America.
It is because of this
that slaves are plenty in America.

They call them American Negroes.

(1981)

II

10. Origins: The Parchman Women's Blues

What I had learned in Africa was that there was a musical language which had been part of the journey to America, but what I had also learned was that it was a language of melody and harmony that had become part of every new musical idiom that took root in the new world, from the American spiritual to Jamaican reggae, to the Puerto Rican danza, or the Brazilian samba. The same vocal intonations, the same shift toward gapped five-tone scales, the same concepts of polymetric rhythm had left their characteristic imprint on every new style of music, as they continue to do today. One of the misunderstandings of some American blues enthusiasts is to separate the blues from this complex, interwoven body of African American musical expression. As I wrote elsewhere, no one should forget that every blues artist did their first singing in their church.

I realized that for a specific musical form, like the blues, I had to return to its own society, to trace what the relationship was to the music that was there. The roots of the Puerto Rican danza may be African, but the new style took its form in Puerto Rico, and that's where I had to look to find it. In the United States I had found that in the South there had been so many upheavals as the African American community fled its root environment in the southern farms and plantations and scattered throughout the United States, that there was no strongly defined 'cultural heartland.' Where should I look, so many years after the flight to the northern cities that was termed the 'Great Migration' by social historians?

Just as researchers and field collectors found a wealth of old English and Scottish folk songs and ballads in the isolated mountain communities of the Appalachians, the collectors searching for a distinctive American music were equally certain there was as rich a bounty of African American song to be found if they could trace black communities that, like the people of Appalachia, had lived in isolation. For field collectors in the South it soon became evident that the place where isolated black communities could most easily be found were the southern prisons, where black prisoners were kept entirely segregated, except for their armed white guards, and where there had been a continuing tradition of work songs and individual singing for many decades. A number of documentary recordings were made in southern prisons in the 1930s and hundreds of work songs and folk ballads were collected. In the Parchman Prison Farm in Mississippi, the recordings by men in the barracks documented the same kind of group singing that was characteristic of other southern prisons. However, Parchman also had a separate women's barracks and some of the songs that were found were clearly a kind of 'root' blues – a kind of 'proto-blues.' This may be as close as we can ever come to the origins of the blues – this small community of lonely women sitting by themselves at rows of sewing machines in Parchman's stifling prison workshop, singing to themselves to make the endless days pass.

The article is a discussion of an important album of women's prison songs from the Parchman Prison Farm released by Rosetta Reitz on her own Rosetta Label in New York City, with the assistance of the Mississippi Department of Archives and History, in 1987. The article was written in 1995.

Women's Blues from Parchman Prison Farm
Jailhouse Blues, Rosetta Records

When I returned to Gambia from a journey into Mali in 1975 and sat in another bare hotel room that smelled of mold and damp plaster, and looked at what I had found in my search through the slave areas of West Africa for the roots of the modern American blues song, I wrote, in a summary chapter in the book *The Roots of the Blues*:

> As I looked at the tapes and notes that lay over the dirty concrete floor of the room I understood, finally, that in the blues I hadn't found music that was part of the old African life and culture. I could hear things in the blues that had come from the tribal musicians of the old kingdoms, but as a style the blues represented something else. It was essentially a new kind of song that had begun with the new life in the American South. Instead of looking for the roots of the blues in Africa, I should have been looking in the American South.

I realized then, late in the 1970s, that I didn't have any clear idea of where to look, since the South has changed so radically in the last half century. The small clusters of shacks at the ends of the dirt roads near the Mississippi levees where I travelled in the 1950s were now mostly deserted. The small towns that once had a Saturday market day had been stripped of their stores and small businesses by the relentless pressures of low price imported merchandise, and the sweeping tide of large retailers, like Wal-Mart, which leave nothing standing in a community they appropriate.

I should have understood that somewhere in the stream of recordings that had been made in the South before the second World War we would be able to find some traces of blues roots, since the blues – as a distinct form – was the closest contemporary of the important African American musical styles to emerge after Emancipation. For me, the answer came in an LP album that I found in a list of available folk song collections on an obscure label with a sympathetic feminist agenda. The album was titled *Jailhouse Blues* and it was released a few years ago by a small, independent company, Rosetta Records, with an address on W 16th Street in New York City. The company's owner, Rosetta Reitz, issued it as one of a 'Woman's Heritage Series.' It was the seventeenth album in the series. A number of the albums had presented blues by women blues singers, but the album released just before this one was *Mae West, Queen of Sex*, subtitled 'Foremothers, Vol. 7,' and it was followed by *Sister Rosetta Tharpe*, 1940s, 'Foremothers, Vol. 8.' The record business clearly needs more independent women like Ms. Reitz, and the album she released is indispensable to blues scholarship.

The music on the album came from a woman's camp inside Parchman itself. In her section of the extensive notes to the album Ms. Reitz writes that in 1936, at the time of the first recordings, Parchman had almost 3000 prisoners. The prisoners were strictly segregated by race and gender, and of the 2,675 male prisoners, 2,104 were black and 571 were white. Parchman was a unique prison experiment – it was, literally, a farm, and that same year the cotton crop extended over most of the 16,000 acres used for growing. For the women, as Ms. Reitz notes, the situation was different from the men's.

Camp 13 was the women's camp where white and black women occupied separate wards. The women's primary work was making clothes for the prisoners, mattresses and bedding for 3,000 beds and field sheets for collecting cotton. The women also did the canning, and in 1935 they canned 15,000 cans of produce from the prison gardens. They also helped out in the fields.

The women worked in a sewing room, with a long table at one side for cutting materials, and lines of sewing machines at small work benches. In appearance it was like a small sweatshop sewing factory in New York's Lower East Side, except for the southern sunshine that brightened the room. The first recordings with the women prisoners were done by John A. Lomax in the summer of 1936 in the sewing room, with the machines pushed back against the wall. Lomax, however, had always had misgivings about the blues, which he considered another form of contemporary popular music and not the kind of traditional folk song that was the focus of his collecting activities for the Library of Congress. He did, however, document the singing of Elinor Boyar, and her 'Gonna Need My Help Some Day' is a beautifully sung example of what was clearly the blues song form that was the women's distinctive singing style.

Three years later, in 1939, Herbert Alpert returned to the sewing room, and this time there were a significant number of blues recorded. Ms. Reitz described the circumstances of the recordings, and she writes that the women were simply asked to sing any song they liked, without 'restrictions about length or subject.' As she concluded:

In spite of their being prisoners, there is an aura of innocence about these songs. The women carried with them, into the prison, their own transportable private worlds, and their music is from that world, which contains beauty, idealism and humanity as well.

The three women Alpert encouraged to perform their blues in front of the inmates crowded into the small room, Mattie Mae Thomas, Beatrice Perry and Eva White, each sang without accompaniment, and their voices were light and clear. The similarity of intonation and melodies suggests that they could have learned from each other, but Eva White learned her dramatic 'No Mo' Freedom' when she was a prisoner in Jackson, Mississippi's Hinds Country Jail. When Mattie Mae Thomas, who was clearly moved by Eva White's performance, asks Alpert if she can add verses to the song, she continues the general theme of the other woman's blues, but she sings verses with a different melody. Thomas was in prison for the third time when Alpert recorded her. She had learned her 'Workhouse Blues' in 1925, when she was in the Reverend Thomas workhouse. As she says of the song in her poignant introduction, 'A made up song. Just about being in prison alone.' She learned another of her songs included on the album, 'Big Mac From Macamere,' when she was in the Sheridan County Workhouse. In one of the lines she dates the year of the song to 1909, '... In the year 1909, I was a little young hobo.' It was about that period that one of the pioneers of the classic blues style, Gertrude 'Ma' Rainey, remembered hearing a young woman sing a blues for the first time when she was touring with a tent show in Mississippi.

The lyrics of the blues that the women sang for Alpert seem to have welled up from the same isolation and despair that was associated with the earliest of the blues songs. Verses and phrases surface that also made their way into commercial blues recordings. In 'No Mo Freedom' Eva White, who was just 24 years old, sings,

> Don't tell me the moon looks pretty, shining down through the willow tree.
> I can see my baby, but my baby can't see me.

Charlie Patton recorded a variant of the same verse in his 'Poor Me,' and the image found its way into other Mississippi songs of the period. In Mattie Mae Thomas's 'Dangerous Blues' she allows us to glimpse her anger, as well as her resignation.

> They keep on talkin' 'bout the dangerous blues.
> If I had me a pistol, I'd be dangerous too.

> You may be a bully, but I don't know.
> But I'll fix you so you won' gimme no mo' trouble in the
> world I know...

> My knee bone hurt me and my ankle swell.
> Says I may get better, but I won't be well...

She finishes with a verse that clearly reflects the reality of their prison lives, and in the background the other women in the room can be heard laughing uncomfortably.

Say Mattie had a baby and he's got blue eyes.
Say might be the captain, he's hangin' roun' (laughter)
Say might be the captain, keepa hangin' roun'
Keep on hangin' roun'.

What is so important about the blues songs of the women in their Parchman barracks is that they didn't sound like the blues that were being sung on recordings or over the radio in the Depression years. While his recording equipment was set up in the sewing room Alpert also recorded the usual range of ring-game songs, ballad fragments, and gospel songs, and the performances have many similarities to the documentary recordings made in other parts of the South. It was the blues the women sang that had a more distinctive sound. By 1939 the commercial blues had been a widely available sales item in the rural South for almost twenty years. Most of the commercial recordings fell into the familiar pattern of three lines and three chords that was repeated in a thousand songs. The women in Parchman certainly could have used these songs as a model. What they sang, instead, was a form of blues that predated anything they would have heard through a commercial source. Their melodies were clearly influenced by the pentatonic models of African song, as contoured through the individual field song, the 'holler.' In her note to the album, Dr. Bernice Johnson Reagon suggests that Mattie Mae Thomas's 'Dangerous Blues' is '...just one step away from the field holler. And one value of this connection of unaccompanied songs is that we get to hear revealed wonderful relationships between song forms, that are sometimes obscured in harmony and accompanied singing.'

The Parchman women's blues use two line verses, sometimes with rhyme, sometimes with rhymes stretched as far as they'll go to suggest a common sound. What moves them even further away from the recorded blues is that they are not only sung without accompaniment, they have been conceived as songs that could not be sung with an accompaniment. There is no room anywhere in the melodic line for a guitar rhythm, or for any rhythm that insists on a fixed pulse. The haunting melodies are repeated in each verse, with the two lines following in a simple, unadorned narrative. It is a form stripped to its essentials, but there could be no more powerful expression of this earliest form of blues song than Eva White's impassioned cry, 'No Mo Freedom.'

No mo freedom,
No mo good times in this wide, wide world for me.

Oh, I'm (beat?) from my feelings
And I'm sick as I can be.

Someday, yes someday, someday I will go free,
I'm goin' treat all you people just like you treated me.

(1995)

11. The Legacy of the Blues

When I moved with my family to Sweden in January 1971, I thought that the blues recording and writing I had been doing for several companies for nearly twenty years would come to an end. But after I had been working for several months in Stockholm with a Swedish company, Sonet Records, one of its managing directors, Dag Haeggqvist, who had brought us to Sonet, asked if it would be possible to produce a blues series for the new Sonet subsidiary that the company had set up in London. What I suggested was a series that would include as many styles of the blues as we could find, and that we work with major artists as much as possible and present the albums as a larger perspective of the blues itself. The twelve albums that made up the series were titled *The Legacy of the Blues*. Since we were more serious in our planning, the notes that I wrote were longer and more ambitious than the usual commercial notes I had written for other albums. I conceived the notes as essays that would present the individual artists, and also set them into the context of their style of the blues. When the series was completed, after almost four years of recording, selecting, and licensing the material for the albums, I expanded the notes into the chapters of a book with the same title as the series, which was published in 1975. One of the chapters is included, the portrait of Robert Pete Williams, and also an album note describing a 'blues night' with Champion Jack Dupree at a rural British agricultural college.

Champion Jack Dupree

Somehow it all felt a little like those trips through the South in the early 1950s, driving through farm country in an old car, asking people directions, stopping for a sandwich at a roadside stand, trying to follow the directions I'd been given with a map folded up in the glove compartment – looking for a blues singer out in the country again. Only this was the 1970s, the landscape alongside the road was the English county of Shropshire, the 'farm' I was looking for was an agricultural college outside of the small city of Newport, and the blues singer I was hoping to see wasn't one of the forgotten artists who had been lost to sight for many years. It was Champion Jack Dupree, who had driven down in his car from Yorkshire. He was performing for a blues night at the college. It hasn't been all that long since the new young white audience discovered the blues, but in those few years the blues has come a long way.

Jack, himself, has also come a long way with the blues. He's always played the same blues, but he's wandered and worked and sung through most of the United States, and now most of the world. When he was born in New Orleans on the Fourth of July, 1910, it was still a colorful, loose, flamboyant city, spread out in ramshackle neighborhoods of white painted wooden houses spread along the crescent curve of the Mississippi River. It was still an open city, despite the U.S. Navy's decision to close down the red-light district, Storyville, when he was seven. It was an easy town to grow up in, but Jack's early years were painful and difficult. His mother and father were burned to death when he was still a child and he was raised in the same orphanage where Louis Armstrong had been placed only a few years before, 'The Colored Waif's Home For Boys.' When he left the orphanage he was fourteen years old, it was 1924, and music was still one of the most vigorous expressions of the city's life. Some of its finest musicians had moved North – to Chicago and New York, and the New Orleans-style jazz they had taken with them had spread to other cities in America and to most of the countries of the world. Since it was the most exciting thing going on in New Orleans Jack did what a lot of other young boys did, he tried music for himself.

New Orleans was never a strong blues town, and the singers from the Mississippi back country plantations or the Texas crossroads towns who did drift in to the city never stayed long enough to make much of an impression. What New Orleans had exported to the Chicago cabarets were its horn players, its Louis Armstrongs and its King Olivers, its Johnny Dodds and its Jimmy Noones, but it was as much a pianist's town, Jelly Roll Morton's town, as it was a cornetist's town. It was the piano that called to Jack, and he started learning to play when he was still in his teens. His teacher was an older man named 'Drive-Em Down,' and Jack was with him until 1930, when he found himself alone again after the older man's death. Jack was twenty years old.

1930, the chaotic year that introduced the country to the Great

Depression, wasn't a good year for a New Orleans piano player to start some kind of a career, and Jack understood that he had to find something else to keep himself going. He turned to the ring and became a professional boxer – the reason for his nickname, 'Champion.' He still kept playing, working in some of the large cabarets in Midwest cities like Indianapolis that kept going through the Depression years. He finally gave up his ring career after winning a final bout in Indianapolis in 1940. In the late spring of that year, on June 13th, he began his recording career, with eight sides for the OKeh label in Chicago. At least one of the records did well enough for him to go back into studio again. Copies of his modest hit, 'Black Woman Swing' and 'Cabbage Greens No. 1' still keep turning up in New Orleans junk shops.

Jack did three more sessions for OKeh the next year, then with the beginning of the war he enlisted in the Navy. He continued to play and to record, with sessions for Moses Asch, who issued them first on 78rpm singles, then later issued them again as Folkways albums. Jack's career never had any clear pattern. He drifted from job to job, from company to company, from record to record. There was a long stretch for King Records in Cincinatti, which also had Lonnie Johnson as one of its artists. One of Jack's songs, 'Junker Blues', stayed popular enough for him to build his usual club routine around it. It was one of the best of the early narcotics blues, and it took Jack a long way. It was finally one of the songs that took him to Europe.

In 1958 Jack did a series of singles for Atlantic Records that were released on an album that became his first successful LP. After ten years of scuffling with a series of singles that never caused the same excitement as 'Junker Blues' the album was the beginning of a new career with a new audience. A new version of 'Junker' was on the record, along with remakes of some of his older blues, and some of the new songs that he always creates during his sessions. The next year, in the fall, he came to London, and he decided to stay. Since 1959 he has been living in Europe, one of the handful of American bluesmen, notably Memphis Slim in Paris, and Eddie Boyd in Helsinki, who have succeeded in making the break from the racial problems that plagued them in the United States.

Jack still lives and plays with some of his fighter's instincts, even after his years of living in Europe. In the studio, to record for the Legacy of the Blues series, he attacked the piano and pushed his songs with a relentless energy. With him for the afternoon were some of the young British musicians who have been bitten by the blues, drummer Huey Flint, bass player Benny Gallagher, guitarist Peter Curtley, and harmonica player Paul Rowan. Although they were all blues veterans – and Gallagher and Flint had a successful album on the sales charts – they never could stop treating him with an awed respect. It was the kind of freewheeling session that Jack does best – pushing the younger musicians with the same dedication he felt to the blues himself, and expecting them to match some of his energy and drive. There were moments when he was standing up at the piano so he could get more weight into his fingers, times when he was shouting across the studio to Huey and Benny, letting them know what he wanted from them. Then there were moments when he was near tears as he sang about his early life and hard childhood.

And all the time that he was in the studio he never stopped.

Jack went on playing for hour after hour. When everybody else went off to a local pub for some food and a few pints he was still there at the piano, working on something else. If he did stop playing he never stopped talking. Jack and his feelings about his life and his noisy laughter finally seemed to fill all the spaces in the studio. He is one of the great entertainers of the blues. He doesn't have the brooding moodiness of the Mississippi singers, or the vivid technical flash of Chicago's artists. He's just himself, a wiry, intense, sometimes wistful man with a large, crowded sense of life's pains and joys. He is as much at home with an audience as he is when he's sitting around a living room or standing at the bar in a pub. Sometimes his piano playing sounds like he's hitting the piano with a stick, sometimes he gets himself into a blues story that is so tangled he forgets where he started – but somehow he keeps it going, and in the end he's left you a sense that something that matters has happened, whether it was the humor and you're still laughing, or it was the sadness that can quiet the noisiest pub audience.

It was hard to find him that early evening in the middle of Shropshire, at least it was hard to find the little agricultural college. Jack, once he gets someplace, is never hard to find. His car sits parked out front, with his name and occupation, 'Blues Singer.' painted on the side. Jack sits back in a dressing room or in the bar, a beer in his hand, talking to anyone close enough to listen. Jo-Anne Kelly, a fine young English blues artist, was playing the same night, and they hadn't seen each other for months, so they warmed up a little for each other in the dressing room. Jack used her second guitar. He isn't a guitarist, but he is a bluesman, and the sound and the style of his guitar playing was another side of his blues.

There was the usual hassle over money, which lasted later than I expected while the argument got louder and shriller. About midnight Jack finally got on stage. A piano was pushed out halfway toward the audience on the small space and there wasn't much light. The audience was mostly sitting on the floor, in a litter of empty glasses and scattered chairs. Jack sat down in a tense rush, and with a thundering chord on the piano he was playing and singing, probably just about the way he played and sang in New Orleans saloons forty years ago. He sat half turned toward his audience, his body shifting and moving as he sang with all the fire and the enthusiasm of somebody working his first big job in a new club where he'd heard the customers left good tips. Finally there was a last chorus, a final glass of beer, a moment when he stood talking beside his car, then he looked around him at the still country night, waved vaguely toward the building where he'd been working, in case anyone was still watching, and drove off across the darkness of the fields.

Somehow, despite the distances from where he begun so many years before, and despite the incongruity of bringing his club songs and restless piano mood to a little college in the English countryside, it all seemed part of the story of the blues.

(1971)

From *The Legacy of the Blues* (1985)
Robert Pete Williams
'You Can Hear The Sound Of It, Comin' Forth, Soundin' Good'

It had been raining for three days in southern Louisiana – a cold, persistent rain that overflowed the shallow ditches beside the roads and seeped across the uneven street and narrow sidewalks of the small towns. In front of some of the houses there were small lakes where the gardens had been, and around little crossroad grocery stores the water backed up in broad ripples whenever a car drove past. In a small group of houses outside the town of Rosedale – not far from Louisiana's capitol, Baton Rouge – the water streamed in dark rivulets off the raised hump of the tarred road and washed against the front steps of the small, one-storey houses. A school bus had just emptied at one end of the street, its pent-up noise of voices and laughter spilling out across the neighborhood as the students – mostly adolescents – splashed through the puddles on their way home. In a house in the middle of the block, a muscular, dark, quiet man was sitting on a couch close to the front window watching for his own children. His house wasn't much different from any of the others in the neighborhood, and he didn't look much different from the people passing along in the street, but there was a guitar on the couch beside him and some finger picks and strings spread out on a low table. It was the house of one of the countryside's last bluesmen. A poster from a concert was tacked to the wall next to the bedroom door. His name was printed across it, 'Robert Pete Williams'.

His daughters burst into the room, piling books on the table, helping themselves to bread and butter, telling him about the day's excitements and confusions. His wife, Hattie Mae, was in the kitchen, standing at the stove, fixing supper. Robert Pete was listening to his daughters and answering them, but his mind was somewhere else. A recording session had been scheduled for later in the evening in Baton Rouge, and after two days of talking and thinking about material, he was beginning to withdraw into a mood of silent nervousness. It was like being in a room with any creative artist in any medium – a painter, a poet, a composer – and as an idea comes into their minds you can feel them beginning to turn it over and see what can be done with it. Instead of talking he often looked away, and when he did say something it was slow and abstracted, most of his mind sorting through the images of the blues he was going to sing.

Robert Pete has spent his life as a laborer, and he's still solidly built; a short, strong man with a large chest and shoulders. He had changed out of his work clothes into the costume he wears when he's performing; striped, flared trousers and polished high-heeled boots, a short sleeved sport shirt and a broad-brimmed Stetson hat that sits at an angle off his forehead. He stood at the kitchen table with a cup of coffee in his hand. He has high blood pressure now and he has to watch his diet. As he says, 'I talk it over with Hattie Mae now I'm getting old and she say all that's comin' down on you from when you were young.'

Hattie Mae had cooked a big supper – collard greens and neck

Robert Pete Williams, Rosedale, Louisiana, 1973
(Photo: Samuel Charters)

bones, fried gar fish, and mashed potatoes with bits of pickle mixed in. Everyone ate except Robert Pete, who took a little fish, finished his coffee, and went to put his guitar in its case. A pint of vodka went into the case with it. He doesn't drink much when he's in the house, but it helps loosen his fingers, and his imagination, when he's performing. He moved restlessly around the room, went to the door and stood looking out. Friends passing called to him, and he nodded; then turned back to look at the clock. We finished supper, Hattie Mae put away the dishes, and it was time to go to Baton Rouge.

Robert Pete's first recordings were done at the state prison farm at Angola, Louisiana by Dr. Harry Oster in 1959. Oster, a professor of English at Louisiana State University, was recording the music of all of Louisiana's cultural groups, and he'd gone into Angola to record the work gang songs still sung there. He found these songs, and he also found three bluesmen: Hogman Maxey, Guitar Welch and Robert Pete Williams. Robert Pete was not only the most exciting of the three; he was one of the most exciting country bluesmen to be found in years. It wasn't only the intensity of his music that made him unique – it was the spontaneous, free creativity of his blues that was so individual. As he described his music to Oster:

> All the music I play, I just hear it in the air. You can hear the sound of it, comin' forth, soundin' good. Well, all my blues that I put out, that was made up blues. I make up my own blues you see. Why, I may be walkin' along or ridin' in a car and blues come to me, and I just get it all in my head. Well, I come back and I get my guitar and then I play it.

After almost fifteen years of playing and recording, his blues still come to him 'in the air'. He has themes, obsessions, that come back to him again and again, but his songs are always changing, always newly shaping themselves. He is almost, in himself, a definition of the country bluesman – a poet of his own experience; his language and idiom coming from the hard country background that shaped him. To be with him when he's recording is like sharing the experience of his blues.

He was born on March 14th, 1914 in Zachary, Louisiana, another small town not far from Baton Rouge, where his father had a small farm. It was a poor, hard life, and when he was still a boy he was already working for somebody else:

I was in my teenage when I started. I slept in the barn and I laid on sacks and I laid under sacks. I'd get a cup of coffee and a piece of bread for breakfast. When I'd see the light burning in the kitchen I'd be like a dog. I'd know I was getting food. All that for $12 a month.

When he was fourteen he was working in a lumberyard in Scotland, another small town not far from where he lives now. He made himself a guitar when he was twenty, learned a little on it, and finally bought a real one. But it wasn't the blues that he was drawn to first. He told Oster,

Music begin to follow me then. I been trying to stop playing music, thinking about lookin' out for preparing my soul for Jesus. I was a Christian man before I got here. I can play church songs too, just as well as I can blues. What Jesus gave me, He didn't take it away from me. He sent me to be a preacher and I didn't like it…

For the next twenty years his life was poor and uncertain, but there were wives, children – 'I got me eight head of boys' – and he didn't stop living. There were jobs. There were Sundays when he slept late and Saturday nights when he stayed up late. He was at the Curry Lumber Company for a long time, stacking lumber for 75c an hour. He was living in Port Allen with a woman named Dora Lee and their four children. After that he worked at the Standard Oil coopering ship, cleaning metal barrels with caustic soda. He still has scars from acid burns he suffered working with the barrels. He had his day jobs, and he had his night jobs when he played a little guitar and sang.

It wasn't until he was forty-two that Robert Pete's life fell to pieces. Early in 1956 he killed a man in a ramshackle bar called Bradley's Club in Scotlandville. At his trial he claimed it was self-defence, and sitting at his window almost twenty years later he still has a clear, tormenting memory of what happened to him that day.

I come to the bar and there was these two fellows there, one with his head back, leanin', and the other one, a big man, and I was standin' there and he says, 'Where you from?' and I say 'Zachary,' and he says 'You lyin',' and I says, 'No, I'm from Zachary,' and I got myself a quart of beer and I went over to a table with it to drink there with some boys I knew and after a minute the big one comes after me again, sayin' something, and I gets up, and he says to the one leanin' 'I'm goin' take care of this…' and grabs my arm, grabs the sleeve, and I pulls away. I'm just small and I didn't want to fight him. I could have got away, but the door done got blocked, you know, all the people who'd come around to see like they do in a fight. He had a knife, a duckbill kind of knife with a broad blade and he come at me. I had the gun. That's the truth. I did have it. But Scotlandville's a bad place, they got men that won't stop anything they's doin'. If I was to go there today I'd carry a gun. So he come at me and I shot him. In the stomach. But you know, he didn't go down, and it was a .45 I shot him with. He just stumbled over a little and leaned on a table, then he started to come at me again. You know if you hit a man with a .45 and he don't go down he's strong – so I shot him again in the heart.

At the trial he says there were no witnesses for him. The people who'd been in the club weren't going to come to the police for somebody who wasn't from the town, even if it was somebody they knew. Without witnesses to the fight – the police couldn't find the knife and the other man had been shot twice with a .45 – Robert Pete didn't have much of a chance. He was sentenced to life imprisonment, and he went into Angola to begin serving his sentence on April 6th, 1956.

He tried, from the beginning, to get out. When Oster found him in the prison three years later he he'd already made three efforts to get paroled, only to be turned down each time. He didn't give up the music, though there was a shortage of instruments, and the prisoners had to pass around what they had. When Oster came through the wire gates with his recording equipment Robert Pete was ready. He still remembers how hard it was to bring himself to play.

It was so hard to play when Dr. Oster came there – everybody was so close and standing behind you and you gets so nervous. Some of them men look like they could eat barbed wire and sleep sound all night.

But he played. Oster and other people began to work to get him out, writing to Louisiana's governor, Earl Long. Their appeals were successful and he was freed on December 1st, 1959, but it was a conditional freedom and he was technically a parolee to be held in the custody of a white farmer with land outside of Denham Springs, Louisiana. He was kept almost as a field slave – the small salary he was paid was the only difference between what he had to endure and what the men and women before him had to endure before 1865. He says about it, with a flare of anger, 'If I had to go back on parole, I'd rather do my time in the penitentiary.'

In the summer of 1964 he was finally free – in time for the Newport Folk Festival. If he was confused at finding himself suddenly in a massed crowd of young white college students who were excited at seeing him play, he didn't show any sign of it. He was in a new suit and a straw hat, talking casually with anyone who came up to him, but his eyes shifted from face to face as people came close to talk, his own face, for a moment, almost expressionless. Then he would glance around him and his face would open up with a smile that was like the sunrise. And he sang with the same free creativity as he had on the session he'd done for Oster five years before, Newport's loudspeakers blaring his voice and guitar through the grey, damp air over the faces staring back at him.

Rosedale is west of Baton Rouge, on the drier country that lifts out of the swamps below the Mississippi River and New Orleans' Lake Ponchartrain. The land is still flat and muddy, with meandering bayous crossed with small bridges as the roads criss-cross over the weed-choked waters. The house Robert Pete built for himself and Hattie Mae is outside of Rosedale – in a small black community straddling the railroad tracks just beyond a large lumber company where a lot of the men work. He built the house out of materials and lumber he found around the countryside as he worked with his own truck, picking up scrap metal. The house is one-storey, painted white, with a small front porch. His truck is usually pulled into a small driveway alongside.

Hattie Mae was driving when it was time to go into the studio, a friend sitting in the car with them. The music has made it possible for Robert Pete to add some things to his life, and their car was new – a big sedan that Hattie Mae drove easily through the darkness. The small back roads opened out onto the double lane highway going east toward Baton Rouge, and the double lanes lifted up onto the curve of the long bridge over the Mississippi and dropped down into the city. The streets were outlined with lights, glaring with lights, but like most small

American cities the night streets were empty. Most of the people have moved out to clutches of suburb at the ends of the road. The few drifters still in the business section were sitting in the movies, or in one of the bars, or in a hotel lobby in front of the TV.

Robert Pete has no trouble with studios or microphones now. He was still in his mood of withdrawn concentration, making every motion with the slowness of a man watching himself in a mirror. The bottle of vodka went beside his foot – he spent a lot of time tuning the guitar. The guitar didn't need all the time, but he did, still getting lines and verses spread out in his head, staring across the studio as he tried out rhythms and fingerings. He uses a slide now. He learned from Fred McDowell, the Mississippi bluesman who was also at Newport when Robert Pete first left the South. They'd become good friends. 'If Fred had a nickel, I had a nickel, and if I had a nickel, Fred had a nickel.' He brought the slide – a piece of metal tubing – out of the guitar case, took a sip of the vodka, then nodded to the engineer, Bill Triche, that he was ready to start.

At its most uninspired the blues can fall into restricted, tight patterns, monotonously closed into its three line verse form and repetitive harmonies like a horse wheeling around and around a threshing stone. To break out of it there has to be a certain individuality, a rough determination to shape the form into something more personal. The legacy of the blues of Robert Pete Williams is their direct responsiveness to what he's thinking and feeling. He begins with the blues forms, then once they're set he moves easily and freely around them, staying close enough to get back to the forms if he senses that he's begun to drift, but still loose enough to use them in any way he chooses.

Themes persist in his blues, but even the same experience becomes new again when he returns to it. In 1959, when he sang about his imprisonment for Dr. Oster, his dominant concern was understandably his effort to get paroled. In 1973 the emphasis had changed to the trial itself, and his feelings at his sentencing.

Lord, I had a fall, I had a fall in 1955.
Lord, I had a fall, babe, 1955.
The police picked me me up, handcuffed me, carried me to jail.

Locked me down, they tried me for my life,

April the 6th, 1956, they sent me to Angola.
Not to lie, not to lie, they tried me for my life.
Cried, let's keep the poor boy.

You know, I called out, you cannot keep me, no, no.
I said I got a man in here in this courthouse with all power in his hand.
They asked me what man you talkin' 'bout,
I was lookin' dead down at the Bible you know,
I said God above got all power over me.

Yeh, you got to send me to your pen, I ain't thinkin' 'bout your
'lectric chair at all.
Oh you got to send me to your pen, and I'm not goin' be there long.
Oh yeh, you got to send me to your pen, Lord, I'm not goin' be there
long.

Uuum, Lord.

You know you got the poor boy your way, but that's alright, that's alright.
One of these ol' days, one of these ol' days,
Lord, I'm goin' walk out this ol' lonesome pen.

You can keep me down in here, but God's got his eyes on you.
Yeh, you can keep me down in here, but God's got his eyes on you.

They give me my sentence, natural life.
I say, that's alright, that's alright,
I (take ahead) every time.
But I won't be there long. Just tell me the day will I stay, 1956.
'59, '59, I was outside with my kids, yeh, Lord...

He didn't talk much between songs, still concentrating, still thinking about what he was going to sing next. He hardly listened to the occasional playbacks. It was almost as he had said when Dr. Oster first heard him, that the blues came to him as a kind of 'voice,' not as a performance. When he finished a song he was like someone who's just finished telling a long story. He doesn't want to listen to it again, he wants to get on to the next story. Hattie Mae sat on a couch in the control room quietly listening. It was only as he sensed that he

211

was coming close to the end of the session that his mood began to lighten. He'd shaken off some of the intensities that had gone into creating the songs. As he stood up to stretch, he was smiling. He took a last sip out of the bottle before Hattie Mae came into the studio to wait for him to get his things packed up and get ready to leave. It was raining again when we went out into the darkness – a light mist of rain blowing across the cars, the bright shine of the lights gleaming over the empty streets.

Robert Pete Williams' blues have come out of the life and the country backgrounds that have been his only reality. But like other artists who have created their own identity, he is no longer enclosed within that reality. The expression of it – his blues – has set him outside it. But he doesn't feel himself estranged – the voice that he hears that becomes the blues for him still continues. When he thinks about his own small community he says thoughtfully:

> I don't go out to these little places here to play because you know I got in that little trouble and people think of that and they might get shooting around me and I'd get a bullet. I went out last Christmas and played with a man, you know, played violin, but that was the only time. It's just too rough, those places back on those little roads…

But those 'places back on those little roads…' have been his life, both as a man and as an artist, and they will go on being part of his blues.

(1985)

Each of the blues artists whose stories became part of *The Legacy Of The Blues* had led checkered, tumultuous lives that were so rich in detail the difficulty was to compact their experience into the pages I could give them in the book. Robert Pete Williams was particularly talkative about his imprisonment on murder charges, a story he had told many times, but he also could talk for hours about local spirits – 'hants' – and about the people and the customs of the towns around him. He still was part of the small, isolated society where he had grown up and he had absorbed all of its lore. I planned for some time that I would go back and spend weeks with him there in his home in Rosedale and have him relate for me on tape the story of life as he understood it in his stretch of bayou Louisiana. Like many hopeful plans, however, there was no opportunity to carry it out. Robert Pete died in 1980 at the age of sixty-six, with so many stories still to tell.

12. Lightnin' Again

One of the problems of writing in one musical field is that you're often asked to do something more about an artist or a theme, when you've already said everything that needed to be said. I was, though, pleased when Bill Belmont of Fantasy Records called me in 1999 and asked if I wanted to be involved in a new Lightnin' Hopkins project. I had already written about Lightnin' in the notes to the first album we did together in 1959, as well as the chapters about him in *The Country Blues* the same year, but his career had been so long and colorful that there was always something to add to the story. Also it was going to be a boxed set. Bill, who is a vice-president of Fantasy Records in Berkeley, which bought the old Prestige catalog, was planning to release a collection of the eleven albums Lightnin' had recorded for Prestige between 1960 and 1964. When I asked Bill how long the notes should be, he shrugged. 'Just give us a bunch of pages,' he suggested, 'Whatever you think.'

One of the perennial problems with writing notes for an album is the length – there's never enough room to do more than begin writing a sketch. With a boxed set there's space to create a portrait or present a complicated idea. The boxed set gave me an opportunity to return to a great – and complicated – blues artist who was also an old acquaintance.

When I read over what I had written for this set and then looked back at the notes I'd written for the first LP Lightnin' and I had recorded in 1959, I could see that I had repeated some of the things I had included the first time. I decided that I would keep a little of this material in the new notes anyway, since it helps give some of the background to this larger portrait of Lightnin'. My hope, also, is that this might give even more of a sense of the way someone like myself works. We rephrase, reconsider and sometimes even reintroduce some of the same material, since it is the artist that we're trying to bring to life, and often it is just these touches that help fill in the expression of the face or the tone of a musical phrase.

When Lightnin' and I sat down for our long interview in 1967 – it was released as the entire side of an LP – he also found he wanted to

Lightnin' Hopkins, Houston, 1974
(Photo: Samuel Charters)

fill in more of the story he had told me that first afternoon eight years earlier. I was the first one to ask him about those early years and at that point he hadn't given those moments in his past a lot of thought. By now he had been asked some of the same questions so often, and he had found – as we all do when we look steadily back into our past – that he now remembered so much more.

Po' Lightnin'
The Prestige Sessions, 1960 – 1964

When I think about Lightnin' Hopkins, I have a whole kaleidoscope of impressions. Sometimes I think of him as wary, suspicious and uncomfortable; the way he was when I managed to track him down – broke and shabby – in a rented room off Dowling Street in Houston's ghetto in the late 1950s. Sometimes I think of him as moody and unpredictable – the way he could become in the recording studio when he was drunk and tired and all he could think of was getting out of there, and he'd retreat into a sodden 'Po Lightnin'' imitation as the day wound down. Just as often, though, I think of him as easy and casual, the way he was the last time we did an album together, a few years before he died. I was in Houston again, and we were sitting on the sidewalk outside of his apartment drinking beer from cans he'd bought for us at the weathered grocery store across the street. We kept the cans in their paper bags so we wouldn't bring down the tone of the neighborhood.

Mostly I'd dropped around because I had to take his picture for the cover of the album, and since we'd finished the recording the night before and he'd gotten his money we didn't have much to do except sit in the sun – it was hot – fan ourselves against the humidity – it had rained earlier in the afternoon and the air was still muggy – and sip our beer. Lightnin' joked with the girls who walked past, called out to friends, and occasionally a big, new car would drive up, stop a little way down the block, and Lightnin' would amble off to carry on a mumbled conversation with the driver. He never bothered to tell me what the conversations were about, and I kept my eyes on my sweating can of beer in its crumpled paper bag and never thought to ask.

The sun was hot, and the light was hazy with the overcast of exhaust fumes that Houston accumulates late in the afternoon. The neighborhood around us – a few blocks of one-storey frame houses and empty backyards with some lawns and patchy gardens, some two-storey apartment buildings, some vacant lots – was still and breathless, just starting to stretch out from the afternoon's rain. But in front of us, a block away, a bare concrete entry ramp swept up from the downtown business district to the freeway going out to the suburbs where most of Houston's white families lived. The commuters were sitting in unending lines in their cars, creeping with a noticeable lack of enthusiasm up the humid, exhaust-plumed ramp. Even with the air conditioning that closed all of them in they still looked hot. Sometimes we could see a driver wiping his face. Lightnin' watched them inch along for a while, then gestured with his beer can.

'It take a lot out of a man to sit caught up like that every day. Never could do it myself.'

Lightnin' was a lean, rawboned man when I first met him, and he stayed about the same over the years – tall and skinny, with the feeling of the country about him. He moved with a watchful casualness. Even when he was upset about something he didn't bother hurrying. What I still feel so vividly about him is the sense that most of the time he was completely at ease with himself. He had the usual complicated vanities that any performer builds up over the years, but there was none of the studied theatricality that some other blues singers try to project. As he said once about his listeners,

'I know whatever I do, they're going to listen. And that's the way I want it. I want them to be listening.'

I never had the feeling that he even thought about what he was going to play when he performed for an audience. He just played it. If he was going to do a recording session he just sat down in front of the microphone and made up songs until somebody told him there was enough on the tape. I don't remember ever seeing him come into the studio with a piece of paper or with even much of anything planned out ahead. On the folk blues circuit he had a reputation as a ferocious guitarist, but he seemed to consider his guitar playing with the same casualness that he regarded his other skills. Playing the guitar was as easy for him as tying his shoes. He had developed three or four ways of accompanying himself that worked for whatever song came into his mind and he didn't think anymore about it. When I rented a guitar for him for the first recordings we did together – his was in a pawn shop – the guitar had a broken string so we drove off to buy a new set. We passed some teenage girls on the street and Lightnin' leaned back over the seat, picked up the guitar and went into a version of 'Good Morning Little School Girl' that was more casually exciting than the playing of nearly any other guitar player using all six strings.

At the same time, I remember talking with him again about guitar playing later that day. There are a lot of Mexican guitar players in south Texas, and Lightnin' knew what he was up against. I said something about their guitar style, thinking in a way that this might flatter him, but he shrugged laconically.

'Don't mess with those Mexicans with a guitar. They'll kill you with it.'

For most of the new white audience that followed Lightnin' around in the 1960s he was the symbol of the country bluesman, but he was able to be as casual as he was because in many ways he wasn't what we like to think of as a bluesman at all. He didn't wander from town to town – in fact it was hard to get him out of Houston. He hated to fly and only did it when he had to earn some money. When he did, he got himself a seat in the back and scrunched down with the half pint of whiskey that he always managed to smuggle on to the plane. He didn't drift from woman to woman. His younger life was stormy, but he was married in 1944 and despite some periods when he and his wife were separated in the 1950s they began living together again when he was able to make a living with his music. When he did stay in town he had a long-standing relationship with a local woman of some wealth who considered him her 'kid-man,' but it was all within the bounds of everyday conventions, as he defined them. His sister was in Houston, and despite occasional breaks they kept in touch with each other. In his own way, which certainly could be undependable, he was close to his brother Joel and to his mother. When you think of all the associations that the term 'bluesman' brings up, Lightnin' doesn't seem to qualify. He didn't live like a bluesman – he just sounded like one.

If anybody has a secret about their lives – and most people like to think they do – then that was Lightnin's secret. When he picked up his guitar, looked out at his wide-eyed audiences, and began to string together verses for whatever song he felt like singing at that moment – he was everything that everyone who was listening to him had ever dreamt about the country blues.

Lightnin' was still lean and hard, and he looked younger than he was when I first saw him in 1959, but he was almost fifty and he had paid all the necessary dues to sing the blues. He was born in the country, on March 15th, 1912, in a little town called Centerville, north of Houston on Route 75. It's rolling country, with a stretch of small hills that keep the backroads twisting and turning to find their way from one little crossroads to the next. The houses are modest, most of them made out of wood and painted white. In 1959 Centerville had the usual country store and a gas station and not much else. His mother, Frances Sims, was still living there in a room near the feed store. Lightnin' remembered it was good country for farming.

'Rich land, God knows. Black land. Anything you wanted to raise, you could raise, from cotton to corn.'

Lightnin' was one of six children. His father, Abe, was a musician, who worked as a farmer to eke out a living. Two of his brothers, John Henry, who was eleven years older, and Joel, a half brother who was eight years older, were both blues musicians, and they recorded with him at the peak of the folk blues revival in the 1960s. His father died – Lightnin' sometimes said he was murdered – when he was three and the family moved five miles away to the town of Leona, where he was raised by relatives. By the time he was eight he had started with a homemade cigar box guitar, and his brothers were already teaching him how to play it.

Like everyone who lived out in the country in the South at that time, he ran across the blues early. When he heard Blind Lemon Jefferson at a picnic in Buffalo, Texas, even though he was still a boy Lemon let him play along with him. As he remembered it years later:

'This is true. When I was in Centerville, Texas, just seventeen miles from Buffalo, Texas, I was eight years old when I went with my guitar. It was near 'bout as big as me. That big. I went to the Buffalo Association and met this here big blind man, Blind Lemon Jefferson. That man was picking that guitar and I just felt it was in me. I told them, I say, "I can play what that man's playin'." They knowed I could play, all them young boys there; so I got up there with my little old guitar and I hit it. Blind Lemon looked, he – you know – turned around. He got the sound from me. He say. "Who is it?" and they say, "This here boy can play a guitar." And he called at me, "Boy, you got to play it right," and I was scared a little bit, you know, but when I said something he heard I was just little and he say, "Let me hear you play that guitar a little bit, boy." I hit his note, runnin' through there like he was, you know. He say, "Boy, what's your name?" I told him, "Sam Hopkins." He say, "You know, I believe you can play," and he hit his guitar and I was in tune, 'cause I tuned it out there. Man, he put me up on top of that truck where he was sitting and we had a association! I played on top of that truck and he told me, said, "Boy I didn't think you could play like that..." '

There's a lot of empty countryside around small towns in Texas, and for farm families like Lightnin's it was the extended string of cousins, aunts, uncles, grandmothers, stepfathers and stepmothers that helped somebody get from one place to another in their lives. It was a cousin, Alger Alexander, who took Lightnin' through his apprenticeship as a blues man. Alger recorded for most of the major blues labels in the 1920s under the name 'Texas' Alexander. Lightnin' first met him at a baseball game in another little town close to Centerville in the 1930s.

'Well, I met Texas Alexander in Leon County at a place you call Normangee, Texas. They had a little old do down there, what you call, I don't know, a picnic, and they had a ball game, see… So I got down there and… I seen a man standing up on a truck with his hand up to his mouth, and man, that man was singing so and he like to broke up the ball game… All his people was living in Normangee, most of them, you know, his mother and them at that time was living, and he had gone kind of like I did and stayed for a while and he come back. That's the way he come back, you understand, he come back ready. I mean he come back ready with that singing. He couldn't play no music. He never played an instrument in his life. But he'd tote a guitar. He'd buy a guitar, and he'd tote it in case that he'd run up on you or me or somebody could play and he'd sing…'

'I accompanied him for quite a bit here in Crockett, Texas, Grapeland, Patterstein, Oakwood, and Buffalo and Centerville, Normangee, Flynn, and Marquez and back in them places. I never followed Texas no further than Houston for a long time 'cause he was a man to get up and go. First Cadillac that I ever known to be, you know, one of them expensive, bad cars – he went somewhere and he come to Normangee in a Cadillac and it was the longest ugly old car, old long Cadillac, one of them there old first made. But it was new! He got over there and everybody admired him, you know, because colored people didn't have nothing. They didn't even have T-Model Fords then and you know he come in a Cadillac. Yeah, Texas was doing all right for himself…'

You can hear phrases from Texas Alexander's singing in Lightnin's later recordings, and Texas, like his younger cousin, sang a lot of songs in a loose field holler style, which meant he didn't worry about what the guitar was supposed to be doing. Among the musicians who accompanied him on record was Lonnie Johnson, who was one of the finest blues and jazz guitarists of the 1920s. The songs Alexander recorded with Lonnie were brilliant examples of how a guitarist can fill behind a singer who isn't bound much by regular rhythm patterns. It's easy to hear parallels between these early recordings – done for OKeh Records in the late 1920s, when Lightnin' was a teenager – and the casual sense of chord changes that was the despair of musicians trying to play along with Lightnin' in the 1960s.

Lightnin' started wandering when he was still in his teens, but he didn't get much further than the small towns close to where he'd grown up. He got married in his twenties – which came the same time as the Depression years – and for several seasons he worked with his 'uncle', a friend of the family called Lucien Hopkins. He kept his music for weekends and back porch parties. In 1945 or 1946, Lucien sat him down and told him he should stop doing farm work and get into Houston. He was in his mid-thirties, and if he was going to make it as a singer he should get started. Lucien gave him money to help him buy a new guitar, and Lightnin' and his wife moved to Houston. Once there it was his family ties that helped him again. His cousin Texas Alexander was in town, and for a while Lightnin' worked with him in the little clubs where he was to go on playing for the rest of his life.

Lightnin' first made it into a recording studio in 1946, and for the next few years it didn't seem like he spent much time anywhere else. It was a woman named Lola Anne Cullum, who was looking for blues artists for one of the new labels springing up everywhere in the country in the post-war years, who heard about him and drove him out to Los Angeles to record his first release, with 'Thunder' Smith playing the piano behind him. This was Hopkin's first release for Aladdin Records – 'Can't You Do Like You Used to Do' and 'West Coast Blues', and the name someone gave the duo – 'Lightnin'' Hopkins and 'Thunder' Smith – stayed with Lightnin' for the rest of his career.

Lightnin's early years in the recording studios were often a little disorganized, but they were productive. Between 1946 and 1953 he recorded at least two hundred titles for a variety of small R&B labels in cities as far apart as Los Angeles and New York. The best of the sessions, not surprisingly considering Lightnin's hometown roots, were recorded in Houston for a small company called Gold Star, run by World War II veteran Bill Quinn. Lightnin' had come back to town from California, and the story is that somebody working for Gold Star heard him sitting on a curbstone with his guitar, playing for some children.

Even in those first post war years, when local releases with hometown artists often sold large numbers of records, Lightnin' was a major success. The first single Quinn put out, 'Short Haired Woman' and 'Big Mama Jump,' sold between forty and fifty thousand copies, which for a local R&B label, without much distribution, was a major hit. It didn't seem to matter that a few weeks earlier, Lightnin' had recorded both of the songs for the Aladdin label in Los Angeles. In those years the local companies had distribution systems that seemed to end about the point where their salesmen got tired of hauling the records around in their station wagons.

Nearly everything of Lightnin's that Quinn put out sold at least forty thousand copies, with the hits like 'Baby, Please Don't Go,' selling more than eighty thousand. The problem was that Lightnin' always needed money. He was earning a lot, but he let it all slip through his hands. Some people also said that he was involved with local gamblers in a successsion of small scams. It was during these years that he was picked up a number of times by the Houston police. It was a richly creative period for Lightnin' as a musician, but the rest of his life was a little frayed. Quinn finally tried giving the money he was earning to Lightnin's wife, but after a few months that situation had got completely out of hand. When in February 1948 Lightnin' recorded for Aladdin again, Quinn decided he had had enough and sold all the remaining masters he had recorded to other companies.

For the next few years Lightnin's singles were a staple of R&B radio fare, even if his records didn't sound much like anybody else's. As I wrote in the chapter about him in *The Country Blues* in 1959:

When radio stations played Lightnin's records on Gold Star, there would usually be an awkward silence after the record was finished while the announcer tried to think of something to say. Usually there would be a nervous laugh and he'd say something like, 'That Lightnin', he sure is something, isn't he!' Lightnin' was a little bewildering to most people who heard him. He was accompanying himself on an unamplified guitar. There was no piano, no drums, no bass. He was one of the first blues singers to work without a group in ten years. His singing was very free, almost disorganized. Some verses were twelve measures long, some were thirteen and a half, some were ten. Lightnin' sang in the same unmeasured, harsh style that Lemon Jefferson and Texas Alexander had recorded twenty years before. The guitar trailed along, echoing the words, droning in a rhythmic drumming on a lower string, then ringing above the voice between the lines and carrying off painfully intense, lyric passages between the verses. Even the blues themselves, rough and direct, were a far cry from the recordings of other blues singers. Lightnin' was one of the roughest singers to come out of the South in years…

Styles were changing so quickly that since Lightnin' didn't really change his style his popularity would have faded anyway, but his habit of drifting from company to company and recording the same songs over and over again meant that he didn't have any kind of solid relationship with any of the companies, and by 1953 no one was interested in recording him. He was still living in Houston, and he had occasional jobs in small clubs like Irene's or the Sputnick Bar, but these were scuffling years for him, and he was as close to the 'Po' Lightnin'' image of himself as he was ever to come. He'd stopped living with his wife, and he was drifting around a series of rented rooms in the shabby neighborhood around Dowling Street. His guitar was in and out of pawn, and whatever money he made came as much from small deals and hustles as it did from his music. His wary, guarded expression in the photographs taken of him in the late 1950s reflects these hard years.

But at the same time that the sun was setting on Po' Lightnin's career as an R&B artist, there was already a stirring of interest in a different kind of blues. A number of enthusiasts had begun to listen to the old country blues. In the early 1950s I'd already travelled through southeast Texas looking for Robert Johnson and Blind Willie Johnson, and in the summer of 1954 I heard a record of Lightnin's, 'Contrary Mary', playing on a jukebox on Girod Street in New Orleans, and decided that some day I'd have to try to find him. It was, however, to be several years before a car he was riding in drove up beside mine at a stop light on Dowling Street and Lightnin' found me.

By the end of that first day I met Lightnin', I managed to rent a guitar for him, we bought some new strings and a bottle of gin, and went back to the bare, drab room where he was staying. In the next three or four hours we recorded his first 'folk blues' album. It was the first album Lightnin' had ever recorded, and there were more and more uneasy questions about why we had to have so many songs. It was a grey day outside and the room was in shadow and he was moody and guarded, but despite his mood he was singing magnificently. He hadn't recorded in a long time, and we went from song to song without any delay for discussions or retakes. I was holding the microphone in an outstretched hand so I could move it down for the guitar solos and then back up for the singing. I could also hold it far enough from his mouth so we didn't have a problem with distortion. There was enough gin for him to forget I was sitting on the end of his bed in the shabby room with him, but his playing never lost its brilliance or its inventiveness, and his singing never slipped into cliches. I kept asking him for old songs, and thinking about what he had heard when he was a boy seemed to bring out a level of intense creativity to the blues he was singing. When the afternoon was over I gave him the money I had – $200 – and before I was out of the room his sister, his sister's boyfriend, a younger girl, and a friend of Lightnin's were already there, waiting for him to take them to the bar on the corner. Lightnin' walked along behind them, tired, his shoulders slumped, looking thin and worn and alone.

When Folkways released the record a few months later Lightnin's life changed overnight. The blues revival was just beginning, and here was a great country bluesman, still playing in a traditional style. I had insisted that he play an acoustic guitar for the session, and the wiry sound of the open strings was even closer to the older blues than most of his recordings for the R&B labels. He had time – between the session we did together and the fall of 1960, when he signed a contract with Prestige Records – to record another eighty-six titles for a number of companies, often with Mack McCormick producing the sessions.

The contract with Prestige lasted until 1964, and there were eleven albums, as well as an interview we did together that took the entire side of an LP. Prestige tried to hold him to the exclusive contract by recording him every chance they could, but Lightnin' couldn't change his old habits, and there were the usual sessions for other companies, often of the same material. Some of the Prestige sessions were done live at a concert, others were recorded in the studios. Several albums were described as having been recorded in Rudy Van Gelder's studio a few miles from Prestige's small building in Bergenfield, New Jersey. This was to explain the presence of the bass and drum accompaniment by Leonard Gaskin on bass and Herbie Lovelle on drums. Sometimes Lightnin' did record there in the studio with them, but just as often the tapes were recorded by Mack McCormick in Houston. Whoever was working for Prestige at the time – I followed Paul Rothchild as folk A&R producer there from the fall of 1963 to the beginning of 1965 – was responsible for getting the advances to Mack for new sessions (Lightnin' usually got an advance of $1000) and then had to keep pressing Mack to get Lightnin' into the studio and send the tapes back to New Jersey. When the tapes came in our job was to dub the rhythm accompaniment. Sometimes I was the one who drew the job, sometimes it was jazz producer Ozzie Cadena, who had a gospel record shop in Newark and supervised Prestige's dates with soul artists like organist Jack McDuff.

Occasionally, when Lightnin' was in New York, there was a session with everyone in the studio at Rudy Van Gelder's, but it was just as difficult for Herbie and Leonard to follow Lightnin's grandly irregular phrasing when they were sitting on the other side of the microphone from him. Lightnin' didn't play a lot of chords – about three was the usual range – but it was difficult to tell just when he was going to play them. Sometimes he'd sing the chord change, but leave the guitar harmony unchanged, other times it was just the opposite. Sometimes a slow blues would go for a whole chorus without anything unexpected, and then the next chorus would be unknown country again.

Herbie and Leonard, and the other musicians Prestige used, worked out their own ways of dealing with the uncertainties. The drum style Herbie decided on was anachronistic. Instead of the crashing back beat that Lightnin' was used to on his club dates, Herbie found it was safer to play a pattering sound with the brushes, since he was never sure where the back beat might come. It was a comforting sound, like rain on an awning, that somehow managed to be reassuring, without intruding.

Leonard had a much more difficult problem following Lightnin' on the bass, since he had to guess what chord was coming next. The usual patterns didn't work, so even if he cautiously edged into one he would usually have to break out of it before he'd gone more than a few bars. When you listen to what he's doing it's obvious that the notes he's playing often have only a tenuous connection with what Lightnin's playing. The effect, however, is something like Herbie's drumming: it's reassuring. To blur the lack of coordination between them Leonard had found a way of playing notes that had no clear pitch. They were a kind of vague thud, and they might have been the note Lightnin' was playing – or they might not have been. No one was paying much attention to those kinds of details. Once when I was commiserating with Leonard about the problems he laughed and shrugged his shoulders.

'I've been playing with Lightnin's all my life.'

Since the Prestige sessions came at a vigorous moment in Lightnin's long blues odyssey, and he was free to follow any ideas that he had in the studio, the music he recorded reflects all of his moods and styles. Here is Lightnin' happy and here is Lightnin' sad. Here is Lightnin' composing a blues out of something as newsworthy as the space flight of astronaut John Glenn, and here is Lightnin' without much of anything on his mind except getting to the end of the session. Here is Lightnin' sober and here is Lightnin' drunk – sometimes more than a little drunk. Here is Lightnin' who was one of the blues' most facile guitarists, and here is Lightnin' who remembers a line or a verse from every blues he ever heard. What is obvious from all of it is that he was one of the greatest country blues artists who ever sat down in front of a microphone.

Lightnin' has often been described as a blues minstrel, and that isn't a bad term for his music. He always could think of something for his audience, and even if it was a song he'd performed over and over again in one form or another, he still sang it as if it had some real meaning for him. In his slow blues the phrasing and the chording were always a little different and in each version of the text there were unexpected verses and new lines. If his audience seemed to get restless with his slow blues, he'd shift to his shuffle, and he had three or four variants of each of his two main tune structures – the blues and the shuffle – to get him through a long evening.

He was so unique as a performer that it's almost useless to compare him with anyone else, but the classic blues artist Lonnie Johnson also had this way of immediately setting the mood with the first notes of his guitar introduction. When Lightnin' was deep into his blues – which was almost all the time – he only had to play a few decisive chords or an elusive run on the guitar to get the audience's attention. Even though he worked within a loose, idiosyncratic formula of chords and guitar fills, the pattern was different each time. Like something moving past the surface of an irregular mirror, whatever he played seemed to be perpetually changing, even if it echoed the mood of something he'd played five minutes before. When he was at his best, every note he sang or played sounded as if he couldn't have chosen any other note – and it sounded like he had just discovered it.

One of the sessions that Lightnin' did for Prestige in 1962, 'This Road By Myself', included one of his most inventive and popular songs for the company, 'Happy Blues for John Glenn.' As McCormick described the day in his album notes, Lightnin' had spent the morning – February 20th, 1962 – sitting in front of his landlady's TV set watching astronaut John Glenn make the first American orbital space flight, and Lightnin' decided to do something to acknowledge all the excitement. This was also the only time that anyone noticed Lightnin' getting something ready before he started to record. McCormick wrote:

...He arrived at the studio an hour early, in itself a rare event presaging things to come. As members of his entourage unloaded instruments and ran his errands, he sat out back in his car. At one point he asked for a piece of paper, and, with a nod at the Gettysburg address legend, a torn envelope was provided. His making notes was essentially a symbolic act for a half-hour later the envelope contained only three marks resembling hex signs. Nonetheless he insisted on propping it up in front of him as he took his place beneath the microphone. In some way the cryptic marks identified for the him the incidents he wished to touch upon, and with it in place he was ready to extemporize. He called a last minute conference to confirm Glenn's first name and whispered his question because, child-like, he intended to surprise those present (including the musicians who accompany him) with his song's subject. The surprise and the first take were ruined by a sudden short in the guitar amplifier. It had been a moody blues set to the same tune as the bitter protest 'Tim Moore's Farm.' While the repairs were in progress, Lightnin' read a newspaper account of Glenn's flight and some detail there seems to have altered his concept for when he launched into the song again it was definitely a happy blues. This is one of those rare times when we can be thankful for an equipment failure in a recording session. Not only was the mood of the song completely changed, Lightnin' changed to a melody that was less familiar, and despite some lapses on his part, when he couldn't remember the chord sequence, the band worked into a strong, grooving rhythm. The text is one of Lightnin's loosest and freshest.

People was all sittin' this morning with this
on their minds.
There ain't no man living can go around the world
three times,
But John Glenn did it!
Yes he did!
He did it and I'm talkin' about it,
Only he did it just for fun.

But John Glenn did it!

An album from 1962, *Smokes Like Lightnin'*, produced by McCormick in the Gold Star Studio in Houston with Lightnin's usual local back-up band, became the outlet for the frustrations Mack was having in his relationship with his artist, and which had been hinted at in the tone of some of his earlier album notes. For this album he vented all of his problems in the liner notes. Probably Prestige was the only record company that would have printed what he wrote, since they were the most hostile set of notes anyone has ever written as a back liner for an album, but with all the anger they did paint a reasonably accurate picture of Lightnin's life at this point.

McCormick began by saying that people keep asking him, now that Lightnin's gotten so famous, 'Has he changed?' He answers,

> ...in direct reply to the question: no he has not changed. He is just the same as he has been all his adult life: a natural born easeman, consumed by self-pity and everlastingly trying to persuade the world that it is his valet...

It is clear that after spending two or three years trying to pick up after Lightnin' – whom McCormick had sympathetically supported as an artist since they first met – Mack had had enough. Writing about Lightnin's gambling, Mack describes how he would take advantage of his friends with elementary dice tricks:

> ...then, his ego bolstered, proceed to a hangout of professional gamblers who promptly drain him of hundreds of dollars. He is a joke to the gamblers of Houston's Third Ward, who eagerly await his visits...

He was as scathing in his dismissal of Lightnin's pose as a man mistreated by women.

> Lightnin' sings endlessly of being mistreating by women though in fact he has been the pampered daytime pet of a married woman for fourteen years. She often accompanies him on trips out of town, and is then introduced as his wife, but in Houston a triangle is maintained with everyone keeping carefully to their own corner...

He was dismissive of Lightnin's daytime entourage.

> He spends most of his time surrounded by a coterie of 'helpers,' restless young men who envy him on the one hand and on the other answer his incessant demands for attention, accept his

drunken tongue lashing, and let him maneuver them into humiliating positions (e.g., clearing a path to the men's room for him). He is lovable and yet tyrannical in the same sad way of a very spoiled child...

McCormick ended his diatribe by describing how Lightnin' left Houston to avoid having to take care of his sister's funeral, leaving his harmonica player Billy Bizor to take care of the details. When Bizor drove Lightnin's brother Joel and their eighty-eight year old mother back to their home from the funeral they found the gas and electricity had been disconnected for nonpayment of the bills.

...Resting herself on the steps of the rickety two-room cabin, the old woman mused by herself: 'I had five children and they could each play music, but the baby couldn't do nothing else but. And he never has been no help to nobody except when you wanted to hear music.' She turned her head to the west, as if seeing the Hollywood nightclub where Lightnin' had gone, and firmly answered the question the fans have been asking: 'I guess he never will change.'

McCormick didn't work with Lightnin' again, but Lightnin' didn't seem to mind what had happened that much. When I saw him a few months later he shrugged and said, 'You can manage me for a while – if you got any jobs.'

Lightnin' continued to make albums after his contract with Prestige ended, and he had a particularly long and fruitful association with Chris Strachwitz and his Arhoolie label. As rock music more or less took over the music scene in the late 1960s Lightnin' travelled less, though he was considered one of the icons of the blues and he often appeared at both the East Coast and West Coast Fillmore Auditoriums at the height of the Haight-Ashbury psychedelic counter-culture years. In 1970 he was in a serious automobile accident and for some time had to wear a neck brace, which restricted his travelling even more. He slowed down as the 1970s passed, but he was living a relatively prosperous and stable life with his wife in Houston. When I saw him in Houston in 1974, he shrugged, 'I'd be out playin' most every night of the week if it weren't for them airplanes. You know one thing Lightnin' don't like to do is fly.'

If he travelled less, he was paid more to do it, and the excesses of gambling and the casualness of his personal relationships that colored his early years became part of the past. It was during this more reflective period in his life that we recorded our last album together for the Swedish label I was working with, Sonet Records, and we sat out in front of his apartment watching the cars inch up the highway ramp.

He made his last major appearance at a Carnegie Hall concert in 1979, and then in the next year he began his struggle against the cancer that killed him a short time later. He died in Houston on January 30th, 1982. If he had lived two more months he would have been seventy years old.

There was so much to Lightnin' – so many recordings, so many stories and myths and disagreements and opinions – that we still haven't begun to sort all of it out. We still can't say in a few sentences who Lightnin' Hopkins was, or what it was he created. His Prestige recordings, though, are a place to start, and everything that is Lightnin' Hopkins is there somewhere. As you listen to his voice and the guitar you can begin to shape your own image of this contradictory and completely unique artist who was one of the most creative and individual singers and guitarists the blues will ever know.

(1994)

13. Zy-De-Blues

Although I knew Lightnin' Hopkins over many years, my closest friendship with any of the blues artists I recorded was the period of almost ten years when I produced a series of albums with the zydeco artist Alton Rubin – who was always known as Rockin' Dopsie, and despite the spelling the name was pronounced Doop-sie. Most of the albums were recorded in his own small city of Lafayette, in western Louisiana, and I would move into a cheap motel across town and work on one of my book projects in my free hours as we planned band rehearsals around his steady schedule of dances and club dates. I met the band in places as unlikely as The Hague in Holland, London, Oslo, Stockholm, and in the islands off the coast of Sweden. He was one of the warmest, most open, and most generous men I've ever known in my life, and I have often thought about the many hours I spent with his close, friendly family, and about our adventures together, in the decade that has passed since his death.

Since I wrote so often about Dopsie I have included one of the notes by 'Freddie Crozier' which was written for the final album we did together in 1984. The long selection 'Zy-De-Blues' is adapted from the chapter 'A Prince of Zydeco' in the forthcoming book *A Language of Song: Journeys in the Musical World of the African Diaspora.*

'Freddie Crozier' on Good Rockin' Dopsie

Dopsie's album *Good Rockin'* was the sixth or seventh we'd done together, so it didn't feel like it was necessary to explain everything again, and 'Freddie Crozier' came through with one of his more informal commercial pitches. It is now a matter of long established custom that a note on Louisiana cajun or zydeco music will include a comparison to either 'gumbo' or 'jambalaya,' and I had already used 'gumbo' several times previously, so this time it was 'jambalaya' that was called on to do the job.

Rockin' Dopsie and The Cajun Twisters
on stage at Fort Spriggs, Houston, 1983
(Photo: Samuel Charters)

Here he is again, that 'Good Rockin'' man from Louisiana, Rocking Dopsie & the Cajun Twisters. As usual he's cooked up a real Louisiana jambalaya of R&B, zydeco two-steps, New Orleans style rock and roll, and the blues, and to help him get the seasoning right he's brought in four new members for the Twisters. His son David has picked up the rub board and joined his older brother, drummer Alton Jr., in the rhythm section, along with new bass player Ray Moulton. Ray was born in Lafayette, but he's spent a lot of time in New York with modern jazz groups. He played the guitar with Billy Cobham's group at the Montreux Jazz Festival in 1978, and in Lafayette these days he often rehearses with his own recording group, when he isn't busy with Dopsie on the bass.

To give the Twisters even more of a heavy, downhome beat Dopsie has brought in two of Louisiana's finest zydeco guitarists. Russell Gordon comes from the little town of Cecelia, not far from Lafayette, and he appeared on all the recordings by Buckwheat Zydeco. He has grown up with the French language, and it's Russell who does the inimitable French vocals on three of the numbers. The other guitarist is Paul Senegal – better known as 'Little Buck' – who is well remembered for all those brilliant guitar breaks he contributed to Clifton Chenier's recordings. For the final flavoring Dopsie asked a good friend, blues singer and local d.j. Joshua Jackson Sr. to do two numbers with the band, and his original number 'I'm A Country Boy', written with Rick Darnell, is one of the best new blues songs to come along in years.

When you put all of the ingredients together you have one of Rocking Dopsie's most exciting albums. It's like they say about him down in Louisiana – 'When you got Rocking Dopsie you sure got Good Rockin'!'

Freddie Crozier
(1984)

Rockin' Dopsie
'A Prince of Zydeco'
from *A Language of Song*

In the darkness the flat, featureless land on either side of the straight road could have been covered with pieces of board, stretching out until their length was lost in the shadows. Sometimes the van slipped past a house, but if there was a light still burning it was only a dim lamp left on over a porch or in the back by a shed. It was too late for anyone to be up and too early for people who had to get to work. At the occasional roadside stops there were lines of idling trucks with their yellow running lights outlining the bulky shapes of trailer rigs and drivers' cabs. Inside the low ceilinged coffee shops I glimpsed the backs of sweaty work shirts, the heavy shouldered drivers wearing them leaning along counters covered with dirty dinner plates, crumpled napkins and coffee cups. It was too late for us to stop. The van kept up its steady pace, the heater holding off the night chill of the East Texas fields. The men in the seats behind us were sprawled against each other in heavy, restless sleep, their ornate shirts creased, their buckled shoes pushed off.

Good Rockin' Dopsie, the man who was driving, talked in a slow, steady monolog. It was his van and the men inside sleeping were his band. As he had done so many times before, he was driving them home from a dance. He didn't have to be up the next morning for his day job – he stopped doing construction work three or four years ago when the dance jobs started paying better – but some of the musicians in his Cajun Twisters did have to get up, and he was bringing them back home to Lafayette so they could get two or three hours sleep in their beds. They'd be a little red-eyed for their jobs, and there would be a next morning headache to remind them of everything they'd had to drink the night before, but they'd get through their day's work – just as they had done so many times before.

Dopsie didn't usually push himself this hard anymore, but the Twisters had played a little high school gym dance in Lafayette on Thursday night, then they'd driven over to Houston for a weekend of dance jobs. On Friday they played a long night under the strings of dangling, half lit colored bulbs that twined over the bandstand at Fort Spriggs, a shadowy, barn sized dance hall for people from Louisiana looking for a little of their own music. The next day drifted past in visits with friends and relatives – cheerful, busy families with wriggling children scattered over the floor, staring up wide-eyed and open-mouthed at the loud talking, flamboyantly dressed musicians. The people they stopped by to see worked small jobs or ran little businesses and they had made decent lives for themselves in neighborhoods of small frame houses out in the countryside beyond Houston's cramped ghetto.

Dopsie and the band tried to squeeze in a little sleep along with the laughter and the greetings, then there was another noisy dance in a smaller club. Finally, with the job over, the amplifiers tiredly heaved off the bandstand and the instruments shoved on top of them in the back of the van, Dopsie began the drive back over the empty night distances of the East Texas flatlands. The only markers I could see to measure the miles we were driving were the flares of the gas burning off on distant wells – fluttering, yellow-white torches in the darkness – and for the first night hours they slid steadily past us with the measured pace of a stick floating on a river. But it had been a long weekend. Dopsie was tired. I finally felt his foot lighten up on the gas pedal, and he pulled over on the crushed shell slope of the road's shoulder.

'Could you take it for a little?' His voice was scraped sand dry after all the singing, but I could hear his tone of apology.

'You know I didn't want you to have to do some of the driving, but, oh man, I got to rest and I still got to get those boys back. They got their jobs.'

Again the flaring of the gas burnoffs in the distance, sliding slowly past the van, the Interstate empty of everything except for the occasional rig eating up miles toward Houston or back toward New Orleans, sometimes a solitary van like Dopsie's. He couldn't keep himself going with music on the radio, since it would keep the others in the band awake. The only thing he could do to keep himself awake was talk. Now he tried to sleep a little, his head against the door panel, and for a time all I heard was the swish of the tyres and fitful snoring from the figures slumped against each other in the dark shadows of the back seats. After a half hour I heard Dopsie's voice again.

'Wouldn't you know I'd be too tired to sleep. But I don't want to drive just yet. You keep going.' And he picked up the story he had been telling me with a hoarse voice that didn't have much more sound left to it than the breathy swish of the tyres.

The complicated patterns of the music that has emerged in the African diaspora often seem as though they were created out of an inevitable process that is also tantalizingly lost somewhere in the past. With zydeco, however, the unique musical style of the black culture of southwest Louisiana, it's possible to come almost to the moment when the two cultures, the white, French-speaking Cajuns and their black Creole neighbors, exchanged musical languages. Perhaps the cross fertilization is closer here than in any of the other styles that have emerged in the scattering of the African peoples. Once the musical exchange had begun, however, it was musicians like Dopsie, driving their vans out of the little towns like Opelousas or Eunice, the small cities like Lafayette or Lake Charles, setting up their amplifiers and microphones on sagging stages in country dance halls, who kept the music alive. It was bands like the Twisters who carried zydeco out across the empty spaces of western Louisiana, and over into Texas on Interstate 10, a highway that Dopsie had driven so often he felt he could almost – but not quite – drive it in his sleep.

The zydeco that at first only a handful of bands like Dopsie and his Twisters played so joyously in the battered, boomy local dance halls in those years, and that now dozens of other bands carry on out in the Louisiana countryside and beyond that to most of the world, is one of the newest of the African American musical idioms. If nothing else about the music, the name, at least, is more or less standardized. In most of the writing about it it's called 'zydeco.' This doesn't mean that everyone goes along with this way of spelling it. One of the first singles done in the new style was recorded in the late 1940s by Houston's resident blues man Lightnin' Hopkins, who heard the first bands in the nearby 'Frenchtown' section of the city. On the label the name was spelled 'Zolo Go'. To suggest the tone of the new style Lightnin' played the accompaniment on an organ, which had some of the feel of a zydeco accordion. Occasionally the local print shop Dopsie used for the dance posters he handed out to the clubs where he was playing came up with 'zordico.' Other variants of the spelling were zarico, zadacoe, zodogo, zottico, and zadico, and they still stubbornly turn up on occasional local advertisements or posters. What is surprising about the variety of the spellings is not that there is some disagreement. What is surprising is that the sounds of all of the words are so similar. All of them begin with a 'z' and end with some variant of daco, deco or dico.

Although the root source of the term is widely known, what is contained in the word is helpful in understanding the music itself. In the simplest terms, 'zydeco' is a short, slangy way of saying the beginning of the Cajun French phrase '*Les haricots sont pas salés*,' which means, 'The beans aren't salty.' Spoken quickly the first two words come out something like 'lezarico,' which can be further squeezed down to 'zarico,' which turned into zydeco. Haricots are snap beans – everyday food in western Louisiana, and what the expression implies is that whoever was cooking them didn't have enough money to add salt pork to the pot, which would have given them a salty taste. The term began to turn up in songs recorded in western Louisiana after the second World War, first as a term for the kind of fast dance that was done to a brisk, single chord melody that turns up on record with dozens of different names. The title of the song finally came to stand for the whole dance style. The use of a French word for the music emphasizes that the style comes out of the Southwest Louisiana French speaking culture, and the complaint about the taste of snap beans is a reminder that zydeco is poor people's music.

What zydeco is, is a more complicated Louisiana problem. The night I was driving the Twisters' van, the band, in the Houston club we'd left long behind us, had started with a few numbers by the band members themselves. Their job was to warm up the crowd before Dopsie, as the star of the night, made his appearance. They churned through a set of current R&B hits, with the backup guitarist doing the singing. When Dopsie came up on the bandstand to loud shouts and applause with his gold, two row button accordion, the band instantly tightened up, and with Dopsie driving them they steamed into a series of uptempo melodies that still had a little R&B feel, but the R&B was mixed with Louisiana two-steps, Cajun songs, plaintive Cajun blues, and the occasional strongly accented waltz for the dancers.

Dopsie sang every number with a high, piercing, half shouting voice. Even with his microphone to help him he still had to work to make himself heard over the pounding of the band. He never stopped pumping his accordion, and sometimes I'd see him come off the stage leaving wet footprints from the streaming perspiration that had soaked through his shoes as he played. When zydeco had first emerged only ten or fifteen years before, it was still small and acoustic – mostly a button accordion, accompanied by a real washboard – steel was considered to have the best tone. To carry the melodies the musicians relied on their own sturdy voices. Within a few years the style, though, had picked up more of an R&B sound. A band like Dopsie's worked with six musicians – Dopsie's accordian, Major Handy's guitar, John Hart's tenor sax, the electric bass of 'Morris' Francis, Dopsie's son Junior's drums, and the rubboard – the 'frottoir' – played by Chester Zeno, a small, rumpled, wrinkle faced man who had been making music with Dopsie since they were both teenagers. Some of the bands that have followed him have added keyboards, a rhythm guitar and a trumpet.

So much of the zydeco repertoire recycles the R&B mainstream of the 1940s and 1950s that the two styles would seem to be at least close cousins. But zydeco sounds different. The band might be doing a cover of the popular version of 'Lawdy Miss Clawdy,' but by the time the words have made the change into bayou French, the melody has been fitted to a button accordion, and at least one of the rhythms is being scraped out on a frottoir, what comes out over the loudspeakers has turned into a sound that is new and only half familiar. It's also too simple to characterize what the bands play as a local, bayou version of the R&B mainstream. Zydeco takes at least as much of its repertoire from the songs and dances of the surrounding French speaking community. They swap the bouncy two-steps and the sentimental waltzes back and forth with the white Cajun bands of their neighbors. People who don't live in the Southwest parishes use the term 'Cajun' to include everything and everybody that's found there, but the cultural sources of what is locally termed 'French music' are as complicated as the mix of influences that goes into the music.

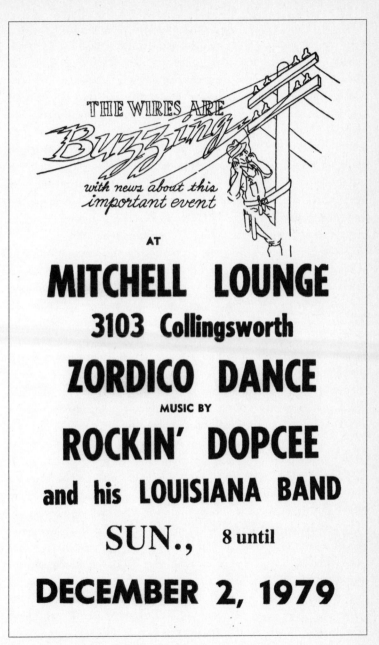

A Rockin' Dopsie 'Zordico' poster, Houston, 1984
(Collection: Samuel Charters)

If you drive west out of New Orleans today, looking for the zydeco bands, the roads have improved, but there is still a wildness about the bayous, a discouraged shabbiness about the small towns. Just west of New Orleans you find yourself crossing miles of flooded land. Off the side of the elevated highway you look down into a darkly tangled cypress forest, and through the branches you can glimpse the moodily glistening surface of the water that floods much of the land. The occasional dry stretches of land are choked with brush and bayou grasses. Narrow, winding channels in the bayous open out like church aisles leading away from the large streams that meander across the hazy countryside. Along the wire fences close to the highway you see the hunched shapes of hawks, and in the air there is a scattering of smaller birds gliding down into the canopy of trees and vines.

Past the swamplands, as you continue driving west, you come to drier ground, and there are narrow rutted roads that go back along the curving mounds of the earth levees that keep the bayous in their channels. Then you reach a stringy growth of cypresses that bring you to a longer, higher elevated roadway over the Atchafalaya basin. The term 'basin' suggests the size of the vast, almost lake-like, spreading stream of water that flows south from the Mississippi River, but it doesn't give an impression of the inexorable power of the water currents below you. If the system of levees closing it off eventually fails, the Atchafalaya will act out its ancient destiny, seize the flooding waters on the other side of the earth walls and become the main channel of a newly directed Mississippi, leaving New Orleans without its river. At the center of the basin's moody currents you can see off to the south almost to the Gulf, with the trees, their straight trunks half sunken into the water, looking as if they'd impulsively started to scatter somewhere in the swamp, then changed their mind and stayed where they were.

A few miles west of the basin you pass the turnoffs to Lafayette, and the land becomes browner, drier. The prairies stretch on either side of the car, the modest, small houses set back away from the road, the flat fields divided into grazing strips with rusted barbed wire. If you continue west, turn off the highway and swing north to a small town like Mamou you find yourself in the old Acadia – a main street with a seedy hotel, a convenience store, two or three gas stations, and the well known Fred's Lounge, its small door opening into a low-ceilinged bar-room that for years broadcast a live Cajun radio show with a band on Saturday mornings. The frame houses of the town were built along the rectangular streets laid out by surveyors when the prairie was opened a century ago. The houses line the neglected streets behind patches of bushes closing in the small lawns, half hidden by the growth of dark trees, their porches shrouded in rusting screens to fend off the mosquitoes.

The weekends when Dopsie and his Cajun Twisters drove over to Houston only occurred every couple of months. It was in this flat stretch of land, in the scattered small towns west of the basin, where the band did most of their playing. Sometimes there were jobs in Lafayette and they didn't have to travel. A school dance, a church hall social, a night on the bandstand at the old Bon Ton Roulay before it burned, the weathered, shambling dance hall close to the center of the city. Not far from Dopsie's house was the dilapidated frame building that housed the Blue Angel Club which functioned as the home club for Clifton Chenier's Red Hot Louisiana Band.

Dopsie drove the band to the jobs in his van, just as he'd done that weekend in Houston, picking them up at their scattered homes and getting them back at the end of the night. The longest drive was for saxophonist John Hart, who lived north of Lafayette in Opelousas. Dopsie's last drive was always that empty stretch of road to John's home in a darkened Opelousas suburb. If Dopsie was doing the driving he knew where everybody was, and he wouldn't have any trouble with somebody going off the road after a night of drinking on the bandstand.

On any Saturday night in the countryside between Lafayette and Lake Charles there could be a dozen zydeco bands like Dopsie's pulling up into the rutted parking lots behind the shadowy dance halls, hauling their amplifiers and microphones up on the battered bandstands and laughing and shouting as they unwound cables, and strung out wires, while the drummer patiently screwed together cymbals and pedals. Buckwheat Zydeco, Fernest Arcenaux and the Thunders, Sampy and the Bad Habits, Nathan Williams and the Zydeco Cha Chas, John Delafose and the Eunice Playboys, The Sam Brothers Five, Boozoo Chavis, Beau Jocque and the Hi-Rollers – so many bands like them out in their vans. Some of the bands had a driver who helped them set up, but a driver had to get some kind of salary, and the jobs didn't pay much. A leader like Dopsie, to keep a band together, had to pay a weekly salary to his musicians, and anything extra came out of the leader's money.

Some of the dance halls where they played were well known, like Richard's, (pronounced in the French manner – Ree-shards), outside of Lawtell, but despite its illuminated sign close to the edge of the road even Richard's was hard to find in the darkness. It's about the size and shape of the large sheds used for storing farm machinery, and the light over the doorway is sometimes the only thing that gives it a different appearance from the other large sheds scattered along the highway. Some of the other places are much harder to find, and even with instructions over the telephone from one of the band members you still can spend frustrating hours driving along the dark, twisting roads and at the end of the drive find yourself in a half-empty, unfamiliar bar-room, with a tinny juke box and a line of regulars on bar stools looking around and wondering what you're doing there.

It was New Orleans that introduced me to Dopsie. There were clubs in the city that were bringing the bands over from west Louisiana, like Tipitina's out on Magazine Street, or the Maple Leaf Club on Oak Street, so the zydeco musicians had some exposure to a larger world. One of the most popular places today is a bowling alley on Carrollton Avenue where the bands play over the rumble and clash of the bowling balls. New Orleans also presents its famed Jazz and Culture Festival out on the grounds of the racetrack every spring. The Festival tries to bring in every kind of Louisiana music – along with every kind of Louisiana handicraft and food. Dopsie played it for several years. On one of his appearances he was mentioned by a popular music journal. A copy of the article, with the name of the band underlined, 'Rocking Dopsie and his Cajun Twisters,' made its way to the company I was working for as a producer. Why not go out to west Lousiana and look up a band with a name that colorful? The name intrigued us as much as the few sentences about the music. I was going to the United States in a few weeks to do some work in a Nashville studio, and I'd produced albums with the Cajun musicians who lived in the same small towns outside of Lafayette, so I could fit in a trip to Louisiana to find Dopsie.

The weekend after I finished in the studio in Nashville, Dopsie was working at Richard's Dance Hall, outside of Lawtell. Four of us drove out from New Orleans. For once there was some moonlight and it was a bright night, and the directions we'd been given took us to the right town. Richard's was just off the road in a pool of light that illuminated the potholed parking lot and the painted boards of the building's sides. If we hadn't been running the car's engine we would have heard the club when we passed on the highway. Dopsie's band was loud. The amplifiers were cranked up, the sound system turned Dopsie's voice into an emergency fire announcement, the drums sounded like someone was trying to break into the club by pounding on the walls, and all of the sound was echoing in the wooden spaces of the club's rafters. Once inside it was a long, pinched, crowded room and the sound boomed out over the dancers. The dance crowd had filled all the tables close to the bandstand, so – still dealing with the volume – we pulled out hard backed wooden chairs at a scarred table back by the door.

The tables were filled by the bandstand, we could see that much, but all we could see were drinks set-ups and plates of food and coats hanging on the backs of chairs. Between us and the band, who were set up behind a painted wood railing ringed by the tight squeezed tables, was a dance floor, and it seemed like everybody from every table was dancing. It was intent, energetic dancing. The men would break away to pull up one pant leg and go into a little country shuffle, a couple up by the bandstand would go into a swinging spin, couples around them would begin to dance with their knees bent, bodies swaying with their loud laughter, women would throw their heads back, pluck up their skirts, and go into their own grinning, eyes-shut circles.

The club was dark, but there were lights over the bandstand. Dopsie and his Twisters were in brightly colored, broad patterned shirts, except for a shorter man in a wrinkled suit in front of the bandstand, who was using a taped spoon to scrape at his ridged metal vest, the frottoir that had only recently replaced the old washboards that had hung from a string around the player's neck. Since Dopsie was leading the band he had on a necktie, but he had pulled it around to the side of his shirt to keep it from tangling in the accordion. He was a medium sized, broad chested, muscular man, his hair cut short and his round, friendly face set in a serious expression until he straightened up and smiled to let us know how much he enjoyed seeing the dancing. On their later tours outside of Louisiana, none of the bands ever got used to audiences that sat staring at them, even if there was a burst of applause when they finished a number. They had worked all their lives trying to get their audiences up on their feet, and if the music didn't have people dancing then they suspected that it was because the band wasn't giving them the music they wanted to hear.

There was no hesitation about the dancers swaying out on the crowded floor at Richard's. Dopsie played the club two or three times a month, and his crowd hadn't come to sit and listen. Most of the couples were in their newest, brightest clothes. Hip tight, shining dresses, elaborate fringed blouses, jewelry and beads, high heels for the women; sport jackets over colorful shirts and slacks for the men. But once the dancing started it was too hot for the jackets, and the women took off any scarves or dressy jackets they'd been wearing. Now they were just dancing, letting the ice melt in drinks back at the tables and the food they'd spread out at their places go cold on the paper plates.

Dopsie's music was solidly in the middle of the zydeco repertory, which meant all the zydeco classics, like 'Ma Negresse' and 'Josephine', whatever current R&B hits the band had gotten around to rehearsing, Cajun two steps, and waltzes sung in French with the same heavy one-two-three downbeat as the big zydeco two-steps. Their 'Zydeco Pas Salé', the old zydeco anthem, had the impetuosity of the wind throwing stones against the side of a building – just Dopsie, the rubboard, and the drums, but the sound of just the three of them roared like the full band, while the dancing jumped into another dimension. I could see handkerchiefs waving, women's arms flinging in circles. In the middle of the second set the band even presented a little show. The rhythm went into a thumping riff and the worn little man playing the frottoir balanced a chair unsteadily upside down above his head, the chair's top rung clenched in his teeth, while he kept up his beat on the frottoir with his spoon. When they finally took a long break I went to find Dopsie. I had already decided to offer him a contract.

For the next several years Dopsie and the band and I spent hours in recording studios as scattered as Baton Rouge, or the small town of Crowley further along the Interstate west of Lafayette, or, once, even in Oslo, Norway. There were completely unpredictable nights at clubs and music halls in places as unlikely as The Hague, London, and Stockholm, along with gritty weekends around Lafayette, in the nearby small towns, and over in Houston. What happened to Dopsie over those years was also happening to the other zydeco bands. Everyone was offered a recording contract, there were suddenly new audiences, and instead of church halls in Eunice, Louisiana, the musicians found themselves playing in concert halls in Paris or Berlin. When I'd sit with the Twisters back at one of the little church halls in Louisiana and they'd meet members of other bands they usually wound up exchanging travel

Rockin' Dopsie at the New Orleans Jazz and Heritage Festival, 1984
(Photo: Samuel Charters)

stories about airports in Switzerland or restaurants in France or the hotels in Germany where they'd stayed on the latest tours.

The leaders of the bands all accepted their role as 'princes' of zydeco, since there was never any question about zydeco's king. The king was Clifton Chenier, who had grown up on his father's sharecropper farm out in the countryside, then spent some years in Lake Charles and Houston after he began leading his band. Finally he had moved not far from Dopsie in Lafayette. It was Chenier, in the 1950s, who put together the first successful zydeco band out of the elements of all the styles he heard around him. With his brother Cleveland on rubboard he defined the zydeco sound, and for the last ten years he'd had a solid relationship with Berkeley's Arhoolie Records and its owner, Chris Strachwitz. To someone not from zydeco country the whole idea of kings and princes seemed like a sort of joke, but Clifton wore his large, glittering crown for years on his jobs, and after his death first Dopsie and then Boozoo Chavis were formally given the title and played at least occasional jobs with shiny crowns of their own.

It was still Clifton who set the height of the bar for the rest of the musicians around the country areas where they all played, but he suffered from diabetes, and for long periods he couldn't perform. He and his wife tried to pay for his dialysis treatments with ideas like 'barbecue breakfasts,' selling barbecue sandwiches out their kitchen window on Sunday mornings. When Clifton didn't have enough jobs to keep his fine band together, Dopsie was able to replace his own saxophone player with John Hart, who had worked with Clifton for years. We called John when we were going into the studio for Dopsie's third album. We recorded it on a Sunday afternoon in Jay Miller's old Excello studio in Crowley, upstairs in a run-down brick building over a street level beauty parlor and an old Ford Model T assembly space. The idea was that if John fit in the band they'd try to work out something to bring him in for the rest of their jobs. After the Sunday afternoon session John never left Dopsie's band.

Sometimes Dopsie tried to explain to me how his life had changed, but it was all beyond anything either of us could have imagined. In our first years of working together he was still doing construction labor. Dopsie had been born in 1932 outside of Lafayette, on a farm close to Carencro, and in those hard years there was never enough money for him to go to school, even if there had been much concern about educating young African Americans in rural Louisiana at that time. He could write his name – Alton Rubin – but he couldn't write anything else and he couldn't read. Construction work was what he could do, and for years he made himself stay awake on the drives back to his day job and then somehow hung on through all of the next day erecting power poles at a new shopping center or breaking up the cement to pave a parking lot. For the first few years that I recorded the band he didn't have a checking account, but when finally I insisted that I couldn't carry so much cash with me around Louisiana we went over to a bank not far from house and asked to talk to the bank manager. He came out with a smile to shake Dopsie's hand. He'd danced to Dopsie's music for years, and also Dopsie had laid the cement floor in the bank. It was his job on the floor that opened the bank's doors for Dopsie. In a moment he had his account.

Dopsie's musical background was as sketchy as his brief schooling. His brother had an accordion – a two row button instrument – and Dopsie used to sneak it away so he could try to teach himself to play it. Since nobody showed him anything he picked it up upside down, and that was the way he played it all his life. He worked out all the zydeco melodies, but he never learned any chords, so his approach to the upside down chord buttons was to hit them in a rough, toneless rhythm that was generally covered by the sound of the rest of the band.

The problem for us with Dopsie's inability to read was that it was very difficult for him to learn new lyrics. For a new album I would come to Lafayette, check into a motel across town, and spend weeks working with him on the songs and doing arrangements with the band. Since I was in Lafayette for such long periods I spent almost as much time at Dopsie's house as I did at the motel. He and his wife Almina had had eight children, and in Dopsie's life I could see reflected so many of the social changes that had come to the South. There had been no education for him, but all of his older children had gone on through high school, and they had continued on to schools that, at least on the junior college level, had been integrated.

When I first met Dopsie he was living with Almina and their children in a cramped house in a mixed neighborhood of mobile homes and small frame buildings on a street that was crowded with cars and trucks. After three or four years he bought a beautiful, modern home in the middle of the block in one of Lafayette's finest neighborhoods. His neighbors were white, but I didn't feel any of the wrenching hostility that had been part of my experience of the South when I first came in 1950. He and Almina had a baby, a large, energetic one-year old named Dwayne, and their next door neighbor, a young white mother with a baby about the same age, was in the house almost every afternoon so the two babies could work out some of their energy on each other. Dopsie was one of the warmest, most generous men I've ever known, and he always seemed to feel pleasantly surprised that life had worked out for him in the way it had.

It would be simple to say that Dopsie didn't have any consciousness of any kind of larger cultural role that his little band was filling as they travelled the Louisiana roads, since he didn't use the sort of language that translates ideas like these into sociological terms, but Dopsie just used other words to say the same thing. When I occasionally asked him about how he felt in his role he would smile his usual quick, warm smile and say something as comfortable as:

'I'm just carryin' on. That's what I'm doing when I'm out there. There's something I got that only me and the other boys like me can keep going with. So that's all I'm doing – that's what we all doing – just carryin' on.'

One night at one of the neighborhood clubs in Houston, I was sitting at a back table with Dopsie while the band was setting up the amplifiers when we suddenly noticed a man in the corner of the dark room, talking in a low voice to the heavy-set man in shirt sleeves who owned the club. The man was in a good looking jacket, but it hung on his shoulders and he had obviously lost some weight since he'd bought it. His hair was processed and he had an air of style about him. It was Clifton Chenier. He had obviously driven over to look for work, and it meant that he had put a band together again. He looked around the room as he talked, and he certainly saw Dopsie, even though he didn't give any sign that he was aware of him. He left without a glance behind him. Dopsie shook his head and sighed,

'The times I've lent that man money.'

For months Dopsie, like the others in the small zydeco community, had done what he could for Clifton, hoping he could go back on the road again.

Clifton had also ended his long relationship with Arhoolie Records. His records weren't selling the way they had been when he was playing regularly in California, but he chose to shift the responsibility for the

Clifton Chenier at the Blue Angel Lounge, Lafayette, 1983
(Photo: Samuel Charters)

smaller sales onto Arhoolie's owner, Chris Strachwitz. Clifton put together a new band, sometimes playing harmonica, and then using a new Italian built electronic accordion that didn't have to be pulled to make it sound. His brother Cleveland was still with him, and his son C. J. Chenier was playing either accordion or saxophone, depending on the arrangement. It was, as always, a tight, exciting band. I followed them up to Chicago and heard them in a club there, and since Clifton was without a contract for the first time in many years I arranged to do an album with him.

Dopsie, with his usual generosity, didn't hold it against me that I was going to record Clifton. He had grown up with Clifton's music and he couldn't have formed his own band without following the path that Clifton had marked. Clifton and I worked out what might go into the album when I met him at jobs around the country, and we did the new album at a studio in Bogalusa, a small town northeast of New Orleans. Clifton was notoriously difficult to work with, but the band was sharp, they'd been out on the road, and he had some strong new songs. I even managed to get a second take on at least one of the songs, and when he blustered about a payment larger than the contract we'd already signed I managed to face him down. The album wasn't his best, or the best record I'd ever done, but it won a Grammy award in 1983. Zydeco was now on a larger world music map.

For the next album with Dopsie we used a studio in Baton Rouge. The studio was in a neighborhood that looked no worse than I was used to, but the band knew better. They wouldn't let me outside the building without one or two of them walking beside me. We had the same problem with Dopsie and new lyrics, but we wanted him to do his version of a local hit by Rocking Sidney, who played out of Lake Charles. The song was an old, traditional children's piece, known under many different titles, but all of them with the general theme of 'Down on the Farm.' The humor of the song is that down on the farm everybody is asking for you. The pigs are asking for you, the are cows asking for you – in this new version the tomatoes ask for you, the potatoes ask for you, the corn asks for you. Dopsie was in an isolated booth for most of the sessions, so his accordion playing wouldn't bleed onto the other instrumental tracks, and I couldn't see him as he was singing. To my surprise he got the name of every vegetable, and he got them in the right order. I went out to the isolation booth to congratulate him and he opened the door with a broad smile.

'I got 'em right here! I didn't miss a one!'

In the morning he'd gone out to a local grocery store and bought one of every vegetable he was supposed to sing about. He had lined them up in front of the microphone and he waved at them, still smiling.

'Every one of them's there – and I got 'em! I got em all!'

The album was nominated for a Grammy the next year, and Dopsie made the trip to New York for what he was certain was the zydeco prize. But this year, to his acute disappointment, the Grammy went to folk guitarist Elizabeth Cotton. Dopsie called me with pain in his voice.

'That prize was supposed to go to zydeco, and they gave it to that old woman!'

Did zydeco change as the bands began travelling outside their bayou world? The essence of this language of song, this language of the African diaspora, is that it continually changes, and it is the artists themselves who carry on the process of change. Some of the zydeco musicians, like Dopsie and Boozoo Chavis, didn't change. Boozoo, three years older than Dopsie, a Lake Charles farmer and horse breeder who wore a plastic apron when he played to keep the sweat from his shirt away from the accordion, had a strong country attachment to his zydeco roots, and he didn't want to change any more than Dopsie did. Out in California, in the Louisiana community there, Queen Ida Guillory and the Bon Temps Band continued to perform in the old bayou style, but it isn't surprising that most of the younger musicians, like Clifton's son, and his keyboard player Stanley 'Buckwheat' Dural, as well as his trumpet player Warren Caesar, played a newer kind of zydeco. The influence now wasn't R&B, it was soul music. When Buckwheat first went on his own, he featured an organ sound with his band and he could handle a smooth motel lounge job anywhere in the country. A few years later, with a contract with England's Island Records and a full brass section, Buckwheat became zydeco's bestselling artist, with a blend of soul, R&B, and rock, all of it with a zydeco tinge. It is the natural progression with any music that grows from a culture that is continually changing and evolving.

The relentless pace of Dopsie's life was too demanding. There was a serious heart attack when he was in his fifties, and a final attack ended his life in 1993, at the age of sixty-one. Of all the memories I have of the years with Dopsie the one that still comes back the most often is a moonlit night in the islands off the west coast of Sweden. The record company had brought Dopsie and the band to Stockholm to help celebrate their twenty-fifth anniversary, and Dopsie was playing on a small, turn of the century, steam driven ferry boat that had been built to take Stockholmers out to their summer homes on the islands. The band was playing with fierce enthusiasm, and Dopsie was pulling his accordion on the jammed middle deck with the perspiration streaming down his face, his shirt and the tops of his trousers streaked with sweat. I went up onto the narrow little deck to catch my breath, and I heard someone calling up to me. I looked over the side and I saw a motorboat, slipping through the water beside us.

'What is that music?' the voice called.

I leaned over the railing and shouted 'Rockin' Dopsie!'

In the half darkness I could make out a head nodding. 'Beautiful,' the voice answered, 'so beautiful!'

Then I straightened up and looked behind us. There in the moonlight, threading through the narrow channels between the islands, was a stream of small boats, all of them edging as close to the little steamer as they could, listening to Dopsie and his music. I could sense what the sound of Dopsie's voice meant to that shining night and to the people listening to him in the stillness, listening almost as though, at that moment, they had forgotten how to breathe.

(2004)

14. The New Blues

In the sixties the blues changed. This was the usual evolving pattern of any popular musical style. The blues of the twenties didn't sound like the ragtime blues of W. C. Handy's pre-WW1 generation, and the jivey blues of the thirties and forties didn't sound anything like the heavy footed classic blues of a decade before. What happened in the sixties was more complex, since it involved a racial shift as well as a musical make-over. The changes that began at that point have broadened and deepened until it is clear now that what happened was a watershed in the role and the position of the blues in American society. It was only a few concert tours down the line before the blues styles of the youngest generation of artists changed to fit the new, emerging pattern. This introduction to the meeting between blues veteran Albert King and a young disciple, Stevie Ray Vaughn, was written in 2001 for Fantasy Records, but the album release was held up by problems of contractual consent, and it remains unissued. The long discussion of the career of Buddy Guy and the changing emphasis on the role of the guitar in the modern blues was written for Vanguard Records in 2003 for a proposed multi-CD set documenting his rich career, but, as with the introduction to the Albert King-Stevie Ray Vaughn album, its release has been delayed by contractual difficulties.

Fathers and Sons
An Afternoon Date with Albert King and
Stevie Ray Vaughn

The chaotic decade of the sixties was a tumultuous moment when all of the world's music changed, and although no one was conscious of it as it was happening, the blues changed along with everything else. In simple terms, the blues that most audiences heard at the beginning of the decade had a black voice, and ten years later many of the the blues artists who had moved onto the rock concert stages were white. It wasn't, however, a repetition of the casual appropriation that had characterised the 19th century's assumption of the right to adopt whatever African American musicians might have created as a white form of entertainment. The new artists who had taken up the blues never lost their sense of a debt that they owed to the African American blues artists who had created the music they were learning to play. What was even more important, there was a kind of apprenticeship, as the new generation learned from the old. For the blues what most decisively effected the change over the sixties and the seventies was a kind of 'father and son' relationship between the blues veterans and the young guitarists and singers who were learning from them.

Fathers and Sons, of course, was the title of one of the seminal blues albums of the era – a meeting between the great black artists of the Chicago blues and the new generation of white blues musicians who had learned at their feet. It was a double LP recorded in 1969 for Chess Records in Chicago; home label to Muddy Waters, Howling Wolf, Chuck Berry, Bo Diddley, and just about every other Chicago artist who worked in the blues idiom. Chess had been trying for three or four years to bring its blues stars into the new era of the sixties, and both Muddy and Wolf had been produced with a South Side version of the 'psychedelic sound.' Wolf's description of his new album was 'dog shit,' and his audience took his word for it. But the album *Fathers and Sons* did take the blues another step, and you still meet people who become emotional when they talk about it.

What was different about it? The difference between these sessions and the 'new era' sounds was that the music the band made in the studio was just the blues. There was no attempt to modernize the blues sound or take it into a new dimension, as Chess had tried to do earlier in the hope that they could continue to reach a black audience. It was hard, scratchy South Side music, but it was no longer shaded toward the old audience that had already left their old fifties blues sounds behind. The new buyers were largely suburban, middle class and white. The 'fathers' on the album were Muddy and his pianist, Otis Spann, drummer Buddy Miles and bass player Sammy Lay. The 'sons' were two young white musicians; harmonica player Paul Butterfield and guitarist Mike Bloomfield, who had been hanging around the blues since they were old enough to ride the Elevated trains down to the South Side by themselves.

There has already been such a long line of white blues guitarists since the 1950s that there could almost be a blues history written around them. Dave Van Ronk, learning to finger pick the John Hurt style; Spider John Koerner and Eric Von Schmidt tracing out their own songs in a blues voice. Then the first electric blues performers – Eric Clapton in England, John Hammond with an electric country sound in New York, Bloomfield in Chicago, Danny Kalb with the Blues Project, Steve Cropper in Memphis, Elvin Bishop – everyone will have names they want to add to the list – and the blues was almost as heavy an influence on a new generation of rock guitarists.

But at whatever point we begin the story of the white musicians who were drawn to the blues, we end up at the same name, Stevie Ray Vaughn. Of all of the people who picked up a guitar and tuned it to a blues chord, Vaughn was the most obsessed by the blues. Everybody else made at least a nod toward other musical styles. Clapton's biggest hits were with reggae, gospel covers, and his own songs; Bloomfield worked with Bob Dylan and tried out the country blues idiom; John Hammond often toured with an R&B band. Rock had turned into an open door for the generation of English guitarists like Keith Richards or Jimmy Page, or Robert Plant, the vocalist with Led Zeppelin, who brought the blues vocal to new levels of baroque extravagance.

With Stevie Ray Vaughn, however, wherever we tune in, we know we'll be in blues country. An exception was his stinging solo on David Bowie's 'Let's Dance,' but Vaughn even made that seem like a blues. If I had to put him up into a blues category, I'd find room for him beside two other guitarists who always seem to take me to this same place, Freddy King and Albert King. Like Stevie, both of them owe a little dues to the other King, B. B., who is the father to that blues generation. It was the music of B. B.'s 'sons' – from Buddy Guy and Otis Rush to Jimmy Dawkins and Robert Cray – that showed the next generation of 'sons' where to put their fingers. Stevie would also have added his brother Jimmy's name to the list – Jimmy Vaughn, the founder of the Fabulous Thunderbirds, and the first Vaughn to burn a club down with the blues.

It isn't too much of a stretch to talk about Albert King and Stevie Ray Vaughn as a father and son, even though Vaughn never toured with one of King's bands. Part of it is the age difference. There was enough of a difference between them that Albert, more than thirty years Stevie's senior, could have been a father to him. Their musical relationship was the central theme of a television program that they recorded for Canadian producer Ian Anderson and the Canadian television network in December 1983, when Vaughn was twenty-eight and King was sixty. If you were fortunate enough to see the program some of what the film caught was an older man passing on advice to a kid. It wasn't advice about playing the guitar. After they exchanged two or three choruses it was as clear as the screech of a high 'e' on the top strings that if Vaughn did have anything to learn from King he'd already learned it years before. Albert said with some consideration that Stevie was 'qualified,' and then he added to it, not really pretending to be serious, 'You already pretty good – pretty good.'

What advice Albert had for Stevie in those years was how to live. It was father to son talk. 'The better you get, the harder you work...' In their 1993 biography of Vaughn, Joe Nick Patoski and Bill Crawford quote Albert telling Stevie, 'You get high when you're working 'cause you're having too much fun and you don't see the people fuckin' you around...you wake up one day back in the clubs without a whole lot to show for what you been through.' On the program Albert suggested 'I'm about ready to turn it over to you.' Stevie protested, 'No, I don't believe that,' but Albert insisted. 'Oh yes, it's true son, it's true. Twenty-eight years long enough. I gotta sit back and watch you...' At one moment during their easy bantering Albert finally admitted, almost with surprise in his voice, 'I didn't think you would ever be as bad as you are.'

For Stevie the figure of Albert went back to his childhood. When he was ten he saw an Albert King poster on a corner in Austin, and he was immediately won over by the what he remembered as the swallow tail guitar in the poster. He said he and Albert met for the first time at Austin's Coliseum Club when he was eighteen, but Albert's version of the story was that when Clifford Antone, owner of famed Austin blues bar Antone's, asked him if Stevie Ray Vaughn could sit in with his band two years later, Albert remembered 'You know, I really didn't know who Stevie Ray Vaughn was.'

Vaughn certainly hadn't forgotten the man he'd seen on the poster playing the swallow tail guitar. When King drove up to Antone's, at the wheel of his tour bus, his pipe firmly clenched in his teeth, Stevie was standing at the curb waiting for him. Clifford Antone had to ask Albert with some persistence if the young Vaughn could sit in, and King finally agreed to give him a chance to play a number. As Patoski and Crawford described what happened, it was as if Stevie, '...had just twisted the cap off the bottle that contained the secrets of all blues and poured every guitar lick known to man right out onstage.' Albert kept him up on the bandstand for the rest of the night.

Stevie's excitement with the blues took the physical form of an almost frightening speed and unflagging invention. He had listened to each of the major blues performers with such dogged persistence that he could continue to develop chorus after chorus with a level of energy that had the feel of someone trying to ride a lightning bolt. In the program with Albert King, the older father figure, however, the mood was often more introspective. The music never lost its intensity, its quality of something very important being handed back and forth, but the tempos were slower, and there was time for each of the guitarists to see where their ideas could take them. One thing musicians all agree about is that it's harder to play a slow tempo than a fast one, and on these duets both guitarists passed the test without hesitation. Part of the success of their extended solos had to go to the very practiced rhythm section of Tony Llorens on keyboards, Gus Thornton on bass and Michael Llorens on drums. They had been backing Albert on his perpetual tours, and they could sense every shift in the mood of the music. Tony, particularly, took some of the solo weight off the two guitarists with his own solo choruses.

One of the pieces they both expanded and considered was Albert's signature piece 'Born Under A Bad Sign', which was the title of his biggest album on the Stax label. Even though he had performed it at least once on every gig he'd done since then, he still presented it with the same measure of excitement and deliberation. He carefully measured out what he intended his audiences to hear each time he played it, and there was always more there than you expected there would be. There were uptempo pieces, most memorably 'Evil', a rocking shuffle featuring Tony Lloren's organ, but most of the set settled down for some blues playing that did seem to lay out everything anybody has ever thought of doing with twelve short bars and three little chords.

It wasn't difficult to tell on the television screen just which one of the guitars was soloing, and which one was laying back, but there were enough differences in their styles, despite the heavy overlay of Albert's influence in some of Stevie's phrasing, that with your eyes closed you still knew who was choking the strings. Albert's tone sometimes sounded as though it were partially choked, and he spent a lot of time in the middle or the lower end of the guitar. His approach to a melodic figure was to worry around it with a series of notes that shifted away from the obvious rhythmic stresses, fluffing out the sound of the guitar until it had some of the character of his voice, which was much lighter than the usual Mississippi growl. (He was from Indianola, in Mississippi's Sunflower County.) Then he slid over to a new little figure and worried around that one with another series of notes, working around the rhythm, but never emphasising it. He spent less time in the upper frets than a lot of other blues guitarists, though he worked his way up the guitar neck when he wanted to build a little tension. Then he would slide back to the middle of the guitar again, or pick through some notes in the bottom strings, as if he'd forgotten something there and he was looking around to see where he left it.

Stevie's tone was clearer than Albert's, and on his solo albums the clear, bright tone was one of the characteristics of his playing. He shaped his choruses up into the higher strings more often than Albert, and there was usually a series of high peaks in his solos, as if he had decided that it would be easier for us to get the point of what he was telling us if he repeated some of it. In these slower blues he gave us the essential Stevie Ray Vaughn, with the occasional suggestion of a little Buddy Guy or Jimmy Hendrix or Otis Rush to make sure we understood what he was laying out for us. The playing from each of them, Albert and Stevie, was the blues at a burnished level of perfection.

Whatever happens on a job, every musician knows that it's only one job, and the next night's crowd will only get up for what happens that night. Albert and Stevie went on to play these pieces again on their solo gigs, and on some nights they must have gotten some of the same fire and focus – but it's also clear, nearly twenty years later, that this was a special moment in the careers of each of the two men. It was evident from the first choruses that they were playing for each other, and that was the best audience either of them would ever have. As can happen in these kinds of friendships, father–son – however it's defined – it was the son who died first. Vaughn died in a helicopter crash in the fog on the way back from a concert in 1990. Albert outlived him by two years. He died of a heart attack in 1992. They didn't meet often, and their careers took different paths, but for anyone who loves their music we can be grateful that for one long day in a television studio they sat down together to this feast of the blues.

(2001)

Buddy Guy
A Cry As Big As The Sky

The tone of the guitar this time is thinner and harder, as though it were being forced through a very small, rough opening. No sound is left to hang in the air, as each note slides away from the guitar with its flesh squeezed dry. Every note is pushed and drawn tight, stripped of any softer implications that might once have been there. Now the silence between the notes has been stretched, so the chorded background becomes a muted scream left to hold the poised line of notes in place. Now when the vocal begins the voice is a whisper, but already by the second line it has swollen into a cry of pain that is as barren and without hope as a crumpled paper bag. What Buddy Guy once sang as a plea to join him in his pain has become a cry of deeper suffering. Now the song acts out a private grief as a public catharsis – with a sound that can be as thin and as harsh as a scraped nail on glass.

The blues has been many things in its long decades, but what the music has become since the 1960s in the hands of a guitar master like Buddy Guy is something that couldn't have seemed obvious even at the beginning of the decade, when the change began. The typical 'now' of one of Buddy's solos is a newer performance of a blues like 'My Time After Awhile', from a 1996 live recording. The back-up group is led by an admirer, G. E. Smith, a blues guitarist himself, who was the musical director for the orchestra of the television program *Saturday Night Live*. For the original version of the song itself, 'My Time After Awhile', the 'once' is the first version, the recording that he made of the piece for a Chess Records single in June, 1964.

The differences between the two performances are a mirror of the blues that the artists of Buddy's generation have helped to create, and it's fascinating to go back and forth between the two versions, thirty-two years apart, and see what has changed and what is still the same. What hasn't changed is the song. Buddy has written very few of his best-known pieces, and this serviceable genre number was composed by the team of Ronald Bager, Robert Geddins, and Sheldon Feinberg. The situation of the song – a man trying to deal with an unfaithful woman – is a staple blues theme, and the verses are as ordinary as something torn out of an old magazine – but the opening line, 'It's your time now, baby, but it's gonna be mine after awhile' serves as an immediately effective setting of the mood. The rest of the text is a series of phrases that have shown up in several generations of blues songs. Sometimes you feel that blues singers hang on to a number like it because at least they can remember the opening line.

The song is the same in the two versions, 1964 and 1996, and surprisingly the instrumentation of the accompaniment groups is just about the same. In 1996 G. E. Smith was providing the musical interludes for the popular show with an augmented blues band, and the original recording used a Chess studio group augmented with horns. The *sound* of the versions, however, or the mood, the style of the verses, is startlingly different. The differences are – as they say – in the details.

And what differences there are! The tempo of the Chess studio recording has been slowed down to a little more than a half of the tempo for the new live version. In a moment of curiosity I timed a line from each version. In 1964 it took about ten seconds for Buddy to sing the first line of the verse. In 1996 he fleshed out the line with three or four additional words – 'It's your turn right now, baby, oh I got a feelin' it's gonna' be my time after awhile' – but at the new tempo the line took about twenty seconds. If you've listened a lot to the singles that Buddy and the rest of the Chess stable of artists released in the sixties, the modern tempo gives a first impression of someone dragging their feet through some sticky mud. On the other hand, if you've been listening a lot to the new tempos, then the old Chess version sounds as though nobody was taking the song very seriously.

Tempos have always been a sensitive point with the blues. One of the musical sources for the blues itself was the field holler, and the introspective, highly personal field melodies have almost no rhythm at all. There is a well-known anecdote from one of the early 1920s New York City appearances of blues singer Bessie Smith, who also dwelled in tempos that sometimes sounded as the though the band had lost its place in the arrangement. One of New York's young jazz stars went to hear her at the Lafayette Theater, and he said afterwards that when she started a verse he had to go take a pee, and when he came out of the toilet she was still singing the same verse. The new blues tempos – which may have edged their way closer to the pace of the old hollers – give their fans considerable time to think about something else between lines.

The biggest difference that you hear, though, is that in the old Chess version the guitar is there for a fifteen second line over the horn riff, and for the rest of the song its role is limited to fills. There is no guitar solo, which for your modern everyday blues recording is a kind of stylistic heresy. At first I thought this had to be an exasperated adjustment to the time limits a single imposed on the arrangement, but to be certain I looked for an album track from that period, and I found a 6' 16" blues that Buddy recorded for Chess in 1961, 'I Found A True Love'. Buddy sings the first choruses, with guitar fills, then steps back for a solo – but the soloist is the tenor sax. He comes back in with the vocal and the guitar fills, then gives way again to a solo, but the soloist this time is the band's other tenor sax. The guitar finally joins the horns for the fade in the last ten seconds.

Buddy's earliest recordings, four songs on Artistic label in 1958, all included a guitar chorus, but somehow over the next few years the guitar's role had been reduced to a filigree of fills. To strengthen the impression that the guitar solo wasn't the essential element of the arrangement, the four titles that he did for Artistic had three different solo guitarists – himself, Otis Rush, or Ike Turner, and it is only a matter of small nuances that helps you tell them apart. It's even more difficult since Rush's solo – on a Willie Dixon number 'Sit and Cry (the Blues)' – was, according to writer Bill Dahl, 'copped verbatim from Jody Williams' then-recent Argo platter "You May" '. But by the 1990s, it was the guitar that had taken over the stage, and Buddy Guy's fervent solos were suddenly in the stage center spotlight.

It wasn't even an essentially different guitar style that took over the new blues. The notes and the phrases of the solos in 1996 are almost identical to the solo lines Buddy had played thirty years before. A burst of notes, a sustained tone on a bent string, an entire phrase played on strings pushed up into the chord a note at a time, clenches of notes, bites of melody. At the newer, slower tempo the phrases of the solos haven't changed – only there is now more space left between them. The backgrounds of most new blues recordings have become a softly chorded fill to sustain the level of sound throughout the solo choruses, often with a piano mixed well back to add a kind of commentary to the more prominently presented fills of the guitar. Like the song and the instrumentation of Buddy's bands in the two versions, so much of what he's doing with the guitar is the same – but it *sounds* different.

Since it's easy to fiddle the sound of a guitar, there are waves of fashion from year to year that leave their imprint on everybody's personal style. Buddy usually names B. B. King, Muddy Waters or

Guitar Slim as influences, but no guitarist came through the fires of the sixties without being seared by Jimi Hendrix, and the harsh sound of Buddy's later work often has the edge of Hendrix, and also some of Hendrix's stylistic quirks. The sound of the later Buddy Guy has certainly picked up some of the sixties mannerisms, if not from Hendrix, then from the stream of raw guitarists who seemed to show up from England every month – from Eric Clapton and Keith Richards to Stevie Winwood, Jeff Beck and Jimmy Page. The new guitar stars often named him as one of their influences, but comparing the guitar sounds from the pre-sixties and the post sixties makes it clear that this has always been a street with traffic going in both directions.

What is also different in the later version of 'My Time After Awhile,' of course, is the new emphasis on the guitar. Each of the blues on the 1996 live date, in fact, opens with a guitar solo, and the only piece that doesn't feature the guitar in the opening chorus is a humdrum pop title, 'Ain't That Loving You.' What I also realized, after working my way through all of Buddy's recordings in the last decades, was that the solo that opens the blues is always essentially the same solo. Like the mood of the lyrics, the arrangement of the song and the harmonies of the verses; the solos are one-size-fits-all.

As I listened to one after another of Buddy's solos I was reminded of the great spaciousness of the solos that Louis Armstrong created in his last decades as a major jazz artist. For both artists the solo had become its own reason for being, and the song itself had dwindled to only another element of the arrangement. Armstrong at least had different melodies, different chords, and the different moods of the lyrics to work with, but what is surprising is that he makes each of the solos an extension of the same emotional setting. It isn't the notes themselves, but the *manner* in which Armstrong presents them. With Buddy's solo it's a hundred tricks of presentation – the tone setting, the volume, the unexpected shifts of phrasing – that make the solo seem new again and again – or at least seem to be newly discovered. On each of the blues tracks on the 1996 live album the opening solo begins with the same introductory phrase, but the audience greets it as though it were a call to an adventure down a road they've never walked before.

I came into Buddy's stylistic journey through solo blues guitar country somewhere around the middle. In the early 1960s, when I was working as an A&R director for Prestige Records, Buddy was working mostly as an automobile mechanic, with a weekend job playing with Junior Wells' quartet at Theresa's, a serviceable corner club in the basement of a South Side tenement. None of Buddy's Chess singles had caught on enough for him to lead his own band, but Junior – who had played harp with Muddy Waters – had a local hit, 'Messin' With The Kid,' and he was enough of a showman to hold on to his weekend job at Theresa's for several years. I would stop by to listen to the two of them, usually with Jack Meyers on bass and Freddie Below Jr. on drums. It was Junior's show, but Buddy's guitar was as much a second voice. He listened and reacted to the sound of the others with such intensity that everything they played together became a densely textured ensemble, even with such minimal instrumental resources.

When I came back to Chicago with my wife Ann as in-house photographer in December 1965 to record the three volume set *Chicago/The Blues/Today!* for Vanguard Records, Junior's quartet was the first group to come into the studio. In that period of the blues each session was essentially a live studio recording. There were no overdubs, no added vocals or guitar lines. It was the quartet I had heard at Theresa's – with that intensity to their silences, and that same quality of *listening* that had kept me breathless through their performances in the little cellar club. Buddy's solo on 'Vietcong Blues' on the 1965 recording has all the elements he was to use again and again, and even with only a bass and drums behind him there is no sense of anything missing in the sound. His sense of the timing of the phrases gives even the silences a place in the solo.

The three albums, issued the next year, were very successful, which meant I could go on and record two additional albums with Junior, including Buddy in what was still Junior's band. After some months I managed to convince Buddy to sign an individual artist's contract with Vanguard. He hesitated mostly because his wife understood that if he moved into the blues mainstream he would spend most of his life on the road. He'd waited too long for some real success, however, and on short trips to Europe he'd gotten some sense of the audience that was out there for him. It was time for him to make a move. In the mid-sixties Buddy was tall, slim, elegant, thoughtful, rambunctious, and as ambitious as he was good looking. He and the very independent Vanguard Records, with artists like The Weavers, Joan Baez and Buffy St. Marie, felt like a good fit.

It was the first album, *A Man and the Blues*, that we recorded in

Chicago in 1966 that gave some measure of reality to Buddy's reputation as one of the most exciting of the younger Chicago guitarists. There were horns, but I kept them in the background, and as a foil for Buddy I brought in a friend, pianist Otis Spann, who had also been featured on the *Chicago/The Blues/Today!* set, and who had done an earlier album for me with Muddy Waters' band in 1964. The one real fly-in-the-microphone with the kind of live-in-the-studio recording we were doing was the problem of the electric guitar. We didn't then have microphones that could block out other studio sounds. If I wanted to record the sound of the piano or the horns with any sensitivity I had to figure out what to do with Buddy's guitar. He couldn't work if he couldn't hear it the way he heard it in a club, and we couldn't work if the sound was leaking into every other microphone in the studio.

There was considerable fumbling before the sound was finally workable. The compromise we agreed on was to set up his guitar amplifier outside the studio in a hallway, but to leave the door slightly ajar so he could hear it. The final sound was so clear that at moments I could hear everyone breathing as they played. With Spann subtly sketching ideas in his piano backgrounds and coloring the spaces that Buddy left in his solo lines, it was with this album that Buddy defined his solo style. Everything that had been there in the small solo spaces he'd had on the Chess singles was here in a more sympathetic setting – now he had enough space, and he filled it. The tempos were the Chicago tempos he was used to, and with Spann giving a shape to the accompaniment he created a classic Chicago album.

It was, however, as a guitarist that Buddy made the biggest impression with his album. As was to happen again and again for the next twenty years, he hadn't created a distinctive repertoire of original material. What he had come into the studio to record was largely a collection of covers and jams. He hadn't written a blues, or any other song, that was different enough in style to define him as an artist with a new emotional dimension. At this point both Buddy and Junior seemed to be completely without a direction as to how they could become blues stars, though their ambition in these years was so intense it was almost physical. Chuck Berry had taken their old formulas and turned them into rock and roll gold, Bo Diddley had begun by working the same clubs they did, and suddenly he was headlining at the new rock concert halls. For Junior and Buddy it was James Brown who had shown them the road they wanted to travel. *A Man and the Blues* sold enough copies to apprentice blues guitarists to give it some respectability – about twenty-five to thirty thousand – but the Berkeley rock band I was recording at the same time, Country Joe and the Fish, had sold three hundred and fifty thousand copies of their first album. That was the level of success Buddy had been aiming for.

Since he had given me the Chicago album I wanted for his first Vanguard release, and it hadn't been the definitive success we'd both hoped for, I let Buddy set up the guidelines for the next album. It was a live album recorded in a Berkeley club, with his Chicago band and an augmented horn section – and the songs he wanted to do were covers of old R&B hits, including James Brown styled-numbers that no one but James Brown could pull off. There was a long, hard stretch of rehearsals and recording, and as he listened back to the final mixes I could tell from his expression that he realized how far the album had missed.

For the next twenty years Buddy spent much of his time on the road, often back with Junior, making occasional solo albums or duet albums featuring their harmonica and guitar. Along the way he was steadily building an audience by opening for most of the major rock stars. His guitar playing didn't change in any way, but he made the adjustments to the big, noisy stadium sound systems that gave the familiar phrases a larger than life presence. And while he was honing his skills, becoming known more and more as a consummate guitarist, the blues itself was changing. Whatever ties the blues had to the every day realities of ghetto life had become stretched so thin as to be almost meaningless. The tempos were too slow for dancing, and the old verities of 'Oh, my baby left me and it hurts me so' really didn't reflect the new patterns of sexual relationships in a rapidly changing America.

By the 1980s it was rap that had effectively reshaped the urban African American audience, just as the blues had performed that role in the 1920s. In the record shops where I buy the newest rap and reggae in Brooklyn today there are thousands of CDs and LPs of rap, reggae, some gospel, a little jazz – but I've never found a single blues album. I have to look for blues records in the stores set up for mostly white teenagers over the Brooklyn Bridge in Manhattan. The new blues audience was almost exclusively white, and this also shifted the attention toward someone like Buddy Guy. For the suburban listeners of the 1960s, the lyrics of the blues now had only a symbolic meaning – they never intended to 'Go to Brownsville and take that right hand road...' and the girls they had crushes on in their high school classes didn't have much relationship to 'Big leg woman gets my pay, skinny woman don't have nothin' to drive my blues away.' Between the end of the 1960s and the end of the 1980s, as one British guitarist after another arrived in the rock concert halls with a different series of guitar licks, the blues became a new kind of social statement.

For Buddy, his stretched, emotionally naked guitar solos had become a larger metaphor for what the *idea* of the blues meant to the new audience, and as he would sing in his blues, 'It's my time now.' When a new record label in New York, Silvertone Records, brought him into the studio for the album *Damn Right, I've Got The Blues* in 1991, among the musicians backing him were guest guitarists Jeff Beck, Eric Clapton and Mark Knopfler. He went on to record a series of excellent albums for Silvertone, he opened a blues club in Chicago and put out a monthly newsletter/magazine for the club that for a time was part of the scurrying blues underground. On one of the *Saturday Night Live* television broadcasts the band went into a riff between sketches and suddenly there was Buddy – unannounced – tearing into a soaring solo. The audience didn't need to be told who had just burst onto the stage – there was a shout that almost drowned out the band. The success he had dreamed of when he first went into a recording studio nearly half a century before had finally showered its rewards over him.

For the newest generation of blues guitarists Buddy had now become a legend – though a vital, still challenging legend. One of the new stars who learned from him was Texan Stevie Ray Vaughn, and although Vaughn's solos could be a fiery medley of everybody's licks – from B. B. King to Jimi Hendrix – in a live performance of Buddy's 'Leave My Girl Alone', released first as a promotional disc, then on a compilation CD *The Real Deal: Volume 2*, Stevie pays the unusual tribute of playing the piece in Buddy's immediately identifiable style. The vocal phrasing – though Stevie's voice is lower and darker – has Buddy's head shaking introspection, and the guitar lead and fills follow Buddy as closely as Stevie's very different temperament will let him. The phrases and the clusters of burning notes are there – but in his excitement his notes spill out in lengthening streams, and most of the silences are filled in.

In the years he had been travelling, Buddy had often run into Stevie, and they'd been close. Vaughn's unexpected death in a helicopter crash in the summer of 1990 stunned the new audience that had grown up for the new kind of blues, and it had a deep personal effect on Buddy.

When he went into the studio for his *Damn Right, I've Got The Blues* album a few months later he ended it with one of his individual and moving solos. It was simply a solo, a long continuing cry of a solo that summed up everything the blues had become and what Buddy's role had been in it. It was titled simply 'Rememberin' Stevie.'

For the track Buddy used only his rhythm section – keyboard, drums, bass, and second guitar – and they play the first chorus at the new slow tempo, using only a simple, repeated riff with the rhythm guitar playing a figure of descending chords again and again, almost like a cry. When Buddy enters he is restrained and thoughtful, and as he sustains his solo over six stunning choruses he finds in each phrase a new figure, and new allusion drawn from all the years he has played the blues. The rhythm behind him sustains the mood with a sound that is drained of histrionics, leaving him free to move in an emotional dimension which he has outlined himself. His playing defines the essence of the blues which now has become symbol and metaphor. The guitar has become a voice beyond the need for any words. As he draws out his familiar phrases and riffs and presents them, one by one, it is almost as though he is laying out each of them as a gift to a friend who was also, like him, a guitarist. The long, sorrowing solo is a summary of everything that today's blues has achieved, and it makes clear how great a role Buddy Guy has played in creating the new idiom. His solo is a despairing cry voiced in the sound of the blues today, and it is a masterpiece.

(2003)

Index